BUDDHA AND THE GOSPEL OF BUDDHISM

BUDDHA AND THE GOSPEL OF BUDDHISM

ANANDA KENTISH COOMARASWAMY

Published by

FacsiMile Publisher
12 Pragati Market
Ashok Vihar, Ph-2
Delhi - 110052, India
Phone: 011-47034999
Email: www.facsimilepublishers.com
info@facsimilepublishers.com

Distribution Network
gyanbooks.com
India, USA, Canada, UK, Australia

ISBN: 978-93-7073-098-4 (PB)
First Published, 1916

2nd Impression 2025

Printed at: Gyan Press, Delhi.

BUDDHA AND THE GOSPEL OF BUDDHISM
Author: ANANDA KENTISH COOMARASWAMY

BUDDHA AND THE GOSPEL OF BUDDHISM

I

THE TEMPTATION OF BUDDHA

NANDA LĀL BOSE

Frontispiece

BUDDHA AND THE GOSPEL OF BUDDHISM

BY

ANANDA COOMARASWAMY D.Sc.

AUTHOR OF "ARTS AND CRAFTS OF INDIA AND CEYLON" "RAJPUT PAINTING" AND "ESSAYS IN NATIONAL IDEALISM" JOINT-AUTHOR OF "MYTHS OF THE HINDUS AND BUDDHISTS"

WITH ILLUSTRATIONS IN COLOUR BY

ABANINDRO NĀTH TAGORE C.I.E.

& NANDA LĀL BOSE

AND THIRTY-TWO REPRODUCTIONS IN BLACK AND WHITE FROM PHOTOGRAPHS

NEW YORK

G. P. PUTNAM'S SONS

1916

PREFACE

THE aim of this book is to set forth as simply as possible the Gospel of Buddhism according to the Buddhist scriptures, and to consider the Buddhist systems in relation, on the one hand, to the Brāhmanical systems in which they originate, and, on the other hand, to those systems of Christian mysticism which afford the nearest analogies. At the same time the endeavour has been made to illustrate the part which Buddhist thought has played in the whole development of Asiatic culture, and to suggest a part of the significance it may still possess for modern thinkers.

The way of the Buddha is not, indeed, concerned directly with the order of the world, for it calls on higher men to leave the market-place. But the order of the world can only be established on a foundation of knowledge: every evil is ultimately traceable to ignorance. It is necessary, then, to recognize the world for what it truly is. Gautama teaches us that the marks of this life are imperfection, transcience, and the absence of any changeless individuality. He sets before us a *summum bonum* closely akin to the Christian mystic conception of 'self-naughting.' Here are definite statements which must be either true or false, and a clearly defined goal which we must either accept or refuse. If the statements be false, and if the goal be worthless, it is of the highest importance that the former should be refuted and the latter discredited. But if the diagnosis be correct and the aim worthy, it is at least of equal importance that this should be generally recognized: for we cannot wish to perpetuate as the basis of our sociology a view of life that is demonstrably false or a purpose demonstrably contrary to our conception of the good.

This book is designed, therefore, not as an addition to our already over burdened libraries of information, but as a definite contribution to the philosophy of life. Our study of alien modes of thought and feeling, if it is to be of any real use to us, must be inspired by other than curious motives or a desire to justify our own system. For the common civilization of the world we need a common will, a recognition of common problems, and to co-operate in their solution. At this moment, when the Western world is beginning to realize that it has failed to attain the fruit of life in a society based on competition and self-assertion, their lies a profound significance in the discovery of Asiatic thought, where it is affirmed with no uncertain voice that the fruit of life can only be attained in a society based on the conception of moral order and mutual responsibility. Let me illustrate by a single quotation the marvellous directness and sincerity of the social ethic to which the psychology of Buddhism affords its sanction: *Victory breeds hatred, for the conquered is unhappy.*

Stories are told of Asiatic rulers paying the price of kingdoms for a single word of profitable counsel. One may well inquire whether any conceivable price could have been too high for Europe to have paid for a general recognition of this truth, ere now. There is, again, a passage of the Ruru-deer Jātaka which is perhaps unique in all literature in its supreme tenderness and courtesy: *For who*—the Bodhisattva asks—*would willingly use harsh speech to those who have done a sinful deed, strewing salt, as it were, upon the wound of their fault?*

It is with gifts such as this that Buddhism, and the Hinduism from which it issues and into which it has again merged, stand over against the world of *laissez faire*, demanding of their followers only the abandonment of all resentment, coveting, and dulness, and offering in return a happiness and peace beyond our reasonable understanding. Can we deny that modes of thought which find expression thus must for ever command our deepest sympathy and most profound consideration? It is not possible that liberation from resentment, coveting, and dulness, should ever be ill-timed: and it is just this liberation which constitutes the ethical factor in Nibbāna, where the psychological part is self-forgetfulness.

It will be plainly seen to what extent I am indebted to the work of other scholars and students, and I wish to make a frank and grateful acknowledgment to all those from whose work I have freely quoted, particularly Professor and Mrs Rhys Davids and Professor Oldenberg, as well as to others to whom I am indebted for the use of photographs. The latter, reproduced in monochrome, illustrate the history of Buddhist art: but beside this, the work of modern Indian painters illustrating Buddhist thought and legend is reproduced in colour.

A few suggestions may be useful as a guide to pronunciation. Vowels generally are pronounced as in Italian: *a* as in *America*, *ā* as in *father*, *e* as *a* in *nave*, *i* as in *it*, *ī* as *ee* in *greet*, *o* as in *note*, *u* as *oo* in *room*, *ū* as *oo* in *boot*: *ai* has the sound of *i* in *bite*, *au* the sound of *ow* in *cow*. Every consonant is distinctly pronounced, and aspirates are distinctly heard. *C* has the sound of *ch* in *church*, while *s* in some cases has the sound of *sh*, *e.g.* in *Siva*, *Īsvara*, *Sankara*, etc. The accent falls on the first syllable or the third, rarely or never on the second.

Certain words, such as *kamma*, *Nibbāna*, *Bodhisatta*, etc., are quoted in these Pāli forms where Hīnayāna Buddhism is in question, and in the more familiar Sanskrit forms *karma*, *Nirvāna*, *Bodhisattva*, where the reference is to Mahāyāna.

ANANDA COOMARASWAMY

LONDON, *February* 8, 1916

CONTENTS

Buddha & the Gospel of Buddhism

PART IV : THE MAHĀYĀNA

PART V : BUDDHIST ART

LIST OF PLATES

Buddha & the Gospel of Buddhism

LIST OF PLATES IN COLOUR

QUOTATIONS

I will go down to self-annihilation and eternal death,
Lest the Last Judgment come and find me unannihilate,
And I be seiz'd and giv'n into the hands of my own Selfhood.

Blake, "*Milton.*"

But, alas, how hard it is for the Will to sink into nothing, to attract nothing, to imagine nothing.

Let it be granted that it is so. Is it not surely worth thy while, and all that thou canst ever do?

Behmen, "*Dialogues.*"

Not I, not any one else can travel that road for you. You must travel it for yourself.

Walt Whitman.

You cannot step twice into the same waters, for fresh waters are ever flowing in upon you.

Herakleitus.

Vraiement comencent amours en ioye et fynissent en dolours.

Merlin.

By a man without passions I mean one who does not permit good and evil to disturb his internal economy, but rather falls in with whatever happens, as a matter of course, and does not add to the sum of his mortality.

Chuang Tau.

Profound, O Vaccha, is this doctrine, recondite, and difficult of comprehension, good, excellent, and not to be reached by mere reasoning, subtile, and intelligible only to the wise; and it is a hard doctrine for you to learn, who belong to another sect, to another faith, to another persuasion, to another discipline, and sit at the feet of another teacher.

'*Majjhima Nikaya,*' "*Sutta 72.*"

PART I : THE LIFE OF THE BUDDHA

His Birth

THE name Buddha, 'the Knower,' 'the Enlightened,' 'the Wake,' is the appellation by which the wandering preaching friar Gautama became best known to his disciples. Of this man we are able to say with some certainty that he was born in the year 563 B.C. and died in 483 B.C. He was the heir of a ruling house of the Sākyas, whose little kingdom, a rich irrigated plain between the Nepalese foot-hills and the river Rapti, lay to the north-east of the present province of Oudh. To the south-west lay the larger and more powerful kingdom of the Kosalas, to whom the Sākyas owed a nominal allegiance. The Buddha's personal name was Siddhattha, his family name Gautama, his father's name Suddhodana, his mother's Māyā. It is only in later legend that Suddhodana is represented as a great king; most likely he was in fact a wealthy knight and land-owner. Siddhattha's mother died seven days after his birth, and her sister Mahajāpatī, another wife of Suddhodana, filled the place of mother to the young prince. He was brought up in Kapilavatthu, a busy provincial capital; he was trained in martial exercises, riding, and outdoor life generally, and in all knightly accomplishments, but it is not indicated in the early books that he was accomplished in Brāhmanical lore. In accordance with the custom of well-to-do youths, he occupied three different houses in winter, summer, and the rainy season, these houses being provided with beautiful pleasure gardens and a good deal of simple luxury. It is recorded that he was married, and had a son, by name Rāhula, who afterwards became his disciple. Siddhattha experienced the intellectual and spiritual unrest of his age, and felt a growing dissatisfaction with the world of pleasure in which he moved, a dissatisfaction rooted in the fact of its transience and uncertainty, and of man's subjection to all the ills of mortality. Suddhodana feared that these thoughts would lead to the loss of his son, who would become a hermit, as was the tendency of the thinkers of the time; and these fears were well founded, for in spite of every pleasure and luxury that could be devised to withhold him, Siddhattha ultimately left his home to adopt the 'homeless life' of the 'Wanderer,' a seeker after truth that should avail to liberate all men from the bondage of mortality. Such enlightenment he found after years of search. Thereafter, during a long ministry as a wandering preacher, he taught the Four Ariyan Truths and the Eightfold Path; attracting many disciples, he founded a monastic order as a refuge for higher men, the seekers for everlasting freedom and unshakable peace. He died at the age of eighty. After his death his disciples gathered together the "Words of the Enlightened One," and from this nucleus there grew up in the course of a few centuries the whole body of the Pāli canon, and ultimately, under slightly different interpretation, the whole mass of the Mahāyāna Sūtras. That so much of the story represents literal fact is not only very possible, but extremely probable; for there is nothing here which is not in perfect accordance with the life of that age and the natural development of Indian thought. We know, for example, that many groups of wandering ascetics were engaged in the same quest, and that they were largely recruited from an intellectual and social aristocracy to whom the pretensions of Brāhmanical priestcraft were no longer acceptable, and who were no less out of sympathy with the multitudinous cults of popular animism. We know the name of at least one other princely ascetic, Vardhamāna, a contemporary of the Buddha, and the founder of the monastic system of the Jainas.

The Legendary Buddha

But while it is easy to extract from the Buddhist books such a nucleus of fact as is outlined above, the materials for a more circumstantial biography of the Buddha, extensive as they are, cannot be regarded as historical in the scientific usage of the word. What is, however, far more important than the record of fact, is the expression of all that the facts, as understood, implied to those to whom they were a living inspiration; and it is just this expression of what the life of Buddha meant to Buddhists, or Bauddhas, as the followers of Gautama are more properly called, that we find in the legendary lives, such as the *Lalitavistara*, which is familiar to Western readers in Sir Edwin Arnold's *Light of Asia*. Here, then, we shall relate the life of Buddha in some detail, from the various sources indicated,[1] regardless of the fact that these presuppose a doctrinal development which can only have taken place after the Buddha's death; for the miraculous and mythological elements are always very transparent and artistic. The history of the Buddha begins with the resolve of the individual Brāhman Sumedha, long ago, to become a Buddha in some future birth, that he might spread abroad saving truth for the help of suffering humanity. Countless ages ago this same Sumedha, retiring one day to the upper chamber of his house, seated himself and fell into thought: "Behold, I am subject to birth, to

[1] Chiefly the *Nidānakathā* (introduction to the Pāli Jātakas), the *Mahā Parinibbāna Sutta*, and the *Lalitavistara*.

decay, to disease, and to death; it is right, then, that I should strive to win the great deathless Nibbāna, which is tranquil, and free from birth and decay, sickness, and woe and weal. Surely there must be a road that leads to *Nibbāna* and releases man from existence." Accordingly, he gave away all his wealth and adopted the life of a hermit in the forest. At that time Dīpankara Buddha appeared in the world, and attained enlightenment. It happened one day that Dīpankara Buddha was to pass that way, and men were preparing the road for him. Sumedha asked and received permission to join in the work, and not only did he do so, but when Dīpankara came Sumedha laid himself down in the mud, so that the Buddha might walk upon his body without soiling his feet. Then Dīpankara's attention was aroused and he became aware of Sumedha's intention to become a Buddha, and, looking countless ages into the future, he saw that he would become a Buddha of the name of Gautama, and he prophesied accordingly. Thereupon Sumedha rejoiced, and, rejecting the immediate prospect of becoming an Arahat, as the disciple of Dīpankara, "Let me rather," he said, "like Dīpankara, having risen to the supreme knowledge of the truth, enable all men to enter the ship of truth, and thus I may bear them over the Sea of Existence, and then only let me realize Nibbāna myself."

Incarnation of the Buddha

When Dīpankara with all his followers had passed by Sumedha examined the Ten Perfections indispensable to Buddahood, and determined to practise them in his future births. So it came to pass, until in the last of these births the Bodhisatta was reborn as Prince Vessantara, who exhibited the Perfection of Supernatural Generosity, and in due time passed away and dwelt in the Heaven of Delight. When the time had come for the Bodhisatta to return to earth for the last time, the deities of the ten thousand world-systems assembled together, and, approaching the Bodhisatta in the Heaven of Delight, said: "Now has the moment come, O Blessed One, for thy Buddhahood; now has the time, O Blessed One, arrived!" Then the Bodhisatta considered the time, the continent, the district, the tribe, and the mother, and, having determined these, he assented, saying: "The time has come, O Blessed Ones, for me to become a Buddha." And even as he was walking there in the Grove of Gladness he departed thence and was conceived in the womb of the lady Mahā Māyā. The manner of the conception is explained as follows. At the time of the midsummer festival in Kapilavatthu, Mahā Māyā, the lady of Suddhodana, lay on her couch and dreamed a dream. She dreamt that the Four Guardians of the Quarters lifted her up and bore her away to the Himālayas, and there she was bathed in the Anotatta lake and lay down to rest on a heavenly couch within a golden mansion on Silver Hill. Then the Bodhisatta, who had become a beautiful white elephant, bearing in his trunk a white lotus flower, approached from the North, and seemed to touch her right side and to enter her womb. The next day when she awoke she related the dream to her lord, and it was interpreted by the Brāhmans as follows: that the lady had conceived a man-child who, should he adopt the life of a householder, would become a Universal Monarch; but if he adopted the religious life he would become a Buddha, removing from the world the veils of ignorance and sin.

It should be told also that at the moment of the incarnation the heavens and the earth showed signs, the dumb spake, the lame walked, all men began to speak kindly, musical instruments played of themselves, the earth was covered with lotus flowers, and lotuses descended from the sky, and every tree put forth its flowers. From the moment of the incarnation, moreover, four angels guarded the Bodhisatta and his mother, to shield them from all harm. The mother was not weary, and she could perceive the child in her womb as plainly as one may see the thread in a transparent gem. The Lady Mahā Māyā carried the Bodhisatta thus for ten lunar months; at the end of that time she expressed a wish to visit her family in Devadaha; and she set out on the journey. On the way from Kapilavatthu to Devadaha there is a pleasure-grove of Sāl-trees belonging to the people of both cities, and at the time of the queen's journey it was filled with fruits and flowers. Here the queen desired to rest, and she was carried to the greatest of the Sāl-trees and stood beneath it. As she raised her hand to take hold of one of its branches the pains came upon her, and so standing and holding the branch of the Sāl-tree she was delivered. Four Brahmā angels received the child in a golden net, and showed it to the mother, saying: "Rejoice, O Lady! a great son is born to thee." The child stood upright, and took seven strides and cried: "I am supreme in the world. This is my last birth: henceforth there shall be no more birth for me!"

At one and the same time there came into being the Seven Connatal Ones, viz., the mother of Rāhula, Ānanda the favourite disciple, Channa, the attendant, Kanthaka, the horse, Kāludāyi, the minister, the great Bodhi tree, and the vases of Treasure.

Kāla Devala

Kāla Devala

When the Bodhisatta was born there was great rejoicing in the heaven of the Thirty-three Gods. At that time also a certain hermit by name Kāla Devala, an adept, sat in trance, visiting the heaven of the Thirty-three, and seeing the rejoicing he learnt its cause. Immediately he returned to earth, and repaired to the palace, asking to see the new-born child. The prince was brought in to salute the great adept, but he rose from his seat and bowed to the child, saying: "I may not work my own destruction"; for assuredly if the child had been made to bow to his feet, the hermit's head would have split atwain, so much had it been against the order of nature. Now the adept cast backward and forward his vision over forty æons, and perceived that the child would become a Buddha in his present birth: but he saw that he himself would die before the Great Enlightenment came to pass, and being reborn in the heaven of No-form, a hundred or even a thousand Buddhas might appear before he found the opportunity to become the disciple of any; and seeing this, he wept. He sent, however, for his nephew, then a householder, and advised him to become a hermit, for at the end of thirty-five years he would receive the teaching of the Buddha; and that same nephew, by name Nālaka, afterwards entered the order and became an Arahat.

On the fifth day the name ceremonies were performed, and the child was call Siddhattha (Siddhārtha). On this occasion eight soothsayers were present amongst the Brāhmans, and of these seven foresaw that the child would become either a Universal Monarch or a Buddha, but the eighth, by name Kondañña, predicted that he would of a surety become a Buddha. This same

Kondañña afterwards belonged to the five who became the Buddha's first disciples.

Then the prince's father inquired: "What will my son see, that will be the occasion of his forsaking the household life?" "The Four Signs," was the answer, "a man worn out by age, a sick man, a dead body, and a hermit." Then the king resolved that no such sights should ever be seen by his son, for he did not wish him to become a Buddha, but desired that he should rule the whole world; and he appointed an innumerable and magnificent guard and retinue to protect his son from any such illuminating omens, and to occupy his mind with worldly pleasures.

Seven days after the child's birth the Lady Mahā Māyā died, and was reborn in the heaven of the Thirty-three Gods, and Siddhattha was placed in the charge of his aunt and stepmother the Matron Gautamī. And now came to pass another miracle, on the occasion of the Ploughing Festival. For while the king was inaugurating the ploughing with his own hands, and the nurses were preparing food, the Bodhisatta took his seat beneath a Jambu-tree, and, crossing his legs like a yogī, he exercised the first degree of contemplation; and though time passed, the shadow of the tree did not move. When the king beheld that miracle he bowed to the child, and cried: "This, dear one, is the second homage paid to thee!"

As the Bodhisatta grew up his father built for him three palaces, respectively of nine, five, and seven stories, and here he dwelt according to the seasons. Here the Bodhisatta was surrounded by every luxury, and thousands of dancing-girls were appointed for his service and entertainment. Taken to the teachers of writing and the other arts, he soon surpassed them all, and he excelled in all martial exercises.

The Prince Marries

At the age of sixteen, the king sought for a wife for his son; for by domestic ties he hoped to attach him still more to the worldly life. The prince had already experienced the desire to become a hermit. But in order, as the books say, to conform with the custom of former Bodhisattas, he consented to marry, if it were possible to find a girl of perfect manners, wholly truthful, modest, congenial to his temperament, and of pure and honourable birth, young and fair, but not proud of her beauty, charitable, contented in self-denial, tender as a sister or a mother, not desiring music, scents, festivities or wine, pure in thought and word and deed, the last to sleep and the first to rise in the house where she should dwell. Brāhmans were sent far and wide to seek for such a maiden amongst the Sākya families. At last the choice fell upon Siddhattha's cousin Yasodharā, the daughter of Suprabuddha of Kapilavatthu. And the king devised a plan to engage the young man's heart. He made ready a display of beautiful jewels which Siddhattha was to distribute amongst the Sākya maidens. So it came to pass: but when all the jewels had been bestowed, Yasodharā came late, and there was nothing left for her. Thinking that she was despised, she asked if there was no gift meant for her. Siddhattha said there was no such thought in his mind, and he sent for other rings and bracelets and gave them to her. She said: "Is it becoming for me to receive such gifts?" and he answered: "They are mine to give." And so she went her way. Then Suddhodana's spies reported that

Siddhattha had cast his eyes only upon Yasodharā, and had entered into conversation with her. A message was sent to Suprabuddha asking for his daughter. The answer came that daughters of the family were only given to those who excelled in the various arts and martial exercises, and "could this be the case with one whose whole life had been spent in the luxury of a palace?" Suddhodana was grieved because his son was considered to be indolent and weak. The Bodhisatta perceived his mood, and asked its cause, and being informed, he reassured his father, and advised that a contest in martial exercises should be proclaimed, and all the Sākya youths invited. So it was done. Then the Bodhisatta proved himself the superior of all, first in the arts of literature and numbers, then in wrestling and archery, and each and all of the sixty-four arts and sciences. When Siddhattha had thus shown his prowess, Suprabuddha brought his daughter to be affianced to the prince, and the marriage was celebrated with all magnificence. Amongst the defeated Sākyas were two cousins of the Buddha, the one Ānanda, who afterwards became the favourite disciple, the other Devadatta, whose growing envy and jealousy made him the life-long enemy of the victor.

The Four Signs

The Bodhisatta is never entirely forgetful of his high calling. Yet it is needful that he should be reminded of the approaching hour; and to this end the cosmic Buddhas made audible to Siddhattha, even as he sat and listened to the singing of the dancing-girls, the message—"Recollect thy vow, to save all living things: the time is at hand: this alone is the purpose of thy birth." And thus as the

The Four Signs

Bodhisatta sat in his beautiful palaces day after day surrounded by all the physical and intellectual pleasures that could be devised by love or art, he felt an ever more insistent call to the fulfilment of his spiritual destiny. And now were to be revealed to him the Four Signs which were to be the immediate cause of the Great Renunciation. The Bodhisatta desired one day to visit the royal pleasure-gardens. His father appointed a day, and gave command that the city should be swept and garnished, and that every inauspicious sight should be removed, and none allowed to appear save those who were young and fair. The day came, and the prince drove forth with the charioteer Channa. But the Devas [1] are not to be diverted from their ends: and a certain one assumed the form of an old and decrepit man, and stood in the midst of the street. "What kind of a man is this?" said the Prince, and Channa replied, "Sire, it is an aged man, bowed down by years." "Are all men then," said the prince, "or this man only, subject to age?" The charioteer could but answer that youth must yield to age in every living being. "Shame, then, on life!" said the prince, "since the decay of every living thing is notorious!" and he turned to his palace in sadness. When all that had taken place was reported to the king, he exclaimed: "This is my ruin!" and he devised more and more amusements, music and plays calculated to divert Siddhattha's mind from the thought of leaving the world.

Again the prince drove out to visit the pleasure-gardens of Kapilavatthu: and on the way they met a sick man, thin and weak and scorched by fever. When the meaning of this spectacle was made clear by the charioteer, the

[1] Devas, the Olympian deities, headed by Sakka, who dwell in the Heaven of the Thirty-three: spiritual powers generally, 'gods.'

Bodhisatta exclaimed again: "If health be frail as the substance of a dream, who then can take delight in joy and pleasure?" And the car was turned, and he returned to the palace.

A third time the prince went forth, and now they met a corpse followed by mourners weeping and tearing their hair. "Why does this man lie on a bier," said the prince, "and why do they weep and beat their breasts?" "Sire," said the charioteer, "he is dead, and may never more see his father or mother, children or home: he has departed to another world." "Woe then to such youth as is destroyed by age," exclaimed the prince, "and woe to the health that is destroyed by innumerable maladies! Woe to the life so soon ended! Would that sickness, age, and death might be for ever bound! Turn back again, that I may seek a way of deliverance."

When the Bodhisatta drove forth for the last time, he met a hermit, a mendicant friar. This Bhikkhu was self-possessed, serene, dignified, self-controlled, with downcast eyes, dressed in the garb of a religious and carrying a beggar's bowl. "Who is this man of so calm a temper?" said the prince, "clothed in russet garments, and of such dignified demeanour?" "Sire," said the charioteer, "He is a Bhikkhu, a religious, who has abandoned all longings and leads a life of austerity, he lives without passion or envy, and begs his daily food." The Bodhisatta answered "That is well done, and makes me eager for the same course of life: to become religious has ever been praised by the wise, and this shall be my refuge and the refuge of others and shall yield the fruit of life, and immortality." Again the Bodhisatta returned to his palace.

When all these things had been reported to Suddhodana, he surrounded the prince's pleasure-palace by triple walls and redoubled the guards, and he commanded the women of the palace to exercise all their charms, to divert the prince's thoughts by music and pleasure: and it was done accordingly. And now Yasodharā was troubled by portentous dreams: she dreamed that the land was devastated by storms, she saw herself naked and mutilated, her beautiful jewels broken, the sun the moon and the stars fell from the sky and Mount Meru sank into the great deep. When she related these dreams to the Bodhisatta, he replied in gentle tones: "You need not fear. It is to the good and the worthy alone that such dreams come, never to the base. Rejoice! for the purport of all these dreams is that the bond of mortality shall be loosed, the veils of ignorance shall be rent asunder, for I have completely fulfilled the way of wisdom, and every one that has faith in me shall be saved from the three evils, without exception."

The Great Renunciation

The Bodhisatta reflected that he ought not to go forth as a Wanderer without giving notice to his father; and therefore he sought the king by night, and said: "Sire, the time is at hand for my going forth, do not hinder me, but permit me to depart." The king's eyes were charged with tears, and he answered: "What is there needful to change thy purpose? Tell me whatever thou desirest and it shall be thine, be it myself, the palace, or the kingdom." The Bodhisatta replied, "Sire, I desire four things, pray thee grant them: the first, to remain for ever in possession of the fresh colour of youth; the second, that sickness may never attack me; the third, that my life may have no term; the last, that I may not be subject to decay." When the king heard these words, he was overcome by grief, for the prince desired what it was not possible for a man to bestow. Then the Bodhisatta continued: "If then I cannot avoid old age, sickness, death and decay, grant at least this one thing, that when I leave this world I may nevermore be subject to rebirth." And when the king could give no better answer, he granted his son's desire. But the next day he established an additional guard of five hundred young men of the Sākyas at each of the four gates of the palace, while the Matron Gautamī established an amazon guard within; for the king would not allow his son to depart with a free will.

At the same time the captains of the Yakkhas[1] assembled together, and they said "To-day, my friends, the Bodhisatta is to go forth; hasten to do him service."

The Four Great Kings[2] commanded the Yakkhas to bear up the feet of the prince's horse. The Thirty-three Devas likewise assembled, and Sakka ordered their services, so that one should cast a heavy sleep on all the men and women and young men and maidens of Kapilavatthu, and another should silence the noise of the elephants, horses, camels, bulls and other beasts; and others constituted themselves an escort, to cast down a rain of flowers and perfume the air. Sakka himself announced that he would open the gates and show the way.

On the morning of the day of the going forth, when the Bodhisatta was being attired, a message was brought to him that Yasodharā had borne him a son. He did not rejoice, but he said: "A bond has come into being, a hindrance for me." And the child received the name of Rāhula or 'Hindrance' accordingly. The same day the Bodhisatta drove again in the city, and a certain noble

[1] Yakkhas, nature spirits.

[2] The Four Kings, Guardians of the Four Quarters.

virgin, by name Kisā Gotamī, stood on the roof of her palace and beheld the beauty and majesty of the future Buddha as he passed by, and she made a song:

> *Blessed indeed is the mother, blessed indeed the father,*
> *Blessed indeed is the wife, whose is a lord so glorious!*

On hearing this the Bodhisatta thought: "She does but say that the heart of a mother, or a father, or a wife is gladdened by such a sight. But by what can every heart attain to lasting happiness and peace?" The answer arose in his mind: "When the fire of lust is extinguished, then there is peace; and when the fires of resentment and glamour are dead, then there is peace. Sweet is the lesson this singer has taught me, for it is the Nibbāna of peace that I have sought. This day I shall relinquish the household life, nothing will I seek but Nibbāna itself." And taking from his neck the string of pearls he sent it as a teacher's fee to Kisā Gotamī. But she thought that the prince loved her, and sent her a gift because of his love. That night the singers and the dancing-girls exerted themselves to please the prince: fair as the nymphs of heaven, they danced and sang and played. But the Bodhisatta, his heart being estranged from sin, took no pleasure in the entertainment, and fell asleep. And the women seeing that he slept, laid aside their instruments and fell asleep likewise. And when the lamps that were fed with scented oil were on the point of dying, the Bodhisatta awoke, and he saw the girls that had seemed so fair, in all the disarray of slumber. And the king's son, seeing them thus dishevelled and disarrayed, breathing heavily, yawning and sprawling in unseemly attitudes, was moved to scorn. "Such is the true nature of women," he thought, "but a man is deceived by dress and jewels and is deluded by a woman's beauties. If a man would but consider the natural state of women and the change that comes upon them in sleep, assuredly he would not cherish his folly; but he is smitten from a right will, and so succumbs to passion." And therewith he resolved to accomplish the Great Renunciation that very night, and at that very time, for it seemed to him that every mode of existence on earth or in heaven most resembled a delay in a house already become the prey of devouring flames; and his mind was irresistibly directed towards the state of those who have renounced the world.

The Bodhisatta therefore rose from his couch and called for Channa; and the charioteer, who was sleeping with his head on the threshold, rose and said: "Sire, I am here." Then the Bodhisatta said: "I am resolved to accomplish the Great Renunciation to-day; saddle my horse." And Channa went out to the stable and saddled Kanthaka: and the horse knew what was the reason of his being saddled, and neighed for joy, so that the whole city would have been aroused, had it not been that the Devas subdued the sound, so that no one heard it. Now while Channa was away in the stable yard, the Bodhisatta thought: "I will take one look at my son," and he went to the door of Yasodharā's chamber. The Mother of Rāhula was asleep on a bed strewn thick with jasmine flowers, and her hand was resting on her son's head. The Bodhisatta stopped with his foot upon the threshold, for he thought: "If I lift her hand to take up my son, she will awake, and my departure will be hindered. I will return and see him after I have attained enlightenment." Then he went forth, and seeing the horse ready saddled,

II

THE DEPARTURE OF BUDDHA

NANDA LÂL BOSE

Page 24

he said, "Good Kanthaka, do thou save me this night, to the end that I may become a Buddha by thy help and may save the worlds of men and gods." Kanthaka neighed again, but the sound of his voice was heard by none.

So the Bodhisatta rode forth, followed by Channa: the Yakkhas bore up the feet of Kanthaka so that they made no sound, and when they came to the guarded gates the angel standing thereby caused them to open silently.

At that moment Māra the Fiend appeared in the air, and tempted the Bodhisatta, exclaiming: "Go not forth, my lord! for within seven days from this the Wheel of Sovereignty will appear, and will make you ruler of the four continents and the myriad islands. Go not forth!" The Bodhisatta replied: "Māra! well I know that this is sooth. But I do not seek the sovereignty of the world. I would become a Buddha, to make tens of thousands of worlds rejoice." And so the tempter left him, but resolved to follow him ever like a shadow, to lay hold of the occasion, if ever a thought of anger or desire should arise in the Bodhisatta's heart. It was on the full-moon day of Āsādha when the prince departed from the city. His progress was accompanied by pomp and glory, for the gods and angels bore myriads of torches before and behind him, and a rain of beautiful flowers was cast down from the heaven of Indra, so that the very flanks of Kanthaka were covered. In this way the Bodhisatta advanced a great distance, until they reached and passed over the river Anomā. When they were come to the other side, the Bodhisatta alighted upon the sandy shore and said to Channa: "Good Channa, the time has come when thou must return, and take with thee all my jewels together with Kanthaka, for I am about to become a hermit and a wanderer in these forests. Grieve not for me, but mourn for those who stay behind, bound by longings of which the fruit is sorrow. It is my resolve to seek the highest good this very day, for what confidence have we in life when death is ever at hand? And do you comfort the king, and so speak with him that he may not even remember me, for where affection is lost, there is no sorrow." But Channa protested, and prayed the Bodhisatta to take pity upon the king, and upon Yasodharā and on the city of Kapilavatthu. But again the Bodhisatta answered: "Even were I to return to my kindred by reason of affection, yet we should be divided in the end by death. The meeting and parting of living things is as when the clouds having come together drift apart again, or as when the leaves are parted from the trees. There is nothing we may call our own in a union that is nothing but a dream. Therefore, since it is so, go, and grieve not, and say to the people of Kapilavatthu: 'Either he will soon return, the conqueror of age and death, or he himself will fail and perish.'" Then Channa too would have become a hermit: but the Bodhisatta answered again: "If your love is so great, yet go, deliver the message, and return."

Then the Bodhisatta took the sharp sword that Channa bore and severed with it his long locks and jewelled crest and cast them into the waters: and at the moment when he felt the need of a hermit's dress, there appeared an angel in the guise of a hunter clad in the russet robes of a forest-sage and he, receiving the white muslin garments of the prince, rendered to him the dark red robes in return, and so departed.

Now Kanthaka attended to all that had been said, and he licked the Bodhisatta's feet; and the prince spoke to him as to a friend, and said: "Grieve not, O Kanthaka, for thy perfect equine nature has been proved—bear with it, and soon thy pain shall bear its fruit." But Kanthaka, thinking: "From this day forth I shall never see my master more," went out of their sight, and there died of a broken heart and was reborn in the Heaven of the Thirty-three. Then Channa's grief was doubled; and torn by the second sorrow of the death of Kanthaka, he returned to the city weeping and wailing, and the Bodhisatta was left alone.

The Search for The Way of Escape

The Bodhisatta remained for a week in the Mango-grove of Anupiyā, and thereafter he proceeded to Rājagaha, the chief town of Magadha. He begged his food from door to door, and the beauty of his person cast the whole city into commotion. When this was made known to the king Bimbisāra, he went to the place where the Bodhisatta was sitting, and offered to bestow upon him the whole kingdom: but again the Bodhisatta refused the royal throne, for he had already abandoned all in the hope of attaining enlightenment, and did not desire a worldly empire. But he granted the king's request that when he had found the way, he would preach it first in that same kingdom.

It is said that when the Bodhisatta entered a hermitage for the first time (and this was before he proceeded to Rājagaha) he found the sages practising many and strange penances, and he inquired their meaning, and what was the purpose that each endeavoured to achieve and received the answer—"By such penances endured for a time, by the higher they attain heaven, and by the lower, favourable fruit in the world of men: by pain they come at last to happiness, for pain, they say, is the root of merit." But to him it seemed that here there was no way of escape—here too, men endured misery for the sake of happiness, and that happiness itself, rightly understood, consisted in pain, for it must ever be subject to mortality and to rebirth. "It is not the effort itself which I blame," he said, "which casts aside the base and follows a higher path of its own: but the wise in sooth, by all this heavy toil, ought to attain to the state where nothing ever needs to be done again. And since it is the mind that controls the body, it is thought alone that should be restrained. Neither purity of food nor the waters of a sacred river can cleanse the heart: water is but water, but the true place of pilgrimage is the virtue of the virtuous man."

And now, rejecting with courtesy the king's offers, the Bodhisatta made his way to the hermitage of the renowned sage Ālāra Kālāma and became his disciple, learning the successive degrees of ecstatic meditation. Ālāra taught, it is clear, the doctrine of the Ātman, saying that the sage who is versed in the Supreme Self, "having abolished himself by himself, sees that nought exists and is called a Nihilist: then, like a bird from its cage, the soul escaping from the body, is declared to be set free: this is that supreme Brahman, constant, eternal, and without distinctive signs, which the wise who know reality declare to be liberation." But Gautama (and it is by this name that the books now begin to speak of the Bodhisatta) ignores the phrase "without distinctive signs," and with verbal justification quarrels with the animistic and dualistic terminology of soul and body: a liberated soul, he argued, is still a soul, and whatever the condition it attains, must be subject to rebirth, "and since each successive renunciation is held to be still accompanied by qualities, I maintain that the absolute attainment of our end is only to be found in the abandonment of everything." [1]

And now leaving the hermitages of Rājagaha the Bodhisatta, seeking something beyond, repaired to a forest near to the village of Uruvelā and there abode on the pure bank of the Nairanjana. There five wanderers, begging hermits, came to him, for they were persuaded that ere long he would attain enlightenment: and the leader of these was Kondañña, the erstwhile Brāhman soothsayer who had prophesied at the festival of the Bodhisatta's name day. And now thinking: "This may be the means to conquer birth and death," Gautama for six years practised there an austere rule of fasting and of mortification, so that his glorious body wasted away to skin and bone. He brought himself to feed on a single sesamum seed or a grain of rice, until one day, as he paced to and fro, he was overcome by a severe pain, and fainted and fell. Then certain of the Devas exclaimed "Gautama is dead!" and some reported it to Suddhodana the king at Kapilavatthu. But he replied: "I may not believe it. Never would my son die without attaining enlightenment." For he did not forget the miracle at the foot of the Jambu-tree, nor the day when the great sage Kāla Devala had been compelled to offer homage to the child. And the Bodhisatta recovered, and stood up; and again the gods reported it to the king. Now the fame of the Bodhisatta's exceeding penances became spread abroad, as the sound of a great bell is

[1] We recognize here the critical moment where Buddhist and Brāhman thought part company on the question of the Ātman. Whether Ālāra failed to emphasize the negative aspect of the doctrine of the Brahman, or Gautama (who is represented as so far entirely innocent of Brāhmanical philosophy) failed to distinguish the neuter Brahman from the god Brahmā, we cannot tell. The question is discussed at greater length in Part III, Chapter IV. (p. 198 f.)

heard in the sky. But he perceived that mortification was not the road to enlightenment and to liberation—"that was the true way that I found beneath the Jambu-tree, and it cannot be attained by one who has lost his strength." And so again the Great Being resolved to beg his food in towns and villages, that his health and strength might be restored. This was in the thirtieth year of the life of Gautama. But the Five Disciples reflected that Gautama had not been able to attain enlightenment even by six years of the most severe austerities, "and how can he do so now, when he goes and begs in the villages and eats of ordinary food?"—and they departed from him and went to the suburb of Benares called Isipatana.

The Supreme Enlightenment

Now during the time that Gautama had been dwelling in the forest near by Uruvelā, the daughter of the village headman, by name Sujātā, had been accustomed to make a daily offering of food to eight hundred Brāhmans, making the prayer—"May the Bodhisatta at length, receive an offering of food from me, attain enlightenment, and become a Buddha!" And now that the time had come when he desired to receive nourishing food, a Deva appeared in the night to Sujātā and announced that the Bodhisatta had put aside his austerities and desired to partake of good and nourishing food, "and now shall your prayer be accomplished." Then Sujātā with all speed arose early and went to her father's herd. Now for a long time she had been accustomed to take the milk of a thousand cows and to feed therewith five hundred, and again with their milk to feed two hundred and fifty, and so on until eight only were fed with the milk of the rest, and this she called

III

SUJATA AND THE BOWL OF MILK-RICE

Nanda Lāl Bose

Page 30

"working the milk in and in." It was the full-moon day of the month of May when she received the message of the gods, and rose early, and milked the eight cows, and took the milk and boiled it in new pans, and prepared milk-rice. At the same time she sent her maid Punnā to the foot of the great tree where she had been wont to lay her daily offerings. Now the Bodhisatta, knowing that he would that day attain Supreme Enlightenment, was sitting at the foot of the tree, awaiting the hour for going forth to beg his food; and such was his glory that all the region of the East was lit up. The girl thought that it was the spirit of the tree who would deign to receive the offering with his own hands. When she returned to Sujātā and reported this, Sujātā embraced her and bestowed on her the jewels of a daughter, and exclaimed, "Henceforth thou shalt be to me in the place of an elder daughter!" And sending for a golden vessel she put the well-cooked food therein, and covered it with a pure white cloth, and bore it with dignity to the foot of the great Nigrodha-tree; and there she too saw the Bodhisatta, and believed him to be the spirit of the tree. Sujātā approached him, and placed the vessel in his hand, and she met his gaze and said: "My lord, accept what I have offered thee," and she added "May there arise to thee as much of joy as has come to me!" and so she departed.

The Bodhisatta took the golden bowl, and went down to the bank of the river and bathed, and then dressing himself in the garb of an Arahat, he again took his seat, with his face towards the East. He divided the rice into forty-nine portions, and this food sufficed for his nourishment during the forty-nine days following the Enlightenment. When he had finished eating the milk rice, he took the golden vessel and cast it into the stream, saying "If I am able to attain Enlightenment to-day, let this pot go up stream, but if not, may it go down stream." And he threw it into the water, and it went swiftly up the river until it reached the whirlpool of the Black Snake King, and there it sank.

The Bodhisatta spent the heat of the day in a grove of Sāl-trees beside the stream. But in the evening he made his way to the foot of the tree of wisdom, and there, making the resolution: "Though my skin, my nerves and my bones should waste away and my life-blood dry, I will not leave this seat until I have attained Supreme Enlightenment," he took his seat with his face towards the East.

At this moment Māra the Fiend became aware that the Bodhisatta had taken his seat with a view to attaining Perfect Enlightenment; and thereupon, summoning the hosts of the demons, and mounting his elephant of war, he advanced towards the Tree of Wisdom. And there stood Mahā Brahmā holding above the Bodhisatta a white canopy of state, and Sakka, blowing the great trumpet, and with them were all the companies of gods and angels. But so terrible was the array of Māra that there was not one of all this host of the Devas that dared to remain to face him. The Great Being was left alone.

First of all, however, Māra assumed the form of a messenger, with disordered garments, and panting in haste, bearing a letter from the Sākya princes. And in the letter it was written that Devadatta had usurped the kingdom of Kapilavatthu and entered the Bodhisatta's palace, taken his goods and his wife, and cast Suddhodana into prison and they prayed him to return to restore peace and order. But the Bodhisatta reflected lust it was that had caused Devadatta thus to misuse the women, malice had made him imprison Suddhodana, while the Sākyas neutralized by cowardice failed to defend their King: and so reflecting on the folly and weakness of the natural heart, his own resolve to attain a higher and better state was strengthened and confirmed.[1]

Failing in this device, Māra now advanced to the assault with all his hosts, striving to overcome the Bodhisatta first by a terrible whirlwind, then by a storm of rain, causing a mighty flood: but the hem of the Bodhisatta's robe was not stirred, nor did a single drop of water reach him. Then Māra cast down upon him showers of rocks, and a storm of deadly and poisoned weapons, burning ashes and coals, and a storm of scorching sand and flaming mud; but all these missiles only fell at the Bodhisatta's feet as a rain of heavenly flowers, or hung in the air like a canopy above his head. Nor could he be moved by an onset of thick and fourfold darkness. Then finding all these means to fail, he addressed the Bodhisatta and said: "Arise, Siddhattha, from that seat, for it is not thine, but mine!" The Bodhisatta replied, "Māra! thou hast not accomplished the Ten Perfections, nor even the minor virtues. Thou hast not sought for knowledge, nor for the salvation of the world. The seat is mine." Then Māra was enraged, and cast at the Bodhisatta his Sceptre-javelin, which cleaves asunder a pillar of solid rock like a tender shoot of cane: and all the demon hosts hurled masses of rock. But the javelin hung in the air like a canopy, and the masses of rock fell down as garlands of flowers.

Then the Great Being said to Māra: "Māra, who is the witness that thou hast given alms?" Māra stretched forth his hand, and a shout arose from the demon hosts, of a

[1] *Cf.*, "The sages of old first got Tao for themselves, and then got it for others. Before you possess this yourself, what leisure have you to attend to the doings of wicked men?"—Chuang Tzu. See also p. 126.

thousand voices crying: "I am his witness!" Then the Fiend addressed the Bodhisatta, and enquired: "Siddhattha! who is the witness that thou has given alms?" and the Great Being answered: "Māra thou hast many and living witnesses that thou hast given alms, and no such witnesses have I. But apart from the alms I have given in other births, I call upon this solid earth to witness to my supernatural generosity when I was born as Vessantara." And drawing his right hand from his robe, he stretched it forth to touch the earth, and said: "Do you or do you not witness to my supernatural generosity when I was born as Vessantara?" And the great Earth replied with a voice of thunder: "I am witness of that." And thereat the great elephant of Māra bowed down in adoration, and the demon hosts fled far away in dread.

Then Māra was abashed. But he did not withdraw, for he hoped to accomplish by another means what he could not effect by force: he summoned his three daughters, Tanhā, Rati, and Rāga, and they danced before the Bodhisatta like the swaying branches of a young leafy tree, using all the arts of seduction known to beautiful women. Again they offered him the lordship of the earth, and the companionship of beautiful girls: they appealed to him with songs of the season of spring, and exhibited their supernatural beauty and grace. But the Bodhisatta's heart was not in the least moved, and he answered:

Pleasure is brief as a flash of lightning
Or like an Autumn shower, only for a moment. . .
Why should I then covet the pleasures you speak of?
I see your bodies are full of all impurity:
Birth and death, sickness and age are yours.
I seek the highest prize, hard to attain by men—
The true and constant wisdom of the wise.

And when they could not shake the Bodhisatta's calm, they were filled with shame, and abashed: and they made a prayer to the Bodhisatta, wishing him the fruition of his labour:

That which your heart desires, may you attain,
And finding for yourself deliverance, deliver all! [1]

And now the hosts of heaven, seeing the army of Māra defeated, and the wiles of the daughters of Māra vain, assembled to honour the Conqueror, they came to the foot of the Tree of Wisdom and cried for joy:

The Blessed Buddha—he hath prevailed!
And the Tempter is overthrown!

The victory was achieved while the sun was yet above the horizon. The Bodhisatta sank into ever deeper and deeper thought. In the first watch of the night he reached the Knowledge of Former States of being, in the middle watch he obtained the heavenly eye of Omniscient Vision, and in the third watch he grasped the perfect understanding of the Chain of Causation which is the Origin of Evil, and thus at break of day he attained to Perfect Enlightenment. Therewith there broke from his lips the song of triumph:

Through many divers births I passed
Seeking in vain the builder of the house.[2]

[1] According to other books the temptation by the daughters of Māra is subsequent to the Supreme Enlightenment. In Plate A the Temptation by the Daughters of Māra takes place in the fifth week of the Forty-nine Days.

[2] The house is, of course, the house—or rather the prison—of individual existence: the builder of the house is desire (*tanhā*)—the will to enjoy and possess. See p. 97.

But O framer of houses, thou art found—
Never again shalt thou fashion a house for me!
Broken are all thy beams,
The king-post shattered!
My mind has passed into the stillness of Nibbāna
The ending of desire has been attained at last!

Innumerable wonders were manifest at this supreme hour. The earth quaked six times, and the whole universe was illuminated by the supernatural splendour of the sixfold rays that proceeded from the body of the seated Buddha. Resentment faded from the hearts of all men, all lack was supplied, the sick were healed, the chains of hell were loosed, and every creature of whatsoever sort found peace and rest.

The Forty-nine Days

Gautama, who was now Buddha, the Enlightened, remained seated and motionless for seven days, realizing the bliss of Nibbāna; and thereafter rising, he remained standing for seven days more, steadfastly regarding the spot where had been won the fruit of countless deeds of heroic virtue performed in past births: then for seven days more he paced to and fro along a cloistered path from West to East, extending from the throne beneath the Wisdom Tree to the place of the Steadfast Gazing; and again for seven days he remained seated in a god-wrought pavilion near to the same place, and there reviewed in detail, book by book, all that is taught in the *Abhidhamma Pitaka*, as well as the whole doctrine of causality; then for seven days more he sat beneath the Nigrodha tree of Sujātā's offering, meditating on the doctrine and the sweetness of Nibbāna—and according to some books it was at this time the temptation by the daughters of Māra took place;

1 2 3

4 5

6 7

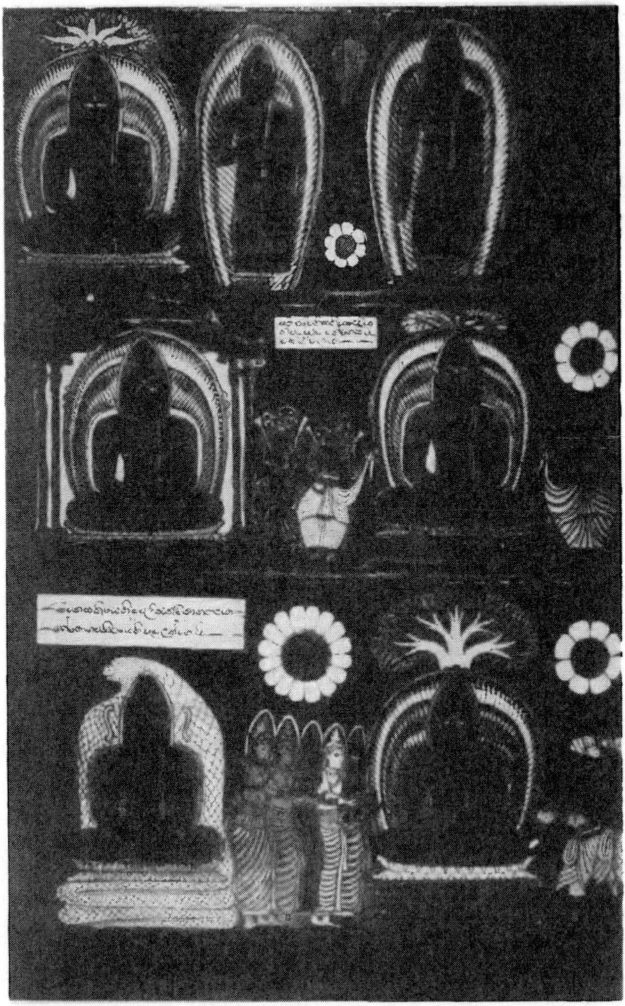

PLATE A 56

THE FORTY-NINE DAYS

From an illustrated manuscript, Sinhalese (18th century)

and then for seven days more while a terrible storm was raging, the snake king Mucalinda sheltered him with his sevenfold hood; and for seven days more he sat beneath a Rājāyatana tree, still enjoying the sweetness of liberation.

And so passed away seven weeks, during which the Buddha experienced no bodily wants, but fed on the joy of contemplation, the joy of the Eightfold Path, and the joy of its fruit, Nibbāna.

Only upon the last day of the seven weeks he desired to bathe and eat, and receiving water and a tooth-stick from the god Sakka, the Buddha bathed his face and seated himself at the foot of a tree. Now at that time two Brāhman merchants were travelling with a caravan from Orissa to the middle country, and a Deva, who had been a blood relation of the merchants' in a former life, stopped the carts, and moved their hearts to make an offering of rice and honey cakes to the Lord. They went up to him accordingly, saying: "O Blessed One, have mercy upon us, and accept this food." Now the Buddha no longer possessed a bowl, and as the Buddhas never receive an offering in their hands, he reflected how he should take it. Immediately the Four Great Kings, the Regents of the Quarters appeared before him, each of them with a bowl; and in order that none of them should be disappointed, the Buddha received the four bowls, and placing them one above the other made them to be one, showing only the four lines round the mouth, and in this bowl the Blessed One received the food, and ate it, and gave thanks. The two merchants took refuge in the Buddha, the Norm, and the Order, and became professed disciples. Then the Buddha rose up and returned again to the tree of Sujātā's offering and there took his seat. And there, reflecting upon the depth of truth which he had found, a doubt arose in his mind whether it would be possible to make it known to others: and this doubt is experienced by every Buddha when he becomes aware of the Truth. But Mahā Brahmā exclaiming: "Alas! the world will be altogether lost!" came thither in haste, with all the Deva hosts, and besought the Master to proclaim the Truth; and he granted their prayer.[1]

The First Turning of the Wheel of the Law

Then he considered to whom he should first reveal the Truth, and he remembered Ālāra, his former teacher, and Uddaka, thinking that these great sages would quickly comprehend it; but upon close reflection he discovered that each of them had recently died. Then he thought of the Five Wanderers who had been his disciples, and upon reflection he saw that they were then residing in the Deer Park at Isipatana in Benares, and he resolved to go there. When the Five Wanderers, whose chief was Kondañña, perceived the Buddha afar off, they said together: "My friends, here comes Gautama the Bhikkhu. We owe him no reverence, since he has returned to a free use of the necessaries of life, and has recovered his strength, and beauty. However, as he is well-born, let us prepare him a seat." But the Blessed One perceived their thought,

[1] "Great truths do not take hold of the hearts of the masses. . . . And now, as all the world is in error, I, though I know the true path—how shall I, how shall I guide? If I know that I cannot succeed and yet try to force success, this would be but another source of error. Better, then, to desist and strive no more. But if I strive not, who will?"—Chuang Tzu. It is highly characteristic of the psychology of genius that when this doubt assails the Buddha he nevertheless immediately responds to a definite request for guidance; the moment the pupil puts the right questions, the teacher's doubts are resolved.

PLATE B

38

THE FIRST SERMON, "TURNING THE WHEEL OF THE LAW," AT BENARES

Gupta period (5th century A.D.), Sārnāth, Benares

and concentrating that love wherewith he was able to pervade the whole world, he directed it specially towards them. And this love being diffused in their hearts, as he approached, they could not adhere to their resolve, but rose from their seats and bowed before him in all reverence. But not knowing that he had attained enlightenment, they addressed him as 'Brother.' He, however, announced the Enlightenment, saying: "O Bhikkhus, do not address me as 'Brother,' for I have become a Buddha of clear vision even as those who came before."

Now the Buddha took his seat that had been prepared for him by the Five Wanderers, and he taught them the first sermon, which is called Setting in Motion the Wheel of the Law, or the Foundation of the Kingdom of Righteousness.

"There are two extremes which he who has gone forth ought not to follow—habitual devotion on the one hand to the passions, to the pleasures of sensual things, a low and pagan way (of seeking satisfaction), ignoble, unprofitable, fit only for the worldly-minded; and habitual devotion, on the other hand, to self-mortification, which is painful, ignoble, unprofitable. There is a Middle Path discovered by the Tathāgata [1]—a path which opens the eyes, and bestows understanding, which leads to peace, to insight, to the higher wisdom, to *Nirvāna*. Verily! it is this Ariyan Eightfold Path; that is to say Right Views, Right Aspirations, Right Speech, Right Conduct, Right mode of livelihood, Right Effort, Right Mindfulness, and Right Rapture.

"Now this is the Noble Truth as to suffering. Birth is

[1] That is by the Arahat; the title the Buddha always uses of himself. He does not call himself the Buddha; and his followers never address him as such.

attended with pain, decay is painful, disease is painful, death is painful. Union with the unpleasant is painful, painful is separation from the pleasant; and any craving unsatisfied, that, too, is painful. In brief, the five aggregates of clinging (that is, the conditions of individuality) are painful.

"Now this is the Noble Truth as to the origin of suffering. Verily! it is the craving thirst that causes the renewal of becomings, that is accompanied by sensual delights, and seeks satisfaction, now here now there—that is to say, the craving for the gratification of the senses, or the craving for prosperity.

"Now this is the Noble Truth as to the passing away of pain. Verily! it is the passing away so that no passion remains, the giving up, the getting rid of, the emancipation from, the harbouring no longer of this craving thirst.

"Now this is the Noble Truth as to the way that leads to the passing away of pain. Verily! it is this Ariyan Eightfold Path, that is to say, Right Views, Right Aspirations, Right Speech, conduct, and mode of livelihood, Right Effort, Right Mindfulness, and Right Rapture." [1]

Now of the band of Bhikkhus to whom the first sermon was thus preached, Kondañña immediately attained to the fruit of the First Path, and the four others attained to the same station in the course of the next four days. On the fifth day the Buddha summoned all five to his side, and delivered to them the second discourse called "On the Non-existence of Soul," of which the substance is related as follows:

"The body, O Bhikkhus, cannot be the eternal soul, for it tends toward destruction. Nor do sensation, perception,

[1] Rhys Davids, *Early Buddhism*, pp. 51, 52.

PLATE C 40

THE FIRST SERMON, "TURNING THE WHEEL OF THE LAW"

Nepalese gilt copper, 8th–9th century A.D.

Author's Collection

the predispositions, and consciousness together constitute the eternal soul, for were it so, it would not be the case that the consciousness likewise tends towards destruction. Or how think you, whether is form permanent or transitory? and whether are sensation, perception, and predispositions and consciousness permanent or transitory? 'They are transitory,' replied the Five. 'And that which is transitory, is it evil or good?' 'It is evil,' replied the Five. 'And that which is transitory, evil, and liable to change, can it be said that 'This is mine, this am I, this is my eternal soul?' 'Nay, verily, it cannot be so said,' replied the Five. 'Then, O Bhikkhus, it must be said of all physical form whatsoever, past or present or to be, subjective or objective, far or near, high or low, that "This is not mine, this am I not, this is not my eternal soul."' And in like manner of all sensations, perceptions, predispositions and consciousness, it must be said, 'These are not mine, these am I not, these are not my eternal soul.' And perceiving this, O Bhikkhus, the true disciple will conceive a disgust for physical form, and for sensation, perception, predispositions and consciousness, and so will be divested of desire; and thereby he is freed, and becomes aware that he is freed; and he knows that becoming is exhausted, that he has lived the pure life, that he has done what it behoved him do, and that he has put off mortality for ever."

And through this discourse the minds of the Five were perfectly enlightened, and each of them attained to Nibbāna, so that at this time there existed five Arahats in the world, with the Buddha himself the sixth. The next day a young man of the name of Yasa, together with fifty-four companions likewise attained illumination, and thus there were sixty persons beside the Master himself, who had attained to Arahatta. These sixty the Master sent forth in diverse directions, with the command: "Go forth, O Bhikkhus, preaching and teaching." But he himself proceeded to Uruvelā, and upon the way he received into the Order thirty young noblemen, and these also he sent forth far and wide. At Uruvelā the Master prevailed against three Brāhmanical ascetics, fire-worshippers, and received them into the Order with all their disciples, and established them in Arahatta. The chief of these was known as Uruvelā Kassapa. And when they were seated on the Gayā Scarp, he preached the Third Sermon called the Discourse on Fire:

"All things, O Bhikkhus are on fire. And what, O Bhikkhus, are all these things that are on fire? The eye is on fire, forms are on fire, eye-consciousness is on fire, impressions received by the eye are on fire; and whatever sensation—pleasant, unpleasant, or neutral—originates in the impressions received by the eye, is likewise on fire.

"And with what are all these on fire? I say with the fire of lust of resentment, and the fire of glamour (*rāga*, *dosa*, and *moha*); with birth, old age, death, lamentation, misery, grief and despair they are afire.

"And so with the ear, with the nose, and with the tongue, and in the case of touch. The mind too, is on fire, thoughts are on fire; and mind-consciousness, and the impressions received by the mind, and the sensations that arise from the impressions that the mind receives, these too are on fire.

"And with what are they on fire? I say with the fire of lust, with the fire of resentment, and the fire of glamour; with birth, old age, death, sorrow, lamentation, misery, and grief and despair, they are afire.

"And seeing this, O Bhikkhus, the true disciple conceives

PLATE D 42

THE BUDDHA TEACHING

Japanese lacquered wood image, 8th century. Kozan-ji Temple, Kyoto.

From the Kokka

disgust for the eye, for forms, for eye-consciousness, for impressions received by the eye, and for the sensations arising therein; and for the ear, the nose, the tongue, and for the sense of touch, and for the mind, and for thoughts and mind-consciousness, impressions, and sensations. And so he is divested of desire, and thereby he is freed, and is aware that he is freed, and he knows that becoming is exhausted, that he has lived the pure life, that he has done what it behoved him to do, and that he has put off mortality for ever." [1]

And in the course of the Sermon upon Fire, the minds of the thousand Bhikkhus assembled there were freed from attachment and delivered from the stains, and so attained to Arahatta and Nibbāna.

Conversion of Sāriputta and Mogallāna

And now the Buddha, attended by the thousand Arahats of whom the chief was Uruvelā Kassapa, repaired to the Palm Grove near by Rājagaha, to redeem the promise that was made to Bimbisāra the king. When it was reported to the king: "The Master is come," he hastened to the grove, and fell at the Buddha's feet, and when he had thus offered homage he and all his retinue sat down. Now the king was not able to know whether the Buddha had become the disciple of Uruvelā Kassapa, or Uruvelā Kassapa of the Buddha, and to resolve the doubt Uruvelā Kassapa bowed down to the Master's feet, saying: "The Blessed Lord is my master, and I am the disciple." All the people cried out at the great power of the Buddha, exclaiming: "Even Uruvelā Kassapa has broken through the net of delusion and has yielded to the follower of the

[1] *Mahāvagga*, I. 21 (a summary of the version by Warren, *Buddhism in Translations*, p. 351).

Buddhas of the past!" To show that this was not the first time that Kassapa the Great had yielded to him the Blessed One recited the *Mahā Nārada Kassapa Jātaka*; and he proclaimed the Four Noble Truths. The king of Magadha, with nearly all his retinue entered the First Path, and those who did not so, became lay disciples. The king gave a great endowment to the Order, with Buddha at their head, and confirmed it by the pouring out of water. And when the Master had thus received the Bambu-grove Monastery, he returned thanks, and rose from his seat, and repaired thither. Now at this time there dwelt two Brāhmanical ascetics near to Rājagaha, by name Sāriputta and Mogallāna. Now Sāriputta observed the venerable Arahat Assaji on his begging round, and remarked the dignity and grace of his demeanour; and when the Elder had obtained alms, and was departing from the city, Sāriputta found occasion to speak with him, and enquired who was his teacher, and what the accepted doctrine. Assaji replied, "Brother, there is a great Sākya monk, to follow whom I left the world and this Blessed One is my teacher, and the doctrine I approve is his." Then Sāriputta enquired: "What then, venerable sir, is your teacher's doctrine?" "Brother," replied Assaji, "I am a novice and a beginner, and it is not long that I have retired from the world to adopt the discipline and Doctrine. Therefore I may only set forth to you the doctrine in brief, and give the substance of it in a few words." Then the venerable Assaji repeated to Sāriputta the Wanderer, the following verse:

What things soever are produced from causes,
Of these the Buddha hath revealed the cause,
And likewise how they cease to be:
'Tis this the great adept proclaims.

And hearing this exposition of the Doctrine, Sāriputta the Wanderer attained to a clear and distinct perception of the Truth that whatever is subject to origination is subject also to cessation.[1] And thus Sāriputta attained to the First Path. Then returning to Mogallāna, he repeated to him the same verse, and he too attained to the First Path. And these two, leaving their former teacher, entered the order established by the Buddha, and within a short time both attained to Arahatta, and the Master made them his Chief Disciples.

Return of the Buddha to Kapilavatthu

In the meanwhile it was reported to Suddhodana that his son, who for six years had devoted himself to mortification, had attained to Perfect Enlightenment, had set rolling the Wheel of the Law, and was residing at the Bambu Grove near by Rājagaha. And he sent a messenger with a retinue of a thousand men with the message "Your father, king Suddhodana, desires to see you." They reached the monastery at the hour of instruction, and standing still to listen to the discourse, the messenger attained to Arahatta with all his retinue, and prayed to be admitted to the Order; and the Buddha received them. And being now indifferent to the things of the world, they did not deliver the king's message. In the

[1] The most essential element of Buddhist doctrine, the full realisation of which constitutes the enlightenment of a Buddha, is here stated in the fewest possible words. The clear enunciation of the law of universal causation—the eternal continuity of becoming—is the great contribution of the Buddha to Indian thought; for it is only with comparative difficulty that the Vedānta is able to free itself from the concept of a First Cause. Assaji's verse is often called the Buddhist Confession of Faith; it is quoted in Buddhist inscriptions more frequently than any other text.

same way the king sent other messengers, each with a like retinue, and all of these, neglecting their business, stayed away there in silence. Then the king prevailed upon his minister Kāludāyin to bear the message, and he consented to do so only upon condition of receiving permission to become a member of the Order himself. "My friend," the king said, "thou mayst become a hermit or not, as thou wilt, only bring it about that I may see my son before I die."

Kāludāyin repaired to Rājagaha, and standing beside the disciples at the hour of instruction, he attained to Arahatta, and was received into the Order. Now at this time eight months had passed since the Enlightenment, and of this time, the first Lent or Rainy Season was spent at the Deer Park in Benares, the next three months at Uruvelā, and two months at Rājagaha. And now the cold season was over, the earth was decked with green grass, and the trees with scarlet flowers, and the roads were pleasant to to the traveller. And on the full-moon day in March, Kāludāyin, a full week since his admission to the Order, spoke with the Buddha, and proposed to him that he should visit his father, who desired to see him. And the Master, foreseeing that salvation of many would result, assented, saying to Kāludāyin: "Well said, Udāyin, I shall go." For it was in accordance with the Rule that the Brethren should travel from place to place. Attended by twenty thousand well-born Arahats, and travelling each day a league, he reached Kapilavatthu in two months. But Kāludāyin went instantly through the air, and informed the king that his son had taken the road, and by praising the virtues of the Buddha every day, he predisposed the Sākyas in his favour.

The Sākyas considered what would be the most pleasant

PLATE E

STANDING IMAGE OF THE BUDDHA

Gupta period (5th century A.D.), Mathurā

place for his residence, and they chose the Nigrodha-grove near by the city. With flowers in their hands, and accompanied by children of the place and the young men and maidens of the royal family, they went out to meet him, and led him to the grove. But regarding him as younger than themselves, as it were a younger brother, a nephew, or a grandson, they did not bow down. But the Buddha, understanding their thoughts, performed the miracle of taking his seat upon a jewelled platform in the air, and so preaching the law. And the king seeing this wonder said: "O Blessed One, when Kāla Devala bowed down to your feet on the day of thy birth I did obeisance to thee for the first time. And when I saw that the shadow of the Jambu-tree remained motionless upon the occasion of the ploughing festival I did obeisance for the second time; and now, because of this great miracle, I bow again to thy feet." And there was not one of the Sākyas who did not bow to the Buddha's feet at the same time. Then the Blessed One descended from the air, and sat upon the throne that had been prepared for him, and there he delivered a discourse, to wit, the story of his former birth as Prince Vessantara.

Conversion of the Sākya Princes

The next day the master entered Kapilavatthu to beg his food, attended by the twenty thousand Arahats. When it was rumoured that the young prince Siddhattha was begging from door to door, the windows of the many storied houses were opened wide, and a multitude gazed forth in amazement. And amongst these was the mother of Rāhula, and she said to herself: "Is it right that my lord, who was wont to go to and from in this town in a gilded palanquin, with every sign of pomp, should now be begging his food from door to door, with shaven hair and beard, and clad in russet robes?" And she reported the matter to the king. He, instantly rising, went forth to remonstrate with his son, that thus he put the Sākya clan to shame. "Do you think it impossible," said he, "that we should provide meals for all your followers?" "It is our custom, O king!" was the reply. "Not so, Master," said the king; "not one of all our ancestors has ever begged his food." "O king," replied the Buddha, "thy descent is in the succession of kings, but mine in the succession of the Buddhas: and every one of these has begged his daily food, and lived upon alms."

And standing in the middle of the street he uttered the verse:

Arise and delay not, follow after the pure life!
Who follows virtue rests in bliss, alike in this
world and the next.

And when the verse was finished the king attained to the Fruit of the First Path. Then the Buddha continued:

Follow after the pure life, follow not after sin!
Who follows virtue rests in bliss alike in this
world and the next.

And the king attained to the Fruit of the Second Path. Then the Buddha recited the *Dhammapāla Jātaka*, and the king attained to the Fruit of the Third Path. It was when he was dying that the king attained to Arahatta: he never practised the Great Effort in solitude.

Now as soon as the king had experienced the Fruit of Conversion, he took the Buddha's bowl and led the Blessed One and all his followers to the palace, and served them with savoury food.

And when the meal was over, the women of the house came and paid homage to the Blessed One, except only the Mother of Rāhula; but she stayed alone, for she thought, "If I have the least value in the eyes of my lord he will come himself to me, and then I will do him homage." And the Buddha went accordingly to the chamber of the Mother of Rāhula, and he was accompanied by the two chief Disciples, and he sat down on the seat prepared for him. Then the Mother of Rāhula came quickly and put her hands upon his ankles and laid her head upon his feet, and so did homage as she had purposed. Then the king said to the Blessed One, "When my daughter heard that thou hadst put on the russet robes, from that day forth she also dressed only in russet garb; and when she heard of thy one meal a day, she also took but a single meal; and when she heard that thou hadst forsaken the use of a high couch, she also slept upon a mat on the floor; and when her relatives would have received her and surrounded her with luxury, she did not hear them. Such is her goodness, Blessed One." "'Tis no wonder," said the Blessed One, "that she exercises self-control now, when her wisdom is matured; for she did no less when her wisdom was not yet matured." And he related the *Canda-kinnara Jātaka.*

On the second day the son of Suddhodana and the Lady Gautamī was to celebrate at the same time his inauguration as crown prince and his marriage with Janapada Kalyānī, the Beauty of the Land. But the Buddha went to his house, and there gave him his bowl to carry; and with a view to his abandoning the world, he wished him true happiness; and then rising from his seat he went his way. And the young man, not venturing to say to the Master, "Take back thy bowl," perforce followed him to the place of his retreat: and the Buddha received him all unwilling as he was, into the Order, and he was ordained.

Upon the morrow the Mother of Rāhula arrayed the child in all its best and sent him to the Blessed One, saying to him: "Look, my dear, at yonder Monk, attended by so many Brethren: he is your father, who was the possessor of a great treasure, which we have not seen since he left us. Go now and say, 'O Father, I am thy son, and I have need of the treasure—give me the treasure, for a son is heir to his father's property.'" And even so the child went up to the Blessed One and stood before him gladly and cheerfully. And when the Blessed One had finished his meal, he arose and went away, and the boy followed him, saying, as his mother had taught him, "O Monk! give to me my inheritance." Then the Blessed One said to Sāriputta, "Well, then, Sāriputta, receive Rāhula into our Order."

But when the king learnt that his grandson had been ordained he was deeply grieved; and he made known his grief to the Master, and won from him the promise that henceforth no son should be received into the Order without the leave of his father and mother.

Now, after the King Suddhodana had attained the Fruit of the Third Path, the Blessed One, together with the company of Brethren, returned to Rājagaha, and took up his residence in the Sītā Grove.

But between Kapilavatthu and Rājagaha the Master halted for a short time at the Mango Grove of Anupiyā. And while he was in that place a number of the Sākya princes determined to join his congregation, and to this end they followed him thither. The chief of these princes were Anuruddha, Bhaddiva, Kimbila, Ānanda, the

IV

YASODHARĀ AND RĀHULA

NANDA LĀL BOSE

Page 50

Buddha's cousin, who was afterwards appointed personal attendant, and Devadatta, the Buddha's cousin, who was ever his enemy.

Conversion of Anāthapindika

Now in these days there was a very wealthy merchant, by name Anāthapindika, and he was residing at the house of a friend at Rājagaha, and the news reached him that a Blessed Buddha had arisen. Very early in the morning he went to the Teacher, and heard the Law, and was converted; and he gave a great donation to the Order, and received a promise from the Master that he would visit Sāvatthi, the merchant's home. Then all along the road for the whole distance of forty-five leagues he built a resting-place at every league. And he bought the great Jetavana Grove at Sāvatthi for the price of as many pieces of gold as would cover the whole ground. In the midst thereof he built a pleasant chamber for the Master, and separate cells for the eighty Elders round about it, and many other residences with long halls and open roofs, and terraces to walk by night and day, and reservoirs of water. Then did he send a message to the Master that all was prepared. And the Master departed from Rājagaha, and in due course reached Sāvatthi. And the wealthy merchant, together with his wife and his son and two daughters in festal attire, and accompanied by a mighty train of followers, went out to meet him; while the Blessed One on his part entered the new-built monastery with all the infinite grace and peerless majesty of a Buddha, making the grove to shine with the glory of his person, as though it had been sprinkled with dust of gold.

Then Anāthapindika said to the Master: "What should I do with this monastery?" and the Master answered:

"Bestow it upon the Order, whether now present or to come." And the great Merchant, pouring water from a golden vessel into the Master's hands, confirmed the gift in these terms. And the Master received it and gave thanks and praised the uses of monasteries and the gift of them. The dedication festival lasted nine months. In those days there also resided at Sāvatthi, the chief town of Kosala, the lady Visākhā, the wife of the wealthy merchant Punnavaddhana. She made herself the patroness and supporter of the Order, and was also the means of converting her father-in-law, who was previously an adherent of the naked Jainas; and for this reason she got the surname of the mother of Migāra. Beyond this was her dedication to the Order of the monastery of Pubbārāma, the value and splendour whereof were second only to those of the monastery erected by Anāthapindika himself.

The Buddha averts a War

Now three rainy seasons were spent by the Lord in the Bambu Grove. It was in the fifth season, when he was residing in the Kūtāgāra Hall of the Great Forest near to Vesāli that there arose a dispute between the Sākyas and the Koliyas regarding the water of the river Rohinī, which, because of a great drought, did not suffice that year to irrigate the fields on both banks. The quarrel rose high, and matters were come nearly to battle, when the Buddha proceeded to the place, and took his seat on the river bank. He enquired for what reason the princes of the Sākyas and Koliyas were assembled, and when he was informed that they were met together for battle, he enquired what was the point in dispute. The princes said that they did not know of a surety, and they made enquiry of the commander-in-chief, but he in turn knew not, and sought information

PLATE F

52

ROCK-CUT IMAGE OF THE BUDDHA

Chinese, Long-men (6th century, A.D.). After Chavannes, *Mission archæologique dans la Chine septentrionale*

from the regent; and so the enquiry went on until it reached the husbandmen, who related the whole affair. "What then is the value of water?" said the Buddha. "It is but little," said the princes. "And what of earth?" "That also is little," they said. "And what of princes?" "It cannot be measured," they said. "Then would you," said the Buddha, "destroy that which is of the highest value for the sake of that which is little worth?" and he appeased the wrath of the combatants by the recital of sundry Jātakas. The princes now reflected that by the interposition of Buddha much bloodshed had been avoided, and that had it not been so, none might have been left to report the matter to their wives and children. And since, had he become, as he might if he had so pleased, a universal monarch, they would have been his vassals, they chose two hundred and fifty of their number, from each party, to become his attendants, and join the Order. But these five hundred were ordained at the wish of their parents, and not by their own will, and their wives were filled with grief for their sake.

The Admission of Women

About this time Suddhodana fell ill with a mortal sickness, and as soon as this was reported to the Blessed One, he proceeded to Kapilavatthu and visited his father. And when he had come before him, he preached to him the instability of all things, so that Suddhodana attained to the Fruit of the Fourth Path; to Arahatta, and Nibbāna, and thereafter he died.

After the death of her husband the widowed queen, the Matron Gautamī, decided to adopt the life of the hermitage, cut off her hair, and proceeded to the place where the Buddha was residing. She was accompanied by the wives of the five hundred princes who had been ordained on the occasion of the imminent battle at the Rohinī river; for these considered that it was better for them to retire from the world, than to remain at home in widowhood. The Matron Gautamī said to the Buddha that as Suddhodana was now dead, and Rāhula and Nanda were both ordained Brethren, she had no wish to reside alone, and she asked that she might be admitted to the Order, together with the princesses who were with her. But this request the Buddha refused, a first, a second, and third time, for he reflected that if they were admitted, it would perplex the minds of many who had not yet entered the Paths, and would be the occasion of evil speaking against the Order. And when they were still refused, the women feared to ask a fourth time, and they returned to their homes. And the Buddha returned to the Kūtāgāra hall, near Vesāli.

Then the Matron Gautamī said to the other princesses: My children, the Buddha has thrice refused us admission to the Order, but now let us take it upon ourselves to go to him where he now is, and he will not be able to deny us." They all cut their hair, adopted the garb of religieuses, and taking earthen alms-bowls, set out for Vesāli on foot; for they considered that it was contrary to the discipline for a recluse to travel by car. Then they who in all their life had walked only on smooth pavements, and regarded it as a great matter to ascend or descend from one story of their palaces to another, trod the dusty roads, and it was not until evening that they reached the place where the Buddha was. They were received by Ānanda. And when he saw them, their feet bleeding and covered with dust, as if half dead, his breast was filled with pity and his eyes with tears, and he enquired the meaning of their journey. When this was made known he informed the Master, describing all that he had seen. But the Buddha merely said: "Enough, Ānanda, do not ask me that women retire from the household life to the homeless life, under the Doctrine and Discipline of Him-who-has-thus-attained." And he said this three times. But Ānanda besought the Blessed One in another way to receive the women into the homeless life. He asked the Blessed One: "Are women competent, Reverend Sire, if they retire from the household to the homeless life, to attain to the Fruits of the First, the Second, the Third, and the Fourth Paths, even to Arahatta?" The Buddha could not deny the competence of women. "Are Buddhas," he asked, "born into the world only for the benefit of men? Assuredly it is for the benefit of women also." And the Blessed One consented that women should make profession and enter the Order, subject to the conditions of the Eight Duties of Subordination to the Brethren. "But," he added, "if women were not admitted to the Order, then would the Good Law endure for a thousand years, but now it will stand for five hundred years only. For just as when mildew falls upon a field of flourishing rice, that field of rice does not long endure, just so when women retire from the household to the homeless life under a Doctrine and Discipline, the norm will not long endure. And just as a large reservoir is strengthened by a strong dyke, so have I established a barrier of eight weighty regulations, not to be transgressed as long as life shall last." And in this way the Matron Gautamī and the five hundred princesses were admitted to the order; and it was not long before Gautamī attained to Arahatta, and the five hundred princesses attained the Fruit of the First Path.

And this took place in the sixth year of the Enlightenment.

The Sixth to the Fourteenth Years

The sixth rainy season was spent at Sāvatthi, and thereafter the Blessed One repaired to Rājagaha. Now the name of king Bimbisāra's wife was Khemā,[1] and such was her pride in her beauty that she had never deigned to visit the Master: but on a certain occasion the king brought about a meeting by means of a stratagem. Then the Buddha performed a miracle for her; he produced a likeness of one of the beautiful nymphs of Indra's heaven, and while she beheld it, he made it pass through all the stages of youth, middle age, old age, and death. And by this terrible sight the Queen was disposed to hear the Master's teaching, and she entered the First Path, and afterwards attained to Arahatta.

During the Master's residence in Rājagaha a wealthy merchant of that place became possessed of a piece of sandal wood, and he had a bowl made of it. This bowl he fastened to the tip of a tall bamboo, and raising it up in this way, he announced: "If any Wanderer or Brāhman be possessed of miraculous powers, let him take down the bowl." Then Mogallāna and other of the Brethren egged each other to take it down, and that other by name Pindola-Bhāradvāja, rose up into the sky and took the bowl, and moved three times round the city ere he descended, to the astonishment of all the citizens. When this was reported to the Buddha, he remarked: "This will not conduce to the conversion of the unconverted, nor to the advantage of the converted." And

[1] For other mention of the Bhikkunī Khemā, see p. 223.

he prohibited the Brethren from making an exhibition of miraculous powers.

The Buddha met with opposition to his teaching, particularly from six heretical teachers, each of whom had a large train of adherents. Of these heretical teachers one was Sanjaya, the former master of Sāriputta and Mogallāna, and another was Nigantha Nātaputta, who is better known as Vardhamāna, the founder of the sect of the Jainas, whose history in many respects recalls that of Buddhism, while, unlike Buddhism, it still numbers many adherents in India proper. These various teachers failed to find any support in the realm of Bimbisāra, and therefore betook themselves to Sāvatthi, hoping to secure greater influence with King Prasenajit. Now Sāvatthi was the place were all former Buddhas have exhibited their greatest miracle, and remembering this the Buddha proceeded thither with the intention of confounding his opponents. He took up his residence in the Jetavana monastery. Very soon afterwards he exhibited to the people, the six teachers, and King Prasenajit, a series of great miracles, creating a great road across the sky from East to West, and walking thereon the while he preached the Good Law. By these means the heretical teachers were overcome.

Following upon the Great Miracle, the Buddha departed to the Heaven of the Thirty-three, and there preached the Law to his mother, Mahā Māyā. The Buddha remained in the Heaven of the Thirty-three for three months, and during that time he created a likeness of himself, that continued the teaching of the Law on earth, and went every day upon his rounds begging food. When the Buddha was about to descend from heaven, Sakka commanded Vissakamma, the divine architect, to create a triple ladder, the foot of which was set down near the town of Sankissa. And the Buddha descended at this place, attended by Brahmā on the right and Sakka on the left. From Sankissa the Master returned to the Jetavana monastery near Sāvatthi. Here the heretical teachers induced a young woman of the name of Cincā so to act as to arouse the suspicion of the people regarding her relation to the Master. After many visits to the monastery, she contrived a means to assume the appearance of a woman far gone in pregnancy, and in the ninth month she brought an open accusation, and required that the Master should provide a place for her confinement. The Buddha answered with a great voice, "Sister, whether thy words be true or false, none knoweth save thou and I." At that very moment the strings gave way, wherewith the woman had bound upon herself the wooden globe by means of which she had assumed the appearance of pregnancy. Pursued by the indignant people, she disappeared in the midst of flames rising from the earth, and descended to the bottom of the lowest Purgatory.

The ninth retreat was spent in the Ghositārāma at Kausambī. Here there arose violent disagreements among the Brethren on matters of discipline, and the Buddha's wisdom and kindness availed not to restore peace. He therefore left the Brethren and proceeded to the village of Bālajalonakāra with the intention of residing alone as a hermit. He met on the way Anuruddha, Nandiya and Kimbila, who were living in perfect unity and content, and he rejoiced their hearts by a religious discourse. Then proceeding to the Rakkhita Grove at Pārileyyaka, he dwelt alone.

After residing for some time at Pārileyyaka, the Lord proceeded to Sāvatthi. Now the contumacious Brethren of Kausambī had received such signal marks of disrespect from the laity of that city that they resolved to proceed to Sāvatthi and lay the matter in dispute before the Master, and they abode by his decision, and peace was restored.

During the eleventh retreat the Master resided at Rājagaha. There he saw one day a Brāhman, by name Bhāradvāja, superintending the cultivation of his fields. The Brāhman, seeing the Buddha subsisting upon the alms of others, said: "O Wanderer, I plough and sow, and so find my livelihood. Do thou also plough and sow to the same end?" But the Buddha replied: "I, too, plough and sow, and it is thus that I find my food." The Brāhman was surprised, and said: "I do not see, O reverend Gautama, that you have a yoke, ploughshare, goad, or bullocks. How, then, say that thou too labourest?" Then the Lord said: "Faith is the seed I sow; devotion is the rain; modesty is the ploughshaft; the mind is the tie of the yoke; mindfulness is my ploughshare and goad. Energy is my team and bullock, leading to safety, and proceeding without backsliding to the place where there is no sorrow." And Bhāradvāja was so much affected by this parable that he was converted and made confession and was admitted to the Order.

In the thirteenth year, during his stay at Kapilavatthu, the Buddha was subjected to violent insults on the part of his father-in-law, Suprabuddha, and he uttered the prediction that within a week Suprabuddha would be swallowed alive by the earth. And, notwithstanding Suprabuddha spent the whole week in the tower of his palace, the earth opened and he was swallowed up in accordance with the prophecy, and he sank into the lowest Purgatory.

The Lord returned from Kapilavatthu to the Jetavana monastery at Sāvatthi and thence proceeded to Alavī, a place that was haunted by a man-eating ogre who was accustomed to devour the children of the place day after day. When the Buddha appeared before him, he was received with threats, but the Master, by gentleness and patience, succeeded in softening his heart, and was able also to answer the questions propounded by the ogre, who became a believer and mended his life. The fierce robber Angulimāla, too, he won over to the Good Law, and notwithstanding his evil life he quickly attained to Arahatta.

About this time the pious Anāthapindika gave his daughter in marriage to the son of a friend residing in Anga, and as the Anga family were supporters of the heretical teacher Nigantha, he gave his daughter a train of maidservants to support her in the right faith. The young wife refused to do honour to the naked Jaina ascetics, and she awakened an eager desire in the heart of her mother-in-law to hear the preaching of the Master: and when he arrived the whole family together with many others were converted. Leaving the completion of the work of conversion to Anuruddha, the Buddha returned to Sāvatthi.

The Buddha's Daily Life

In this way there passed by year after year of the Buddha's wandering ministry, but the events of the middle years cannot be chronologically arranged with exactitude; it will suffice if we give a general description of the Master's daily life at this time.[1]

"From year to year the change from a period of wandering to a period of rest and retirement repeated itself for Buddha and his disciples. In the month of June when, after the

[1] What follows is quoted from the admirable summary of Oldenberg.—*Buddha*, English translation by W. Hoey.

dry, scorching heat of the Indian summer, clouds come up in towering masses, and the rolling thunders herald the approach of the rain-bearing monsoon, the Indian to-day, as in ages past, prepares himself and his home for the time during which all usual operations are interrupted by the rain: for whole weeks long in many places the pouring torrents confine the inhabitants to their huts, or at any rate, to their villages, while communication with neighbours is cut off by rapid, swollen streams, and by inundations. 'The birds,' says an ancient Buddhist work, 'build their nests on the tops of trees: and there they nestle and hide during the damp season.' And thus also, it was an established practice with the members of monastic orders, undoubtedly not first in Buddha's time, but since ever there was a system of religious itinerancy in India, to suspend itinerant operations during the three rainy months and to spend this time in quiet retirement in the neighbourhood of towns and villages, where sure support was to be found through the charity of believers. . . . Buddha also every year for three months 'kept vassa, rainy season,' surrounded by groups of his disciples, who flocked together to pass the rainy season near their teacher. Kings and wealthy men contended for the honour of entertaining him and his disciples, who were with him, as guests during this season in the hospices and gardens which they had provided for the community. The rains being over, the itinerating began: Buddha went from town to town and village to village, always attended by a great concourse of disciples: the texts are wont to speak in one place of three hundred, and in another of five hundred, who followed their master. In the main streets, through which the religious pilgrims, like travelling merchants, used to pass, the believers who dwelt near had taken care to provide shelter, to which Buddha and his disciples might resort: or, where monks who professed the doctrine dwelt, there was sure to be found lodging for the night in their abodes, and even if no other cover was to be had, there was no want of mango or banyan trees, at the feet of which the band might halt for the night. . . .

"The most important headquarters during these wanderings, at the same time the approximately extreme points, to the north-west and south-east of the area, in which Buddha's pilgrim life was passed, are the capital cities of the kings of Kosala and Magadha, Sāvatthi, now Sahet Maheth on the Rapti, and Rājagaha, now Rājgir, south of Bihar. In the immediate neighbourhood of these towns the community possessed numerous pleasant gardens, in which structures of various kinds were erected for the requirements of the members. 'Not too far from, nor yet too near the town,' thus runs the standard description of such a park given in the sacred texts, 'well provided with entrances and exits, easily accessible to all people who enquire after it, with not too much of the bustle of life by day, quiet by night, far from commotion and the crowds of men, a place of retirement, a good place for solitary meditation.' Such a garden was the Veluvana, 'Bambu Grove,' once a pleasure-ground of King Bimbisāra, and presented by him to Buddha and the Church: another was the still more renouned Jetavana at Sāvatthi, a gift made by Buddha's most liberal admirer, the great merchant Anāthapindika. Not alone the sacred texts, but equally also the monumental records, the reliefs of the great Stūpa of Bharhut, recently explored, show how highly celebrated this gift of Anāthapindika's was from the earliest days in the Buddhist Church. . . . If it is possible to speak of a home in the homeless wandering life of Buddha and his disciples, places like the Veluvana and Jetavana may of all others be so called, near the great centres of Indian life and yet untouched by the turmoil of the capitals, once the quiet resting-places of rulers and nobles, before the yellow-robed mendicants appeared on the scene, and 'the Church in the four quarters, present and absent,' succeeded to the possession of the kingly inheritance. In these gardens were the residences of the brethren, houses, halls, cloisters, storerooms, surrounded by lotus-pools, fragrant mango trees, and slender fan-palms that lift their foliage high over all else, and by the deep green foliage of the Nyagrodha tree, whose roots dropping from the air to earth become new stems, and with their cool shady arcades and leafy walks seem to invite to peaceful meditation.

"These were the surroundings in which Buddha passed a great part of his life, probably the portions of it richest in effective work. Here masses of the population, lay as well as monastic, flocked together to see him, and to hear him preach. Hither came pilgrim monks from far countries, who had heard the fame of Buddha's teaching, and, when the rainy season was past, undertook a pilgrimage to see the Master face to face. . . .

"The fame of Buddha's person also drew together from far and near crowds of such as stood without the narrower circles of the community. 'To the ascetic Gotama,' people remarked to one another, 'folks are coming, passing through kingdoms and countries, to converse with him.' Often, when he happened to halt near the residences of potentates, kings, princes, and dignitaries came on wagons or on elephants to put questions to him or to hear his doctrine. Such a scene is described to us in the opening of the 'Sūtra on the fruit of asceticism,' and reappears in pictorial representation among the reliefs at Bharhut. The Sūtra relates how King Ajātasattu of Magadha in the 'Lotus-night'—that is, in the full moon of October, the time when the lotus blooms—is sitting in the open air, surrounded by his nobles on the flat roof of his palace. 'Then,' as it is recorded in that text, the king of Magadha, Ajātasattu, the son of the Vaidehi princes, uttered this exclamation, 'Fair in sooth is this moonlight night, lovely in sooth is this moonlight night, grand in sooth is this moonlight night, happy omens in sooth giveth this moonlight night. What Samanā [1] or what Brāhman shall I go to hear, that my soul may be cheered when I hear him?' " One counseller names this and another that teacher: but Jīvaka, the king's physician, sits on in silence. Then the king of Magadha, Ajātasattu, the sun of Vedehī, spake to Jīvaka Komārabhacca: "Why art thou silent, friend Jīvaka?"—"Sire, in my mango grove he resteth, the exalted, holy, supreme Buddha, with a great band of disciples, with three hundred monks; of him, the exalted Gotama, there spreadeth through the world lordly praise in these terms: He, the exalted one, is the holy, supreme Buddha, the wise, the learned, the blessed, who knoweth the universe, the highest, who tameth man like an ox, the teacher of gods and men, the exalted Buddha. Sire, go to hear him, the exalted one: perchance, if thou seest him, the exalted one, thy soul, O sire, may be refreshed"—and the king orders elephants to be prepared for himself and the queens, and the royal procession moves with burning torches on that moonlight night through the gate of Rājagaha to Jīvaka's mango grove, where Buddha is said to have held with the king the famous discourse, 'On the fruits of asceticism,' at

[1] A begging friar, *Bhikkhu*.

the end of which the king joined the Church as a lay-member. . . .

" A frequent end of these dialogues is, of course, that the vanquished opponents or the partisans of Buddha invite him and his disciples to dine on the following day.

The Buddha Teaching in the House of a Layman
(Ajanta Frescoes, after Griffiths)

'Sir, may it please the Exalted One and his disciples to dine with me to-morrow.' And Buddha permits his consent to be inferred from his silence. On the following day, about noon, when dinner is ready, the host sends word to Buddha: 'Sire, it is time, the dinner is ready'; and Buddha takes his cloak and alms-bowl and goes with his disciples into the town or village to the residence of his host. After dinner . . . at which the host himself and his family serve the guests, when the customary hand-washing is over, the host takes his place with his family at Buddha's side, and Buddha addresses to them a word of spiritual admonition and instruction.

"If the day be not filled by an invitation, Buddha, according to monastic usages, undertakes his circuit of the village or town in quest of alms. He, as well as his disciples, rises early, when the light of dawn appears in the sky, and spends the early moments in spiritual exercises or in converse with his disciples, and then he proceeds with his companions towards the town. In the days when his reputation stood at its highest point and his name was named throughout India among the foremost names, one might day by day see that man before whom kings bowed themselves, walking about, alms-bowl in hand, through streets and alleys, from house to house, and without uttering any request, with downcast look, stand silently waiting until a morsel of food was thrown into his bowl.

"When he had returned from his begging excursion and had eaten his repast, there followed, as the Indian climate demanded, a time, if not of sleep, at any rate of peaceful retirement. Resting in a quiet chamber or, better still, in the cool shades of dense foliage, he passed the sultry close hours of the afternoon in solitary contemplation until the evening came on and drew him once more from holy silence to the bustling concourse of friend and foe."

The Appointment of Ānanda

During the first twenty years of the Buddha's life, his personal attendants were not such permanently. The

PLATE C

STANDING IMAGE OF THE BUDDHA ATTENDED BY ĀNANDA AND KASSAPA AND TWO BODHISATTAS

Chinese stele, Wei dynasty, 6th century A.D.

Collection of Mr Victor Goloubew

Brethren took it by turns to carry the Master's bowl and cloak, and he did not favour one more than another. But one day he addressed the Brethren and said: "O Bhikkhus, I am now advanced in years:[1] and some Bhikkhus, when they have been told 'Let us go this way,' take another way, and some drop my bowl and cloak on the ground. Do ye know of a Bhikkhu to be my permanent body-servant?" Then the venerable Sāriputta arose and said: "I Lord, will wait upon thee." Him the Exalted One rejected, and Mogallāna the Great, also. Then all of the foremost disciples said: "We will wait upon thee." Only Ānanda remained silent: for he thought "The Master himself will say of whom he approves." Then the Exalted One said: "O Bhikkhus, Ānanda is not to be urged by others: if he knows it of himself, he will wait upon me." Then Ānanda stood up and said: "If, Lord, thou wilt refuse me four things, and grant me four things, then I will wait on thee." Now the four things that Ānanda wished to be denied were special favours, for he did not wish it to be said that his service was undertaken for the sake of clothes, or good fare, or lodging, or that he might be included in invitations. And the four boons that he desired were that the Buddha would accept any invitation received through Ānanda, that he would be easy of access to such as Ānanda should bring to speak with him and to Ānanda himself, and that he would repeat to Ānanda such doctrines as he desired to hear again: for Ānanda did not wish it to be thought that the Buddha made no account of him, nor that men should say that the Buddha's immediate attendant was not well versed in the doctrine. All these boons were granted by the Blesssed One, and thenceforward until the day of his death, Ānanda remained the

[1] The Buddha was at this time fifty-six years of age.

permanent attendant of the Buddha.[1] It was not, however, until after the Buddha's death that Ānanda attained to Arahatta.

The Enmity of Devadatta

In the picture of Buddha's daily life described a few pages previously, mention is made of Ajātasattu, King of Magadha. This Ajātasattu was the son of Bimbisāra, the chief of the Buddha's royal supporters. When Ajātasattu was conceived, it was indicated by an omen and a prophecy that he would be the slayer of his father. And this came to pass at the instigation of Devadatta. One day when the Buddha was teaching in the Bambu Grove, Devadatta proposed that because of the Master's advanced age, the leadership of the Congregation should be vested in himself. From the time when this suggestion was plainly refused, Devadatta's enmity and ill-will greatly increased. Because of what had taken place the Buddha issued a decree against Devadatta as a renegade whose words were not to be recognized as proceeding from the Buddha, the Law, or the Community. The angry Devadatta now betook himself to Ajātasattu, King Bimbisāra's son and heir, and persuaded him to murder his father and usurp the throne, while Devadatta should kill the Master and become Buddha. Bimbisāra however discovered his son's intention, and so far from punishing him in any way, abdicated the throne and gave over the kingdom to his son. Nevertheless, upon Devadatta's representing that Bimbisāra might desire to recover the throne, Ajātasattu brought about his death by starvation.

[1] Personal service on the Buddha implied to bring his water and toothbrush, wash his feet, accompany him abroad, bear his bowl and cloak, sweep his cell, and act as chamberlain.

PLATE H 68

THE QUELLING OF MĀLĀGIRI

Amarāvatī, 2nd century A.D.

Then Devadatta secured the new king's consent to the murder of the Buddha, and he hired thirty-one men to carry out his purpose. All these men, however, notwithstanding they were notorious criminals, were so affected by the majesty and loving kindness of the Master, that they could not raise hand against him, but on the contrary, experienced conversion, and joined the Community. Devadatta was now convinced that the Buddha could not be slain by any human being, and determined to let loose upon him the fierce elephant Mālāgiri. This beast was accustomed to drink eight measures of spirituous liquor every day, but Devadatta commanded the keeper to give it sixteen measures the next day, and to let it loose against the Buddha as he proceeded through the streets. The Buddha was informed of what was to be done, but he refused to change his usual procedure, and he entered the city at the usual hour, accompanied by a company of Bhikkhus. Soon afterwards the elephant was let loose upon him, and at once it raged through the streets, working havoc. The Bhikkhus entreated the Master to escape, but as he would not, they sought to walk before him, in order that he might not be the first to meet the savage beast, but this the Buddha forbade, albeit in the case of Ānanda, his doing so was only prevented by the exercise of miraculous power. At this moment the elephant was about to destroy the mother of a child who had run into the street in ignorance of the danger: but the Buddha called to it: "It was not intended that you should destroy any other being than myself: here am I: waste not your strength on any less noble object." On hearing the voice of Buddha, the elephant looked towards him; and immediately the effects of the liquor passed away, and the elephant approached him in the gentlest fashion and kneeled before him. The Master charged him to take no life in future, but to be kind to all people: and the elephant repeated the five precepts before the assembled crowds. Thus the rage of Mālāgiri was subdued, and had he not been a quadruped, he might have entered the First Path.[1] As Buddha had thus performed a miracle, he reflected that it would not be becoming to seek alms in the same place, and he therefore returned to the Jetavana monastery, without proceeding on his usual course.

Following upon this, Devadatta attempted to create a schism in the Order. Together with certain other Bhikkhus he requested the Buddha to establish a more severely ascetic rule for the Brethren, as that they should clothe themselves only in cast-off rags, that they should dwell as forest-hermits, accept no invitations, and abstain from fish and meat. The Master refused to concede these demands, declaring that those who wished might adopt this more severe rule, but that he would not make it binding upon all. Devadatta, who expected this refusal, made it the occasion of division within the Order. Together with a party of five hundred recently ordained Brethren, he made his way to Gayā Scarp. But as he was preaching there, he happened to see Sāriputta and Mogallāna in the audience, and thinking them to be of his party, he requested Sāriputta to preach, while he himself slept. Sāriputta and Mogallāna now addressed the assembly and persuaded the five hundred schismatics to return to the Master. When Devadatta awoke and learnt what had taken place, the hot blood broke from his mouth in anger. Devadatta lay sick for nine months: and at the end of this time he determined

[1] Animals may keep the precepts, gods may enter the Paths, but only human beings can attain to Arahatta and Nibbāna.

to seek the Buddha's forgiveness, for he knew that the Master felt no ill-will toward him. His disciples endeavoured to dissuade him, knowing that the Buddha would not see him: but he had himself conveyed in a palanquin to the Jetavana monastery. The Bhikkhus informed Buddha of his approach, but the Master answered: "He will not see the Buddha: for his crimes are so great that ten, or a hundred, or even a thousand Buddhas could not help him." When they reached the monastery, the disciples of Devadatta laid down the palanquin: and then, despite his weakness, Devadatta rose and stood. But no sooner did his feet touch the ground, than flames arose from the lowest hell, and wrapped him in their folds, at first his feet, then his middle, and then his shoulders. Then in terror he cried aloud: "Save me, my children, I am the cousin of the Buddha. O Buddha, though I have done so much against thee, for the sake of our kinship save me!" And he repeated the formula of taking refuge in the Buddha, the norm, and the order. By this he received the help of the Three Gems at last, and in a future birth he will become the Private Buddha Sattisara, notwithstanding he now went to hell and received a body of fire.

Now King Ajātasattu, who had murdered his father, felt the pangs of conscience. He found no comfort in the doctrines of the six heretical teachers who were the Lord's opponents. And then, on the advice of his physician Jīvaka—as related previously—he sought the Buddha himself, and heard his teaching and became a convert to the true faith.

Destruction of the Sākyas

Not long after this, in the seventh year of Ajātasattu's reign, the son of the king of Kosala dethroned his father and, to revenge himself for a slight received, he marched on Kapilavatthu. Almost the whole of the Sākya clan was destroyed in the ensuing war, while the party of the Kosalas perished in a great flood.

When the Lord had reached his seventy-ninth year—being the forty-fifth year following the Enlightenment—Ajātasattu undertook an unsuccessful war upon the Vajjians of Vesālī. The Buddha was consulted upon the likelihood of victory, and in this connection we are informed what is the Master's view of polity, for he declares that he himself has taught the Vajjians the conditions of true welfare, and as he is informed that the Vajjians are continuing to observe these institutions, he foretells that they will not suffer defeat. And these conditions are stated in the following terms: "So long, Ānanda, as the Vajjians meet together in concord, and rise in concord, and carry out their undertakings in concord—so long as they enact nothing already established, abrogate nothing that has been already enacted, and act in accordance with the ancient institutions of the Vajjians, as established in former days—so long as they honour and esteem and revere the Vajjian elders, and hold it a point of duty to hearken to their words—so long as no women or girls belonging to their clans are detained among them by force or abduction—so long as they honour and esteem and revere and support the Vajjian shrines in town or country, and allow not the proper offerings and rites, as formerly given and performed, to fall into desuetude—so long as the rightful protection, defence, and support shall be fully provided for the Arahats amongst them, so that Arahats from a distance may enter the realm, and the Arahats therein may live at ease—so long may the Vajjians be expected not to decline, but to prosper."

Following upon this pronouncement the Master in like manner assembled the Brethren, and set forth forty-one conditions of welfare of a religious Order, of which conditions several relating to concord and to the observance and maintenance of existing regulations and obedience and respect to elders are identical with those which are given for the secular society. Amongst others we may note the following:

"So long, O Bhikkhus . . . as the Brethren delight in a life of solitude . . . shall not engage in, be fond of, or be connected with business . . . shall not stop on their way to Nibbāna because they have attained to any lesser thing . . . shall exercise themselves in mental activity, search after truth, energy, joy, peace, earnest contemplation, and equanimity of mind . . . shall exercise themselves in the realization of the ideas of the impermanency of all phenomena, bodily or mental, the absence of every soul . . . shall live among the Arahats in the practice, both in public and in private, of those virtues which are productive of freedom and praised by the wise, and are untarnished by desire of a future life or the faith in the efficacy of outward acts . . . shall live among the Arahats, cherishing, both in public and private, that noble and saving insight which leads to the complete destruction of the sorrow of him who acts according to it—so long may the Brethren be expected not to decline, but to prosper."

And at Rājagaha, on the Vulture's Peak, the Master taught the Brethren, and again at Nālanda in the same manner. "Such and such is upright conduct; such and such is earnest contemplation; such and such is intelligence.[1] Great becomes the fruit, great the advantage of

[1] *Sīla*, *samādhi*, and *paññā*, something like the 'works,' 'faith,' and 'reason' of Christianity. The formula above quoted appears repeatedly as a familiar summary of the Buddha's discourse.

earnest contemplation, when it is set round with upright conduct. Great becomes the fruit, great the advantage of intellect, when it is set round with earnest contemplation. The mind, set round with intelligence, is set quite free from the Intoxications, that is to say, from the Intoxication of Sensuality, from the Intoxication of Becoming, from the Intoxication of Delusion, from the Intoxication of Ignorance."

The gift of a garden by Ambapālī

Then the Master proceeded to Vesālī. At this time, also, there was dwelling in the town of Vesālī a beautiful and wealthy courtesan whose name was Ambapālī, the Mango-girl. It was reported to her that the Blessed One had come to Vesāli and was halting at her Mango Grove. Immediately she ordered her carriages and set out for the grove, attended by all her train; and as soon as she reached the place where the Blessed One was, she went up toward him on foot, and stood respectfully aside; and the Blessed One instructed and gladdened her with religious discourse. And she, being thus instructed and gladdened, addressed the Blessed One and said: "May the Master do me the honour to take his meal with all the Brethren at my house to-morrow." And the Blessed One gave consent by silence. Ambapālī bowed down before him and went her way.[1]

Now the Licchavi princes of Vesālī also came to know that the Blessed One had come to the town, and they too proceeded to the Mango Grove where he was halting.

[1] The picture of the wealthy and truly pious courtesan, 'gladdened by religious discourse,' remains true to Indian life in old-fashioned cities even at the present day. The whole episode exhibits a beautiful tolerance, recalling the like stories of the Christian Magdalene. For Ambapālī's 'Psalm,' see p. 285 seq.

And as they went they met with Ambapālī returning, and she drove up against them axle to axle, and wheel to wheel, so that they all exclaimed: "How comes it, Ambapālī, that thou drivest up against us thus?" "My Lords," she made answer, "I have just invited the Blessed One and his Brethren for their to-morrow's meal." Then the princes replied: "O, Ambapālī, give up this meal to us for the sum of a hundred thousand." "My Lords," she said, "if you were to offer to me all Vesāli with its subject territory, I would not give up so honourable a feast." Then the Licchavis cast up their hands and exclaimed: "We are outdone by the Mango-girl!" and they went on their way to the Mango Grove. And when they, too, had greeted the Blessed One and had hearkened to his instruction, they addressed the Master and said: "May the Blessed One do us the honour to take his meal, with all the Brethren, at our house to-morrow." But the Buddha replied: "O, Licchavis, I have promised to dine to-morrow with Ambapālī the courtesan." And again the princes exclaimed: "We are outdone by the Mango-girl!"

The next day Ambapālī served the Lord and all the Brethren with her own hands, and when they would eat no more she called for a low stool and sat down beside the Master and said: "Lord, I make a gift of this mansion to the Order of which thou art the chief." And the Blessed One accepted the gift; and after instructing and gladdening Ambapālī with religious discourse, he rose from his seat and went his way.

The last Retreat

From Vesālī the Master went to the neighbouring village of Beluva, where he spent the last Retreat. There a severe sickness came upon him. But the Exalted One, considering that his time was not yet come, and that it was not right that he should pass away without taking leave of the Order, "by a great effort of the will bent that sickness down again, and kept his hold on life till the time he fixed upon should come: and the sickness abated upon him." Now when he had quite recovered, he came out from his lodging, and sat down upon a seat, and there Ānanda came to him and saluted him and said: "I have beheld, Lord, how the Exalted One was in health, and I have beheld how the Exalted One had to suffer. And though at the sight of the sickness of the Exalted One my body became weak as a creeper, and the horizon became dim to me, and my faculties were no longer clear, yet notwithstanding I took some little comfort from the thought that the Exalted One would not pass away until at least he had left instructions as touching the Order,"

"What then, Ānanda," said the Buddha, "does the Order expect that of me? I have preached the truth without making any distinction between exoteric and esoteric doctrine; for in respect of the truths, Ānanda, He-who-has-thus-attained has no such thing as the closed fist of a teacher, who keeps some things back. Surely, Ānanda, should there be anyone who harbours the thought, 'It is I who will lead the brotherhood,' or 'the Order is dependent upon me,' it is he who should lay down instructions in any matter concerning the Order. Now He-who-has-thus-attained, Ānanda, thinks not that it is he who should lead the brotherhood, or that the Order is dependent upon him. Why then should he leave instructions in any matter concerning the Order? I too, O Ānanda, am now grown old, and full of years, my journey is drawing to its close, I have reached my sum of days, I am turning eighty

V

BUDDHA AND ANANDA

NANDA LĀL BOSE

Page 76

years of age; and just as a worn-out cart, Ānanda, can be kept going only with the help of thongs, so, methinks, the body of Him-who-has-thus-attained can only be kept going by bandaging it up. It is only, Ānanda, when the Tathāgata, by ceasing to attend to any outward thing, becomes plunged by the cessation of any separate sensation in that concentration of heart which is concerned with no material object—it is only then that the body of Him-who-has-thus-attained is at ease.

"Therefore, O Ānanda, be ye lamps unto yourselves. Be ye a refuge to yourselves. Betake yourselves to no external refuge. Hold fast to the Truth as a lamp. Hold fast as a refuge to the Truth. Look not for refuge to anyone besides yourselves. . . . And whosoever, Ānanda, either now or after I am dead, shall be a lamp unto themselves, shall betake themselves to no external refuge, but holding fast to the Truth as their lamp, and holding fast as their refuge to the Truth, shall look not for refuge to anyone besides themselves—it is they, Ānanda, among my Bhikkhus who shall reach the very topmost Height!—but they must be anxious to learn."[1]

Upon another occasion the Master walked with Ānanda to the Capāla shrine: and he began to speak of his coming death. And when Ānanda was grieved, and would have besought him to remain on earth, he said:

"But now, Ānanda, have I not formerly declared to you that it is in the very nature of all things, near and dear unto us, that we must divide ourselves from them, leave them, sever ourselves from them? How, then, Ānanda, can this be possible—whereas anything whatever born,

[1] This noble passage—I quote the translation of Professor Rhys Davids—expresses with admirable literary art the pure individualism of Buddhist thought, here so nearly akin to that of Whitman and Nietzsche.

brought into being, and organized, contains within itself the inherent necessity of dissolution—how then can this be possible that such a being should not be dissolved? No such condition can exist! And, Ananda, that which has been relinquished, cast away, renounced, rejected, and abandoned by the Tathāgata—the remaining sum of life surrendered by him—verily with regard to that, the word has gone forth from the Tathāgata, saying: 'The passing away of Him-who-has-thus-attained shall take place before long. At the end of three months from this time the Tathāgata will die!' That the Tathāgata for the sake of living should repent him again of that saying —this can no wise be!"

Thereafter the Buddha set out with Ānanda to go to the Kūtāgāra Hall in the Great Forest. And being arrived there, the Brethren were assembled, and the Buddha exhorted them, and made public announcement of his coming death. "Behold, now, O Brethren, I exhort you, saying: 'All component things must grow old. Work out your salvation with diligence. The final extinction of the Tathāgata will take place before long. At the end of three months from this time the Tathāgata will die!'"

The Last Meal

Thereafter the Buddha proceeded to Pāra, and he halted at the Mango Grove of Cunda, an hereditary smith. And when this was reported to Cunda he hastened to the grove; there the Buddha instructed and gladdened him with religious discourse. And he invited the Master and the Brethren to dine at his house on the morrow.

Early in the morning Cunda the smith prepared sweet

rice and cake and a dish of pork:[1] and he announced the hour to the Exalted One. And he, taking his bowl, proceeded to the house of Cunda the smith, and partook of the meal prepared, and afterward he instructed and gladdened Cunda the smith with religious discourse.

But when the Exalted One had partaken of the meal prepared by Cunda the smith, there fell upon him a dire sickness, the disease of dysentery and sharp pain came upon him, even unto death. But the Exalted One, mindful and self-possessed, bore it without complaint, and when he was a little relieved he said to Ānanda: "Come, Ānanda, let us go on to Kusinara." "Even so, lord," said the venerable Ānanda.

Now the Exalted One turned aside from the path to the foot of a certain tree, and said to Ānanda, "Fold, I pray you, Ānanda, the robe in four, and spread it out for me. I am weary, Ānanda, and must rest awhile." "Even so, lord," said the venerable Ānanda. And when he was seated he asked for water, and Ānanda brought it, from a neighbouring stream—and he found the water of the stream was running clear, notwithstanding that a caravan of five hundred carts had just passed the ford.

Conversion of Pukkusa

Immediately after this there passed by a young man, by name Pukkusa, a disciple of Ālāra Kālāma. And he related to the Buddha how upon a certain occasion this Ālāra Kālāma had been sitting beside the road, and was so absorbed in meditation that five hundred carts passed him by, so nearly that even his robe was sprinkled with the dust: and a certain man was so much impressed by

[1] Or perhaps truffles. But there is nothing contrary to Buddhist practice in eating flesh prepared and offered by others.

this profound abstraction that he became Ālāra's disciple. Upon hearing this story the Buddha replied by relating an occasion of even greater abstraction, on his own part, when, as he was walking to and fro upon a certain threshing-floor at Atumā, the rain fell and lightning flashed, and two peasants and four men were killed by a thunderbolt—and yet though conscious and awake, he neither saw nor heard the storm: and upon that occasion in like manner a certain man was so much impressed by the Master's abstraction that he became a disciple.

Upon hearing this relation, Pukkusa's faith in Ālāra Kālāma faded away, and he resorted to the Exalted One, and to the Law and to the Brotherhood as his refuge, and requested the Exalted One to accept him as a lay disciple. And he sent for two robes of cloth of gold and presented them to the Master, and so went his way. But when Ānanda folded the robes and the Master wore them, the golden cloth seemed to have lost its brightness —and this was because whenever One-who-has-thus attained attains to Perfect Enlightenment, as also on the day when he passes away, the colour of his skin becomes exceeding bright. "And now," said the Master, "the utter passing away of Him-who-has-thus-attained, will take place at the third watch of this night in the Sāla-grove of the Mallians. Come, Ānanda, let us go on to the river Kakutthā." "Even so, lord!" said the venerable Ānanda.

The Exalted One went down into the water of the river Kakuttha, and bathed and drank; and then, taking his seat upon the bank, he spoke with Ānanda concerning Cunda the smith, that none should impute the least blame to him because the Master died after receiving the last meal at his hands. On the contrary, he said, there

PLATE J

THE DEATH (*Pariniblāna*) OF THE BUDDHA
Rock-cut reclining image, Polonnāruva, Ceylon, 12th century A.D.

80

are two offerings of food which are supremely precious—that which is given immediately before One-who-has-thus-come attains to Perfect Insight, and the other before his utter passing away: and "there has been laid up to Cunda the smith a *kamma* redounding to length of life, good birth, good fortune and good fame, and to the inheritance of heaven and of sovereign power; and therefore let not Cunda the smith feel any remorse."

The Master's Death

Then the Exalted One said to Ānanda: "Come, Ānanda, let us go on to the Sāla-grove of the Mallas, on the further side of the river Hiranyavatī." And when they were come there, he said: "Spread over for me, I pray you, Ānanda, the couch with its head to the north, between the Twin Sāla trees. I am weary, Ānanda, and would lie down." "Even so, lord!" said the venerable Ānanda. And the Exalted One laid himself down on his right side, with one leg resting on the other; and he was mindful and self-possessed.

And now there came to pass certain marvels, and the Master spoke of these to Ānanda, and said: "The twin Sāla trees are all one mass of bloom with flowers out of season; all over the body of Him-who-has-thus-attained, these drop and sprinkle and scatter themselves, out of reverence for the successors of the Buddhas of old. And heavenly music sounds in the sky, out of reverence for the successors of the Buddhas of old. But it is not thus, Ānanda, that He-who-has-thus-attained is rightly honoured, and reverenced. But the brother or the sister, the devout man or woman who continually fulfils all the greater and lesser duties, who is correct in life, walking according to the precepts—it is he who rightly honours and reverences the Tathāgata. And therefore, Ānanda, be ye constant in the fulfilment of the greater and the lesser duties, and be ye correct in life, walking according to the precepts; and thus, Ānanda, should it be taught."

Then the Buddha addressed Ānanda, and said to him that he saw a great host of the gods assembled together to behold the Tathāgata upon the night of his final passing away: and a host of spirits of the air and of the earth, "of worldly mind, who dishevel their hair and weep, who stretch forth their arms and weep, who fall prostrate on the ground, and roll to and fro in anguish at the thought 'Too soon will the Exalted One pass away! Too soon will the Exalted One die! Too soon will the Eye in the world pass away!'" "But," the Master continued, "the spirits who are free from passion bear it calm and self-possessed, mindful of the saying—'Impermanent, indeed, are all component things.'"

And the Master made mention of four places that should be visited by the clansmen with feelings of reverence—the place where the Tathāgata was born, the place where he attained Supreme Enlightenment, the place where the kingdom of righteousness was established, and the place where the Tathāgata utterly passed away: "and they, Ānanda, who shall die while they, with believing heart, are journeying on such a pilgrimage, shall be reborn after death, when the body shall dissolve, in the happy realms of heaven."

When Ānanda enquired what should be done with the remains of the Tathāgata, he answered: "Hinder not yourselves, Ānanda, by honouring the remains of Him-who-has-thus-attained. Be zealous, I beseech you, Ānanda, on your own behalf! Devote yourselves to your own good!

There are lay disciples who will do due honour to the remains of the Tathāgata."

Now Ānanda had not yet attained to Arahatta, he was still a student, and he went away to the monastery, and stood leaning against the lintel of the door, weeping at the thought 'Alas! I remain still but a learner, one who has yet to work out his own perfection. And the Master is about to pass away—he who is so kind!' Then the Exalted One summoned the Brethren and said, "Where now, brethren, is Ānanda?" and they answered: "The venerable Ānanda, lord, has gone into the monastery, and is leaning against the lintel of the door, and weeping at the thought 'Alas! I remain still but a learner, one who has yet to work out his own perfection. And the Master is about to pass away—he who is so kind!'." Then the Exalted One called a certain Brother and sent him to Ānanda with the message: "Brother Ānanda, the Master calls for thee." And Ānanda came accordingly, and bowed before the Exalted One and took his seat respectfully. Then the Exalted One said: "Enough, Ānanda! do not let yourself be troubled; do not weep! Have I not already, on former occasions, told you that it is in the very nature of all things most near and dear unto us that we must divide ourselves from them, leave them, sever ourselves from them. How, then, Ānanda, can this be possible—whereas anything whatever born, brought into being, and organized, contains within itself the inherent necessity of dissolution—how, then, can this be possible, that such a being should not be dissolved? No such condition can exist. For a long time, Ānanda, you have been very near to me by acts of love, kind and good, that never varies, and is beyond all measure. You have done well, Ānanda! Be earnest in effort, and you too shall be free from the Intoxications of Sensuality, of Individuality, Delusion and Ignorance." And he praised the able service of Ānanda before the whole assembly.

Then the Master said to Ānanda: "Go now into the village of Kusinārā, and inform the Mallas that the Tathāgata is about to pass away, to the end that they may not afterwards reproach themselves by saying: 'In our own village the Tathāgata died, and we took not the occasion to visit the Tathāgata in his last hours.'" And the Mallas of Kusinārā, with their young men and maidens and wives were grieved and saddened, and betook themselves to the Sāla Grove where the Buddha was lying. And Ānanda presented them to the Master, family by family, in the first watch of the night.

Now there was at this time a wanderer of the name of Subhadda, to whom the Buddha's approaching death was made known: and he desired to speak with the Master, for the dissipation of his doubt. To this end he approached Ānanda: but he refused access to the Master, saying, "The Exalted One is weary, do not trouble him!" But the Exalted One overheard what was said, and desired that Subhadda should be given access: for he knew that the questions to be asked were sincere, and that Subhadda would understand the answers. And this was what Subhadda sought to know—whether the leaders of other schools of thought, the masters of other congregations, such as Nigantha Nātaputta, or Sanjaya the former teacher of Sāriputta and Mogallāna, esteemed as good men by many, had, as they claimed, attained a true understanding of things, or had some of them so attained, and not others? And the Exalted One declared: "In whatsoever doctrine and discipline, Subhadda, the Ariyan Eightfold Path is not found, there is not found any man of true sainthood, either of the first, the second, the third, or the fourth degree. But in that Doctrine and Discipline in which is found the Ariyan Eightfold Path, there are men of true sainthood, of all the four degrees. Void are the systems of other teachers—void of true saints. But in this one, Subhadda, may the Brethren live the Perfect Life, that the world be not bereft of Arahats." And Subhadda's doubt being thus resolved, he resorted to the Exalted One, to the Law, and to the Congregation as his refuge, and he was received into the Order: and "ere long he attained to that supreme goal of the higher life (Nibbāna), for the sake of which the clansmen go out from all and every household gain and comfort, to become houseless wanderers—yea, that supreme goal did he, by himself, and while yet in this visible world, bring himself to the knowledge of, and continue to realize, and to see face to face! And he became conscious that birth was at an end, that the higher life had been fulfilled, that all that should be done had been accomplished, and that after this present life there would be no beyond." Thus it was that the venerable Subhadda became yet another among the Arahats; and he was the last disciple whom the Exalted One himself converted.

Now the Exalted One addressed the Brethren and said thrice, "It may be, Brethren, that there may be doubt or misgiving in the mind of some Brother as to the Buddha, or the doctrine, or the path, or the method. Inquire, Brethren, freely, Do not have to reproach yourselves afterwards with the thought: 'our teacher was face to face with us, and we could not bring ourselves to inquire of the Exalted One when we were face to face with him.'" But none had any doubt or misgiving. And the venerable Ānanda said to the Exalted One: "How wonderful a thing is it, lord, and how marvellous! Verily I believe that in this whole assembly of the Brethren there is not one Brother who has any doubt or misgiving as to the Buddha, or the doctrine, or the path or the method!" And the Buddha answered: "It is out of the fullness of faith that thou hast spoken, Ānanda! But, Ānanda, the Tathāgata knows for certain that in his whole assembly of the Brethren there is not one Brother who has any doubt or misgiving as to the Buddha, or the doctrine, or the path, or the method! For even the most backward,[1] Ānanda, of all these five hundred brethren has become converted, is no longer liable to be borne in a state of suffering, and is assured hereafter of attaining the Enlightenment of Arahatta."

Then again, the Exalted One addressed the Brethren and said: "Decay is inherent in all component things! Work out your salvation with diligence!"

This was the last word of Him-who-has-thus-attained. Then the Exalted One entered the first stage of Rapture, and the second, third, and fourth: and rising from the fourth stage, he entered into the station of the infinity of space: thence again into the station of the infinity of thought: thence again into the station of emptiness: then into the station between consciousness and unconsciousness: and then into the station where the consciousness both of sensations and ideas has wholly passed away. And now it seemed to Ānanda that the Master had passed away: but he entered again into every station in reverse order until he reached the second stage of Rapture, and thence he passed into the third and fourth stages of Rapture. And passing out of the last stage of Rapture he immediately expired.

[1] According to Buddhaghosha this refers to Ānanda himself, and was said for his encouragement.

The Distress of the Brethren

When the Exalted One died, of those of the Brethren who were not yet free from the passions, some stretched out their arms and wept, and some fell headlong on the ground, rolling to and fro in anguish at the thought: "Too soon has the Exalted One died! Too soon has the Happy One passed away! Too soon has the Eye in the world passed away." But those of the Brethren who were free from the passions, to wit, the Arahats, bore their grief collected and composed in the thought: "Impermanent are all component things! How is it possible that they should not be dissolved?"

And the Venerable Anuruddha exhorted the Brethren, and said: "Enough, my Brethren! Weep not, nor lament! Has not the Exalted One formerly declared this to us, that it is in the very nature of all things near and dear unto us, that we must divide ourselves from them, leave them, sever ourselves from them? How then, Brethren, can this be possible—that when dead anything whatever born, brought into being, and organized, contains within itself the inherent necessity of dissolution—how then can this be possible that such a being should not be dissolved? No such condition can exist!"

The Funeral Rites

On the next day Ānanda informed the Mallas of Kusinārā that the Exalted One had passed away; and they too stretched forth their arms and wept, or fell prostrate on the ground, or reeled to and fro in anguish at the thought: "Too soon has the Exalted One died!" And they took perfumes and garlands, and all the music in Kusinārā, and proceeded to the Sāla Grove, where the body of the Exalted One was lying. And they spent there six days paying honour and homage to the remains of the Exalted One, with dancing and hymns and music, and with garlands and perfumes. On the seventh day they bore the body of the Exalted One through the city and out by the Eastern gate to the shrine of the Mallas, there to be burnt upon the pyre. They wrapped the body in layers of carded cotton wool and woven cloth, and placed it in a vessel of iron, and that again in another; and building a funeral pyre of perfumed woods, they laid the body of the Exalted One upon it. Then four chieftains of the Mallas bathed their heads and clad themselves in new garments with the intention of setting on fire the funeral pyre. But lo, they were not able to set it burning. Now the reason of this was that the venerable Mahā Kassapa was then journeying from Pāvā to Kusinārā with a company of five hundred Brethren: and it was willed by the gods that the pyre should not take fire until the venerable Mahā Kassapa together with these Brethren had saluted the feet of the Master. And when Mahā Kassapa came to the place of the funeral pyre, then he walked thrice round about it and bowed in reverence to the feet of the Exalted One, and so did the five hundred Brethren. And when this was ended, the funeral pyre caught fire of itself.

And what was burnt was the flesh and the fluids of the body, and all the wrappings, and only the bones were left behind; and when the body was thus burnt, streams of water fell from the sky and rose up from the ground and extinguished the flames, and the Mallas also extinguished the fire with vessels of scented water. They laid the bones in state in the Council Hall of the Mallas, set round with a lattice-work of spears and a rampart of bows, and

VI

THE FINAL RELEASE

Abanindro Nāth Tagore

Page 88

there for seven days they paid honour and reverence to them with dancing and music and garlands and perfumes. Now these matters were reported to Ajātasattu, and to the Licchavis of Vesāli, and to the Sākyas of Kapilavatthu, and the Bulis of Alakappa, and the Koliyas of Rāmagama, and to the Brāhman of Vethadīpa; and all these, with the Mallas of Kusinārā, laid claim to the remains of the Exalted One, and wished to erect a mound above them, and to celebrate a feast of honour. The Mallas, however, saying that the Exalted One had died in their village, refused to part with the remains. Then a certain Brāhman of the name of Dona reminded the assembled chieftains that the Buddha was wont to teach forbearance, and he recommended that the remains should be divided into eight portions, and that a monument should be erected by each of those who laid claim, in their several territories; and this was done accordingly. Dona himself erected a monument over the vessel in which the remains had been guarded, and the Moriyas of Pippalivana, who made claim to a share when the distribution had already been made, erected a mound above the ashes of the fire. And thus there were eight monuments for the remains of the Exalted One, and one other for the vessel, and another for the ashes.

PART II : THE GOSPEL OF EARLY BUDDHISM

I. DHAMMA, THE DOCTRINE AND DISCIPLINE

Just, O Brethren, as the wide sea has but one taste, the taste of salt, so also, Brethren, have this Doctrine and Discipline one only taste, the taste of Salvation.—*Cullavagga* ix.

THE whole of the doctrine (*dhamma*, Sanskrit *dharma*) of Gautama is simply and briefly capitulated in the Four Ariyan Truths (*Ariyasaccāni*) or axioms: That there is suffering (*Dukkha*), that it has a cause (*Samudaya*), that it can be suppressed (*Nirodha*), and that there is a way to accomplish this (*Magga*), the 'Path.' This represents the application of current medical science to the healing of the spiritually sick. The good physician, seeing Everyman in pain, proceeds to diagnosis: he reflects upon the cure, and commends the necessary regime to the patient —this is the history of the life of Gautama. The sick soul knows its sickness only by its pain; it seeks the cause of its suffering, and the assurance of a remedy, and asks what shall it do to be saved—this is the history of those who take refuge in the Law of the Buddha.

Let us repeat here the essential part of Gautama's first sermon: [1]

"This, O monks, is the Ariyan Truth of Suffering: Birth is suffering, old age is suffering, sickness is suffering, death is suffering, to be united with the unloved is suffering, to be separated from the loved is suffering, not to obtain what one desires is suffering; in short, the fivefold clinging to the earth is suffering.

[1] Here after Oldenberg, *Buddha*, 2nd English ed., p. 206, with a few verbal alterations.

"This, O monks, is the Ariyan Truth of the Origin of Suffering: It is the will to life which leads from birth to birth, together with lust and desire, which finds gratification here and there; the thirst for pleasures, the thirst for being, the thirst for power.

"This, O monks, is the Ariyan Truth of the Extinction of Suffering: The extinction of this thirst by complete annihilation of desire, letting it go, expelling it, separating oneself from it, giving it no room.

"This, O monks, is the Ariyan Truth of the Path which leads to the Extinction of Suffering: It is this sacred Eightfold Path, to-wit: Right Belief, Right Aspiration, Right Speech, Right Living, Right Effort, Right Recollectedness, Right Rapture."

It is the first division of the Eightfold Path, Right Belief, Views, or Faith, which constitute the Gospel of Buddha, the Doctrine of Buddhism, which we shall now set forth systematically. This teaching consists in a knowledge of the world and of man "as they really are." This right knowledge is most tersely summarized in the triple formula of *Dukkha*, *Anicca*, *Anattā*—Suffering, Impermanence, Non-egoity. The knowledge of these principles is a knowledge of The Truth.[1] Let us consider them in order and detail.

Dukkha

The existence of Suffering, or Evil, is the very *raison-d'être* of Buddhism:

"If these things were not in the world, my disciples, the Perfect One, the holy Supreme Buddha, would not appear in the world; the law and the doctrine which the Perfect One propounded would not shine in the

[1] *Majjhima Nikāya*, i, 140.

world. What three things are they? Birth, old age, and death.

"Both then and now, says the Buddha again, just this do I reveal: Suffering and the Extinction of Suffering."

Dukkha is to be understood both as symptom and as disease. In the first sense it includes all possible physical and mental loss, "all the meanness and agony without end," suffering and imperfection of whatever sort to which humanity and all living beings (gods not excepted) are subject. In the second sense it is the liability to experience these evils, which is inseparable from individual existence.

So far Gautama has put forward nothing which is not obviously a statement of fact. It might, indeed, appear that in our life pain is compensated for by pleasure, and the balance must indeed be exact here, as between all pairs of opposites. But as soon as we reflect, we shall see that pleasure itself is the root of pain, for "Sorrow springs from the flood of sensual pleasure as soon as the object of sensual desire is removed."[1] In the words that are quoted on our title-page: *Vraiement comencent amours en ioye et fynissent en dolours*; in the words of Nietzsche, "Said ye ever Yea to one joy? O my friends, then said ye Yea also unto *all* Woe."

According to the *Dhammapada*:

"From merriment cometh sorrow; from merriment cometh fear. Whosoever is free from merriment, for him there is no sorrow: whence should fear come to him? From love cometh sorrow; from love cometh fear. Whosoever is free from love, for him there is no sorrow: whence should come fear to him?"

But not only is pleasure the prelude to pain, pleasure is

[1] *Visuddhi Magga*, xvii.

pain itself; again in the words of Nietzsche, "Pleasure is a form of pain."

For there is for ever a skeleton at the feast: happiness in the positive sense, joy that depends on contact with the source of pleasure external to oneself, cannot be grasped, it cannot endure from one moment to another. It is the vanity of vanities to cling to that which never is, but is for ever changing; and those who realize that all this world of our experience is a Becoming, and never attains to Being, will not cling to that which cannot be grasped, and is entirely void.

Accordingly, the whole of Buddhist psychology is directed to an analysis of consciousness, directed to reveal its ever-changing and composite character.

Anicca

Impermanence is the inexorable, fundamental and pitiless law of all existence.

"There are five things which no Samanā, and no Brāhman, and no god, neither Māra, nor Brahmā, nor any being in the universe, can bring about. What five things are those? That what is subject to old age should not grow old, that what is subject to sickness should not be sick, that what is subject to death should not die, that what is subject to decay should not decay, that what is liable to pass away should not pass away. This no Samanā can bring about, nor any god, neither Māra, nor Brahmā, nor any being in the universe."

Just as Brāhmanical thought accepts the temporal eternity of the Samsāra, an eternal succession and coincidence of evolution and involution, and an eternal succession of Brahmās, past and future: so also Gautama lays emphasis

—and more special emphasis, perhaps—upon the eternal succession of Becoming. The following stanza has indeed been called the Buddhist confession of faith, and it appears more frequently than any other text in Indian Buddhist inscriptions:

Of those conditions which spring from a cause
The cause has been told by Tathāgata:
And the manner of their suppression
The great Samanā has likewise taught.

How essential in Buddhism is the doctrine of the eternal succession of causes appears from the fact that it is often spoken of as *the* gospel:

"I will teach you the Dhamma," says Gautama, "That being present, this becomes; from the arising of that, this arises. That being absent, this does not become; from the cessation of that, this ceases."[1]

We read again that "Dhamma-analysis is knowledge concerning conditions."[2]

What he taught was designed to avoid the two extreme doctrines of realism and nihilism, the belief in phenomenal being and the belief that there is no phenomenal process at all. "Everything *is*: this, O Kaccāna, is one extreme view. Everything *is not*: this is the second extreme view. Avoiding both these extremes, the Tathāgata teaches the Norm by the Mean." This doctrine of the Mean asserts that everything is a Becoming, a flux without beginning (first cause) or end; there exists no static moment when this becoming attains to beinghood—no sooner can we conceive it by

[1] *Majjhima Nikāya*, ii, 32.
[2] *Vibhanga.*

the attributes of name and form, than it has transmigrated or changed to something else. In place of an individual, there exists a succession of instants of consciousness.

"Strictly speaking, the duration of the life of a living being is exceedingly brief, lasting only while a thought lasts. Just as a chariot wheel in rolling rolls only at one point of the tire, and in resting rests only at one point; in exactly the same way, the life of a living being lasts only for the period of one thought. As soon as that thought has ceased, the living being is said to have ceased.

"As it has been said:

"The being of a past moment of thought has lived, but does not live, nor will it live.

"The being of a future moment of thought will live, but has not lived, nor does it live.

"The being of the present moment of thought does live, but has not lived, nor will it live."[1]

We are deceived if we allow ourselves to believe that there is ever a pause in the flow of becoming, a resting-place where positive existence is attained for even the briefest duration of time. It is only by shutting our eyes to the succession of events that we come to speak of things rather than of processes. The quickness or slowness of the process does not affect the generalization. Consider a child, a boy, a youth, a man, and an old man; when did any of these exist? there was an organism, which had been a babe, and was coming to be a child; had been a child, and was coming to be a boy; and so on. The seed becomes seedling, and seedling a tree, and the tree lets fall its seeds. It is only by continuity, by watching the process of Becoming that we can identify the old man

[1] *Visuddhi Magga*, Ch. VIII.

with the babe, the tree with the seed; but the old man is not (identical with) the babe, nor the tree (with) the seed. The substance of our bodies, and no less the constitution of our souls, changes from moment to moment. That we give to such individuals a name and form is a pragmatic convention, and not the evidence of any inner reality. Every existence is organic, and the substance of its existence is a continuity of changes, each of which is absolutely determined by pre-existing conditions.

Why is this law of causality of such great importance for Gautama, whose doctrine is not a mental gymnastic, but "just this: Evil and the Cessation of Evil"? Because this doctrine is precisely the physician's diagnosis of the disease of *Dukkha*. As a constitutional disease, it is set forth in the well-known series of the *Twelve Nidānas*, the interconnection of which is spoken of as the Law of Dependent Origination (*Paticca-samupāda*). The Twelve Nidānas, afterwards called the wheel of causation, are repeated in no less than ninety-six Suttas; and the importance of the series arises from the fact that it is at once a general explanation of phenomena, and an explanation of the special phenomenon of Evil in which the Buddhist were most interested. The effect of the series is to show that *viññāna*, the consciousness of I, does not reside in an eternal soul, but is a contingent phenomenon arising by way of cause and effect. It should be noted, as Professor Rhys Davids has pointed out, that the value of the series does not lie in the fact that it explains Evil, but in the fact that the right understanding of Causal Origination constitutes that very insight by which the source of Evil—consciousness of I and the desires of the I—is destroyed. The 'Wheel of Causation' turns as follows:[1]

[1] *Majjhima Nikāya*, i, 140.

Other lives (past)	Ignorance (*avijjā*)
	Misperceptions (*sankhāra*) or vain imagining, will (*cetanā*)
This present life and	Consciousness (of I, etc.) (*viññāna*)
	Name and Form, *i.e.* Mind and Body, (*nāma-rūpa*)
	Sense organs (*sadayatana*)
	Contact (*spassa*)
	Emotion (*vedanā*)
	Craving (*tanhā*)
	Attachment (*upādāna*)
Other lives (future)	Coming-to-be (*bhava*)
	Rebirth (*jāti*)
	Old age and death, sorrow, lamentation, evil, grief, despair (*jarāmaranam*, etc.)

This list, wherever it occurs, ends with the formula 'Such is the uprising of this entire body of Evil.' It should be noted that the whole series of terms is not always repeated, and not always in the same order; these are rather the spokes of a wheel than its circumference.

If we now ask what is the effect and what cause, it is clear that Ignorance lies at the root of all. From Ignorance arises the thought of entity, whereas there exists but a becoming; from the thought of self as entity, and from the desires of Me, arises life; life is inseparable from Evil.

The diagnosis implies the cure; it is the removal of the conditions which maintain the pathological state. These conditions which maintain Ignorance, are primarily Craving, and the thought of I and Mine, with all its implications of selfishness and superstition. The means to accomplish the cure are set forth in the mental and moral discipline of the Buddhist 'Wanderers.'

Anattā

Practically inseparable from the doctrine of *Anicca* is that of *Anattā*, that there exists no changeless entity in any thing, and above all, no 'eternal soul' in man. Ānanda inquires of the Buddha:

"What is meant, lord, by the phrase, The world is empty?"

The Buddha replies: "That it is empty, Ānanda, of a self, or of anything of the nature of a self. And what is it that is thus empty? The five seats of the five senses, and the mind, and the feeling that is related to mind: all these are void of a self or of anything that is self-like."[1]

Mental states are phenomena like other phenomena, and nothing substantial such as a soul or ego lies behind them; just as the names of things are concepts. The favourite similes are drawn from natural phenomena and from things constructed, such as a river, or a chariot. If you except the water, the sand, the hither bank and the further bank, where can you find the Ganges? If you divide the chariot into its component parts, such as the wheels, the poles, the axle, the body, the seat, and so forth, what remains of the chariot but a name?[2] In the same way it will be found that when the component parts of consciousness are analyzed, there is no residue; the individual maintains a seeming identity from moment to moment, but this identity merely consists in a continuity of moments of consciousness, it is not the absence of change.

"Like a river," says a modern Buddhist, "which still maintains one constant form, one seeming identity, though not a

[1] *Samyutta Nikāya*, iv, 54. [2] See below, p. 296.

single drop remains to-day of all the volume that composed the river yesterday."[1]

It is of the utmost importance to realize this truth, because for the individual possessed with the notion "I am form; form belongs to the I," "through the changing and alteration of form arise sorrow, misery, grief, and despair." The simile of the river emphasizes the continuity of an ever-changing identity. Another simile, drawn from sleep and dream, emphasizes the intermittent nature of consciousness; the ordinary course of organic existence, called *bhavanga-gati*, is compared to the flow of dreamless sleep; consciousness is only awakened when some external stimulus causes a vibration in the normal flow.

The complex elements of conscious existence are spoken of by the Buddhists in two ways—in the first place as *Nāma-rūpa*, literally name and form, that is to say, 'man's nature and fleshly substance'; and in the second place, as the Five aggregates (*khandha*, *skandha*). These two or five embrace the whole of conscious experience without leaving over any activity to be explained by a 'soul.' The relation of the two schemes will appear from the following table:

Mental factor	Physical factor
1. *Nāma*- (synonyms: *viññāna*, *citta*, *mano*, *i.e.* consciousness, heart, mind).	*rūpa*
2. *Vedanā*, *saññā*, *sankhāra*, *viññāna*, (*i.e.* feeling, perception, will, etc., and awareness).	*rūpa*

In both cases *rūpa* is the physical organism (not 'form'

[1] Anuruddha, *Compendium of Philosophy*. Introd. Essay by S. Z. Aung, p. 9.

in a philosophic or æsthetic sense), the fleshly nature; *Nāma* is name or mind; *nāma* and *rūpa*, name (mere words) and body, are just those things by which a 'person,' in fact complex and variable, appears to be a unity. In the second group, which is not, like the first, borrowed directly from the Upanishads, greater stress is laid on the several elements of the mental factor, with the practical object of shutting out any possible loophole for the introduction of the idea of a mind of soul as an unchanging unity.

Vedanā is 'feeling,' with the hedonistic significance of pleasant, unpleasant, and neutral, resulting from contact with the objects of sense, and itself producing *tanhā*, craving or desire. It is emphasized that 'there is no distinct entity that feels,' 'it is only feeling that feels or enjoys,' and this 'because of some object which is in causal relation to pleasant or other feeling' (Buddhaghosha). Buddhist thought knows no subject, and concentrates its attention upon the object.

Saññā is perception of all kinds, sensuous or mental, that is to say, 'awareness with recognition, this being expressed by naming' (Rhys Davids).

The *Sankhāras* form a complex group, including *cetanā*, or will (volition),[1] and a series of fifty-one coefficients of any conscious state.

Viññāna is 'any awareness of mind, no matter how general or how abstract the content.'

It is to be noted that the terms *rūpa* and *viññāna* are used in a more restricted sense in the fivefold classification than when used to embrace the whole of conscious existence. The rather cumbrous system of the *khandhas* was

[1] "I say that *cetanā* is action; thinking, one acts by deed, word, or thought."—*Anguttara Nikāya*, iii, 415.

later on replaced by a division into *citta*, mind, and *cetasikā*, mental properties. All Indian thinkers are, of course, in agreement as to the material, organic nature of mind.

For the serious study of Buddhist psychology the reader must consult either of Mrs Rhys Davids, two works on this subject. All that need be emphasized here is the practical purpose of the Buddhists in making use of these classifications. "Why," says Buddhaghosha, "did the Exalted One say there were five Aggregates, no less and no more? Because these not only sum up all classes of conditioned things, but they afford no foothold for soul and the animistic; moreover, they include all other classifications." The Buddhists thus appear to admit that their psychology is expressly invented to prove their case. The Buddhists were, of course, very right in laying emphasis on the complex structure of the ego—a fact which modern pathological and psychical research increasingly brings home to us—but this complexity of the ego does not touch the question of the Brāhmanical Ātman, which is, 'not so, not so.'[1]

So much, then, for the fundamental statement of 'Right Views.'

The Four Paths

Frequent mention has been made of the Four Paths. This is a fourfold division of the last of the Four Ariyan Truths. The Four Paths, or rather four stages of the one Path, are as follows:

1st. Conversion, entering upon the stream, which follows from companionship with the good, hearing the Law, enlightened reflection, or the practice of virtue. This

[1] For this question see below, p. 198 *seq.*

depends upon a recognition of the Four Ariyan Truths, and is subsequent to the earliest step of merely taking refuge in the Buddha, the Law, and the Order, a formula which is repeated by every professing Buddhist, including the many who have not yet entered the Paths. The First Path leads to freedom from the delusion of Egoity, from doubt regarding the Buddha or his doctrines, and from belief in the efficacy of rites and ceremonies.

2nd. The Second Path is that of those who will only once more return to the world, and in that next birth will attain Final Release. In this Path the converted individual, already free from doubt and from the delusions of self and of ritualism, is able to reduce to a minimum the cardinal errors of lust, resentment, and glamour.

3rd. The Third Path is that of those who will never return to this world, but will attain Release in the present life. Here the last remnants of lust and of resentment are destroyed.

4th. The Fourth Path is that of the Arahats, the adepts; here the saint is freed from all desire for re-birth, whether in worlds of form or no-form, and from pride, self-righteousness, and ignorance. The state of the Arahat is thus described:

"As a mother, even at the risk of her own life, protects her son, her only son, so let there be goodwill without measure among all beings. Let goodwill without measure prevail in the whole world, above, below, around, unstinted, unmixed with any feeling of differing or opposing interests. If a man remain steadfastly in this state of mind all the while he is awake, whether he be standing walking, sitting, or lying down, then is come to pass the saying, 'Even in this world holiness has been found.'"[1]

[1] *Metta Sutta.*

The Four Paths

The following are the Ten Fetters, evil states of mind, or sins from which the aspirant is freed as he treads the Four Paths:

Sakkāya-ditthi, the delusion of self or soul; *Vicikicchā*, doubt; *Sīlabbata pāramāsa*, dependence upon rites; *Kāma*, sensuality, physical desire; *Patigha*, hatred, resentment; *Rūparāga*, desire for life in worlds of matter; *Arūparāga*, desire for life in spiritual worlds; *Māno*, pride; *Uddhacca*, self-righteousness; and *Avijjā*, ignorance.

The aspirant becomes an Arahat when the first five of these are wholly overcome. Freedom from the other five is the 'Fruit of the Fourth Path.'

"They, having obtained the Fruit of the Fourth Path, and immersed themselves in that living water, have received without price, and are in the enjoyment of Nibbāna" (*Ratana Sutta*). It will be noticed that a clear distinction is here drawn between the attainment of Arahatta and the realization of Nibbāna, while in other places the two states are treated as identical. It is clear, however, that if Nibbāna is the *Fruit* of the Fourth Path, those who have merely entered that Path, and are thus Arahats, have not yet attained the last freedom; they have, indeed, still fetters to break.

There is another grouping of the sins from which the Saint is released, known as the Three, or Four Floods, or Intoxications or Taints. The three are: (1) *Kāma āsava*, sensuality; (2) *Bhava āsava*, desire for re-birth; (3) *Avijjā āsava*, ignorance of the Four Ariyan Truths; while the fourth is *Ditthi*, 'views,' or metaphysical speculation. He who is freed from these three, or four, Deadly Taints of Lusts, Will to Life, Ignorance, and Views, has likewise attained release, and for him there is no return.

II. SAMSĀRA AND KAMMA (KARMA)

We are now in a better position to understand the theory of soul-wandering in Early Buddhism. I say particularly Early Buddhism, because in the greater part of pre-Buddhist thought, and in all popular thought, whether Brāhmanical or Buddhist, the doctrine of metempsychosis, the passing of life from one form to another at death, is conceived animistically as the transmigration of an individual soul.

Take for example, such a text as *Bhagavad Gītā*, ii, 22: "As a man lays aside outworn garments and takes others that are new, so the Body-Dweller puts away outworn bodies and goes to others that are new." Here the *language* is plainly animistic. One reader will understand that a soul, an ethereal mannikin, removes from one abode to another; a second reader, observing that This (Body-Dweller) is no other than That which is 'not so, not so,' perceives that empirically speaking nothing—nothing that we can call anything—transmigrates. There is here an ambiguity which is inseparable in the case of all conceptions which are sublimated from experiences originally animistic or sensuous.[1] Brāhmanical thought does not seek to evade this ambiguity of expression, which is, moreover, of historical significance; and this continuity of development has the advantage that no impassable gulf is fixed between the animist and the philosopher.

This advantage is emphasized by Sankara in his distinction of esoteric and exoteric knowledge, *parā* and *aparā*

[1] As, for example, in the analogous case of *rasa*, which meant taste or flavour in the sense of savour, and has come to mean in a technical sense, æsthetic emotion. So with *ānanda*, originally physical pleasure, afterwards also spiritual bliss.

vidyā: to That which is 'not so, not so,' attributes are ascribed for purposes of worship or by way of accommodation to finite thought. This ascription of attributes, on the part of laymen, is regarded by the philosopher with lenience: for he understands that the Unshown Way, the desire for That-which-is-not, is exceeding hard. Those who have not yet won their way to idealism, may not and cannot altogether dispense with idols.[1] Brāhmanism, regarded as a Church, is distinguished from the Buddhism of Gautama—not yet the Buddhism of the Buddhist Church—by this tenderness to its spiritual children:—"Let not him that knoweth much awaken doubt in slower men of lesser wit."[2] Gautama, on the other hand, is an uncompromising iconoclast. He preaches only to higher men, such as will accept the hard sayings of *Dukkha*, *Anicca*, and *Anattā* in all their nakedness. This position enabled him to maintain one single argument with entire consistence; he needed not to acknowledge even the relative value of other forms or degrees of truth; he wished to break entirely with current absolutist and animistic thought.

This position emphasized for him the difficulty of expressing what he wished to teach, through the popular and animistic language of the day; and yet he could not avoid the use of this language, except at the cost of making himself unintelligible. This difficulty may well have

[1] Those spiritual purists who insist that absolute truths, such as *anattā* (non-egoity), and *neti*, *neti* (not so, not so) ought alone to be taught, and who despise all theological and æsthetic interpretation of these realities as false, should consider the saying of Master Kassapa: "Moral and virtuous Wanderers and Brāhmans do not force maturity on that which is unripe; they, being wise, wait for that maturity."—*Pāyāsi Sutta*, *Dialogues of the Buddha*, ii, 332.

[2] *Bhagavad Gītā*, iii, 29.

contributed to the hesitation which he felt in regard to the preaching of the gospel. The method he was forced to adopt, was to make use of the current phraseology, expanding and emphasizing in his own way, and employing well-known words in new uses.

We have therefore to guard ourselves, as Buddhaghosha says, from supposing that the manner of stating the case exactly expresses the fact. The term Samsāra is a case in point; for this 'Wandering' is not for Gautama the wandering of any *thing*. Buddhism nowhere teaches the transmigration of souls, but only the transmigration of character, of personality without a person.

Many are the similes employed by Gautama to show that no *thing* transmigrates from one life to another. The ending of one life and the beginning of another, indeed, hardly differ in kind from the change that takes place when a boy becomes a man—that also is a transmigration, a wandering, a new becoming.

Among the similes most often used we find that of flame especially convenient. Life is a flame, and transmigration, new becoming, rebirth, is the transmitting of the flame from one combustible aggregate to another; just that, and nothing more. If we light one candle from another, the communicated flame is one and the same, in the sense of an observed continuity, but the candle is not the same. Or, again, we could not offer a better illustration, if a modern instance be permitted, than that of a series of billiard balls in close contact: if another ball is rolled against the last stationary ball, the moving ball will stop dead, and the foremost stationary ball will move on. Here precisely is Buddhist transmigration: the first moving ball does not pass over, it remains behind, it dies; but it is undeniably the *movement of that ball*, its momentum, its *kamma*, and not any newly created movement, which is reborn in the foremost ball. Buddhist reincarnation is the endless transmission of such an impulse through an endless series of forms; Buddhist salvation is the coming to understand that the forms, the billiard balls, are compound structures subject to decay, and that nothing is transmitted but an impulse, a *vis a tergo*, dependent on the heaping up of the past. It is a man's character, and not himself, that goes on.

It is not difficult to see why Gautama adopted the current doctrine of kamma (action, by thought, word, or deed). In its simplest form, this doctrine merely asserts that actions are inevitably followed by their consequences, 'as a cart a horse.' So far as the experience of one life goes, it is simply the law of cause and effect, with this addition, that these causes are heaped up in *character*, whereby the future behaviour of the individual is very largely determined.

Kamma must not be confused with mechanical predestination. It does not eliminate responsibility nor invalidate effort: it merely asserts that the order of nature is not interrupted by miracles. It is evident that I must lie on the bed I have made. I cannot effect a miracle, and abolish the bed at one blow; I must reap as 'I' have sown, and the recognition of *this* fact I call kamma. It is equally certain that my own present efforts repeated and well directed will in course of time bring into existence another kind of bed, and the recognition of *this* fact I also call kamma. So far, then, from inhibiting effort, the doctrine of kamma teaches that no result can be attained without 'striving hard.' There is indeed nothing more essential to the Buddhist discipline than 'Right Effort.'

If we combine the doctrine of kamma with that of samsāra, 'deeds' with 'wandering,' kamma represents a familiar truth—the truth that the history of the individual does not begin at birth. "Man is born like a garden ready planted and sown."

> *Before I was born out of my mother generations*
> *guided me. . . .*
> *Now on this spot I stand.*

This heredity is thinkable in two ways. The first way, the truth of which is undeniable, represents the action of past lives on present ones;[1] the second, which may or may not be true, represents the action of a single continuous series of past lives on a single present life. The Buddhist theory of kamma plus samsāra does not differ from its Brāhmanical prototype in adopting the second view. This may have been because of its pragmatic advantage in the explanation of apparent natural injustice; for it affords a reasonable answer to the question, "Who did sin, this man or his parents, that he was born

[1] That the human individual is *polypsychic*, that an indefinite number of streams of consciousness coexist in each of us which can be variously and in varying degrees associated or dissociated is now a doctrine widely accepted even by "orthodox psychology."

G. W. BALFOUR, *Hibbert Journal*, No. 43.

The same thought is expressed more Buddhistically by Lafcadio Hearn: "For what is our individuality? Most certainly it is not individuality at all; it is multiplicity incalculable. What is the human body? A form built up out of billions of living entities, an impermanent agglomeration of individuals called cells. And the human soul? A composite of quintillions of souls. We are, each and all, infinite compounds of fragments of anterior lives." In the Psalm of Ānanda: "a congeries diseased, teeming with many purposes and places, and yet in whom there is no power to persist."

blind?" The Indian theory replies without hesitation, *this man.*

Buddhism, however, does not explain in what way a continuity of cause and effect is maintained as between one life A and a subsequent life B, which are separated by the fact of physical death; the thing is taken for granted.[1] Brāhmanical schools avoid this difficulty by postulating an astral or subtle body (the *linga-sarīra*), a material complex, not the Ātman, serving as the vehicle of mind and character, and not disintegrated with the death of the physical body. In other words, we have a group, of body, soul, and spirit; where the two first are material, complex and phenomenal, while the third is 'not so, not so.' That which transmigrates, and carries over kamma from one life A to another life B, is the soul or subtle body (which the Vedānta entirely agrees with Gautama in defining as non-Ātman). It is this subtle body which forms the basis of a new physical body, which it moulds upon itself, effecting as it were a spiritualistic 'materialization' which is maintained throughout life. The principle is the same wherever the individual is reborn, in heaven or purgatory or on earth.

In this view, though it is not mentioned by Buddhists,[2] there is nothing contrary to Buddhist theory. The validity of the dogma of non-eternal-soul remains unchallenged by the death survival of personality; for that survival could not prove that the personality constitutes

[1] *Vide* T. W. Rhys Davids, *Early Buddhism*, p. 78.

[2] *Vide* T. W. Rhys Davids, *Ibid.* p. 78. That the theory of the subtle body is not mentioned accords with Gautama's general objection to the discussion of eschatology. It is, however, a tribute to the value of Buddhist thought, that even the proof of the survival of the person would not affect the central doctrine of the soul's complexity and phenomenal character.

an eternal unity, nor can it prove that anything at all survived the attainment of Nibbāna. We may indeed say that Buddhism, notably in the Jātakas, takes the survival of personality (up to the time of attaining Nibbāna) for granted; and were it otherwise, there would be little reason for the strong Buddhist objection to suicide, which is based on the very proper ground that it needs something more powerful than a dose of poison to destroy the illusion of I and Mine. To accomplish that requires the untiring effort of a strong will.

III. *BUDDHIST HEAVENS AND HOW TO REACH THEM*

Gautama has not denied the existence of gods or of future states of existence in heavens or hells. Buddhism is atheistic only in the sense that it denies the existence of a First Cause, and emphasizes the conception of the mortality of all divine beings, however long-lived they may be supposed to be. Apart from this, Gautama is represented as not merely acquiescing in popular beliefs, but as speaking of his own intercourse with the gods and visits to their heavens; and, still more important, all those spiritual exercises which do not lead directly to Nibbāna are specially commended as securing the lesser, but still very desirable, fruits of re-birth, in the lower heavens, or in the Brahmā-worlds of Form or No-form. In all this, moreover, there is nothing illogical to the spirit of the Dhamma, which insists on the law of Becoming, but does not necessarily exclude the possibility of other modes of Becoming than those familiar in our order of experience. Spiritualism, in other words, while quite unessential to early Buddhism, does not in any way contradict the Dhamma.

Buddhist Heavens and How to Reach Them

Group	Plane	Description	Heavens
Brahmā-lokas	*Arūpa-lokas*, or Planes of No-form.	The four highest heavens, free from sensuous desire and not conditioned by form. These heavens are attained by practice of the *Four Arūpa Jhānas*.	
Brahmā-lokas	*Rūpa-lokas*, or Planes of Form.	The sixteen heavens free from sensuous desire but conditioned by form. These heavens are attained by practice of the *Four Jhānas*.	
	Kāma-lokas, or Planes of Sensuous Desire (these are also *Rūpa-lokas* but are not Brahmālokas)	The six *Kāmāvacāra deva-lokas*. These heavens are attained by the merit of good works.	*Paranimitta-vasavatti* gods.
			Nimmana rati gods.
			Tusita heaven (where Gautama Buddha resided previous to his last birth and where Metteya now awaits his last birth).
			Yāma gods.
			Tāvatimsa heaven (where reside the Thirty-three gods and their chief Sakka).[1]
			The Four Great Kings (Guardians of the Four Quarters, N., S., E., and W.).
		The five worlds of men, demons, ghosts, animals, and purgatory.	

[1] A hundred of our years make one day and night of the Gods of the Suite of the Thirty-three; thirty such days and nights their month; and twelve such months their year. And the length of their lives is a thousand such celestial years, or in human reckoning, thirty-six million years.—*Pāyasi Sutta*.

The chief of the gods who are commonly spoken of in the Suttas, are Sakka and Brahmā.[1] Sakka, as it were, is king of the Olympians, 'the Jupiter of the multitude,' and is more or less to be identified with the Indra of popular Brāhmanism. Greater than Sakka and more spiritually conceived, is Brahmā, the supreme overlord of orthodox Brāhman theology in the days of the Buddha. Both of these divinities are represented in the Suttas as converts to the Dhamma of the Buddha, who is the 'teacher of gods and men.' A whole group of Suttas has to do with the conversion and exhortation of these gods, and these Suttas are evidently designed to make it appear that the Brāhman gods are really on the side of Gautama, and to this end they are made to speak as enlightened and devout Buddhists.

The Buddhist cosmogony though related to the Brāhmanical, is nevertheless peculiar to itself in detail, and deserves some attention. It will be better understood from the table on page 111 than by a lengthy description. The most essential and the truest part of this cosmogony however (and the only part which is dwelt upon in the more profound passages of early Buddhist scripture), is the three-fold division into the Planes of Desire, the Brahmā Planes conditioned by Form, and the Brahmā Planes unconditioned by Form. There is a profound truth concealed even in the mythological idea of the possibility of visiting the Brahmā worlds while yet living on earth. Does not he rise above the Plane of Desire who in æsthetic contemplation is "*aus sich selbst entrückt?*"[2] does not the geometrician also know the Brahmā Planes of Form? There are phases of experience that can carry us further.

[1] The impersonal Brahman is unknown to Buddhist dialectic.

[2] Goethe, *Faust*, ii, p. 258.

M. Poincaré writes of the mathematician Hermite: "*Jamais il n'évoquait une image sensible, et pourtant vous vous aperceviez bientôt que les entités les plus abstraites étaient pour lui comme des êtres vivants. Il ne les voyait pas, mais il sentait qu'elles ne sont pas un assemblage artificiel, et qu'elles ont je ne sais quel principe d'unité interne.*"[1] Does not Keats, moreover, refer to the Brahmā Plane unconditioned by Form, when he writes in one of his letters: "There will be no space, and consequently the only commerce between spirits will be by their intelligence of each other—when they will completely understand each other, while we, in this world, merely comprehend each other in different degrees"? If it be true that he who does not attain to Nibbāna here and now is reborn in some other world—and this is taken for granted in early Buddhism—then what is more reasonable than to suppose that those who cultivate here on earth those states of mind which we have indicated, viz. the states of self-absorption in the contemplation of beauty or of ideal form, or in the most abstract thought, are reborn in those worlds which they have so often visited? This consideration is maintained as follows in the *Tevijja Sutta:*

---

[1] *La Valeur de la Science.* Mrs Rhys Davids notices the apparent absence of music in the higher Buddhist heavens (*Buddhist Psychology*, p. xlv); but where form must be replaced by 'high fetches of abstract thought,' there also music may be *silent*, and may not need those articulated instruments which are used in the lower heavens of sense. "Pythagoras . . . did not say that the movements of the heavenly bodies made an audible music, but that it was itself a music . . . suprasensible"—(Schelling); "There the whole sky is filled with sound, and there that music is made without fingers and without strings"—(Kabīr). There also, and in the same way, exists eternally the Veda or Dhamma which is only 'heard' in lower worlds.

Having described the Four Sublime Moods, Gautama asks:

"Now what think you, Vāsettha, will the Bhikkhu who thus lives be in possession of women and of wealth, or will he not?"

"He will not, Gautama!"

"Will he be full of anger, or free from anger?"

"He will be free from anger, Gautama!"

"Will his mind be full of malice, or free from malice?"

"Free from malice, Gautama!"

"Will his mind be tarnished, or pure?"

"It will be pure, Gautama!"

"Will he have self-mastery, or will he not?"

"Surely he will, Gautama!"

"Then you say, Vāsettha, that the Bhikkhu is free from household and worldly cares, and that Brahmā is free from household and worldly cares. Is there then agreement and likeness between the Bhikkhu and Brahmā?"

"There is, Gautama!"

"Very good, Vāsettha. Then in sooth, Vāsettha, that the Bhikkhu who is free from household cares should after death, when the body is dissolved, become united with Brahmā, who is the same—such a condition of things is every way possible!"[1]

We must not, however, suppose that the cultivation of the Four Sublime Moods by an ascetic, and according to the strict Buddhist formula, is the only means of attaining to union with Brahmā. Buddhist scripture recognizes beside these ethical exercises other special conditions of intellect and emotion which are attained in the 'Four Jhānas,' and these practices, like those of the Four Sublime Moods, may be followed by householders as well as by ascetics.

[1] T. W. Rhys Davids, *Dialogues of the Buddha*, i, p. 318.

If it should be proved, or come to be generally believed in the modern world that personality survives death—and is it reasonable to suppose that the accident of death should suffice to overcome the individual Will to Life?—then some such classification of the heavens as is indicated in early Buddhist eschatology may well be used; alternatively, we might speak of the three heavens of the Monist—Beauty, Love, and Truth. And we may well believe with the early Buddhists that those who shall reach these heavens are precisely those who have already experienced similar states of consciousness: the various ranks of artists, lovers, and philosophers. The self-devotion and self-forgetfulness of these must lead as surely as the Buddhist trances to the Brahmā-worlds, on the principle that like to like attains. Equally with the Buddhist trances also, must the concentration of the artist, lover and philosopher tend to final emancipation.

IV. NIBBĀNA

"The story admits of being told thus far, but what follows is hidden, and cannot be told in words."—*Jallāluddīn Rūmī.*

Nibbāna is one of the many names for the goal and *summum bonum* to which all other purposes of Buddhist thought converge. What are *Moksha* to the Brāhman, the *Tao* to the Chinese mystic, *Fanā* to the Sūfī *Eternal Life* to the followers of Jesus, that is Nibbāna to the Buddhist. To attain to this Nibbāna, beyond the reach of Evil, is the single thought that moves the Buddhist aspirant to enter on the Paths. Whoever would understand Buddhism, then, must seek to understand Nibbāna: not, that is to say, to interpret it metaphysically—for speculation is one of the Deadly Taints—but to understand its implications to an orthodox Buddhist and its meaning on the lips of Gautama.

Unfortunately, the term Nibbāna (in its Sanskrit form Nirvāna) became familiar to European students long before the Buddhist scriptures had been made accessible; and the early western writers on Buddhism "interpreted Buddhism in terms of their own belief, as a state to be reached after death. As such they supposed the 'dying out' must mean the dying out of 'a soul'; and endless were the discussions whether this meant eternal trance, or absolute annihilation of a soul."[1] How irrelevant was this discussion will be seen when we realize that Nibbāna is a state to be realized here and now, and is recorded to have been attained by the Buddha at the beginning of his ministry, as well as by innumerable Arahats, his disciples; and when we remember that Buddhism denies the existence of a soul, at any time, whether before or after death.

In the *Milinda Panha*, Nibbāna is compared to a "glorious city, stainless and undefiled, pure and white, ageless, deathless, secure, calm and happy"; and yet this city is very far from being a heaven to which good men attain after death:

"There is no spot, O king, East, South, West or North, above, below or beyond, where Nibbāna is situate, and yet Nibbāna is; and he who orders his life aright, grounded in virtue, and with rational attention, may realize it, whether he live in Greece, China, Alexandria, or in Kosala."

[1] But the *Milinda Panha* also speaks (erroneously) of an Arahat as 'entering into' Nibbāna, saying that the layman who attains to Arahatta must either enter the Order or pass into Nibbāna, the latter alternative here implying physical death (as in the case of Suddhodana, the father of Buddha, p. 48).

He enters into this city who 'emancipates his mind in Arahatta.'

The literal meaning of the word Nibbāna is: 'dying out,' or 'extinction,' as of a fire.[1] To understand its technical import we must call to mind the simile of flame so constantly employed in Buddhist thought: "The whole world is in flames," says Gautama. "By what fire is it kindled? By the fire of lust (rāga), of resentment (dosa), of glamour (moha); by the fire of birth, old age, death, pain, lamentation, sorrow, grief and despair it is kindled." The process of transmigration, the natural order of Becoming, is the communication of this flame from one aggregate of combustible material to another. The salvation of the Arahat, the saint, then, is the dying down—Nibbāna—of the flames of lust, hate, and glamour, and of the will to life. Nibbāna is just this, and no more and no less.

Nibbāna (nirvāna) is the only Buddhist term for salvation familiar to western readers, but it is only one of many that occur in the orthodox Buddhist scriptures. Perhaps the broadest term is *Vimokhā*, or *Vimutti*, 'salvation' or

[1] Other etymologies are possible: thus "It is called Nibbāna, in that it is a 'de-parture' from that craving which is called *vāna*, lusting"—(Anuruddha, *Compendium of Philosophy*, iv, 14). It is important to remember that the term Nirvāna is older than Buddhism, and is one of the many words used by Gautama in a special sense. In the Upanishads it does not mean the dying out of anything, but rather perfect self-realization; to those in whom the darkness of ignorance has been dispersed by perfect knowledge, 'as the highest goal there opens before them the eternal, perfect, Nirvānam'—(*Chāndogya Upanishad*, 8, 15, 1). Buddhist usage emphasizes the strict etymological significance of 'dying out;' but even so, it is not the dying out of a soul or an individuality, for no such thing exists, and therefore no such thing can die out; it is only the passions (craving, resentment and delusion) that can die out. As to what remains, if anything, early Buddhism is silent.

'deliverance,' and those who have attained this salvation are called *Arahats*, adept, whilst the state of adeptship is called *Arahatta*. Other terms and definitions include the 'end of suffering,' the 'medicine for all evil,' 'living water,' the 'imperishable,' the 'abiding,' the 'ineffable,' the 'detachment,' the 'endless security.'

The Nibbāna of which we have so far spoken, it will be seen, is essentially ethical; but this Nibbāna involves, and is often used as a synonym for, 'the cessation of becoming';[1] and this, of course, is the great desideratum, of which the ethical 'extinction' is merely the means and the outward sign. Salvation (*vimutti*) has thus also a psychological aspect, of which the most essential element is the release from individuality. Thus we find defined the following Eight Stations of Deliverance: (1) Having oneself external form, one sees forms; (2) unaware of one's own external form, one sees forms external to oneself; (3) æsthetic hypnosis; (4) abiding in the sphere of space regarded as infinite; (5) abiding in the sphere of cognition regarded as infinite; (6) abiding in the sphere of nothingness; (7) abiding in the sphere of neither ideation nor non-ideation; and (8) abiding in the state where both sensations and ideas have ceased to be.[2]

Another way to realize the practical connotation of the Buddhist Nibbāna, is to consider the witness of those Arahats who, beside Gautama, have attained thereto. Two of Gautama's disciples are said to have testified as follows: "Lord, he who is Arahant, who . . . has won his own salvation, has utterly destroyed the fetters of

[1] *Samyutta Nikāya*, ii, 115.

[2] *Mahā Nidāna Sutta*, 35; *Mahāparinibbāna Sutta*, 33. The 4th–7th stations are identical with the Four Arūpa Jhānas by which the Formless heavens are attained—see pp. 111, 147.

becoming, who is by perfect wisdom emancipate, to him there does not occur the thought that any are better than *I*, or equal to *me*, or less than *I*." "Even so," answered Gautama, "do men of the true stamp declare the gnosis they have attained; they tell what they have gained (*attha*), but do not speak of I (*attā*)."[1] The emancipation contemplated in early Buddhism is from *māna*, the conceit of self-reference, the Sāmkhyan *ahamkāra*. Of him that has attained we can truly say that nothing of himself is left in him. Thus we find a dialogue of two disciples; one has a serene and radiant expression, and the other asks, "Where have you been this day, O Sāriputta?" "I have been alone, in first Jhāna (contemplation), brother," is the triumphant answer, "and to me there never came the thought: '*I* am attaining it; *I* have emerged with it!'"[2]

For the effect on life of the experience of Nibbāna, we have the witness of the Brethren and Sisters whose 'Psalms' are recorded in the *Therā-therī-gāthā*.[3] To take the Brethren first: "Illusion utterly has passed from me," says one, "cool am I now; gone out all fire within." Another describes the easy movement of the life of the free:

E'en as the high-bred steer with crested back lightly the plough adown the furrow turns,
So lightly glide for me the nights and days, now that this pure untainted bliss is won."

[1] *Anguttara Nikāya*, iii, 359.

[2] *Samyutta Nikāya*, iii, 235. *Cf.* the Sūfī conception of *Fanā al-fanā*, 'the passing away of passing away,' when even the consciousness of having attained *fanā* disappears.

[3] Written down 80 B.C., and available to English readers in the careful and sympathetic versions of C. A. F. Rhys Davids, *Psalms of the Sisters*, 1910, and *Psalms of the Brethren*, 1913.

Perhaps the prevailing thought is a more or less rapturous delight in the escape from evil and from craving (dukkha and tanhā), from lust, hate, and infatuation, and from the prospect of re-birth—of continued Becoming in any other conditioned life. From the standpoint of will, again, there is emphasis upon the achievement of freedom, self-mastery, and so forth. And the attainment is also expressed poetically—just as the Brahman in Brāhmanical scripture is symbolized as 'bliss,' 'intelligence,' etc.—as light, truth, knowledge, happiness, calm, peace; but the similes are always cool, never suggesting any violent rapture or overmastering emotion. But while we recognize an unmistakable note of exultation in the conquest achieved here and now, we must also clearly recognize that orthodox Buddhist teaching is characterized by "the absence of all joy in the forward view;"[1] and, indeed, no mystic can look forward to greater bliss than has already been experienced:[2] to what more, indeed, can one who has already attained the *summum bonum* look forward, or what can the physical accident of death achieve for him who has already by his own effort reached the goal? Gautama expressly refuses to answer any question relative to life after death, and he condemns all speculation as unedifying: "I have not," he says, addressing the venerable Mālunkyaputta, who desired information on these points, "revealed that the Arahat exists after death, I have not revealed that he does not exist; I have not revealed that he at once exists and does not exist after death, nor that he neither exists nor does not exist after

[1] C. A. F. Rhys Davids, *Psalms of the Brethren*, 1913, p. xlviii.

[2] For: "Paradise is still upon earth—" (Behmen): "When I go hence, may my last words be, that what I have seen is unsurpassable" (Tagore). There is nothing more to be desired.

death. And why, Mālunkyaputta, have I not revealed these things? Because, O Mālunkyaputta, this is not edifying, nor connected with the essence of the norm, nor tend to turning of the will, to the absence of passion, to cessation, rest, to the higher faculties, to supreme wisdom, nor to Nibbāna; therefore have I not revealed it."[1] The early Arahats, refraining loyally from speculation, might have concurred with Emerson in saying: "Of immortality the soul, when well employed, is incurious. It is so well that it is sure it will be well."

It is most explicitly indicated that the state of Nibbāna cannot be discussed:

As a flame blown to and fro by the wind, says the Buddha, goes out and cannot be registered, even so a Sage, set free from name and form, has disappeared, and cannot be registered.

The disciple inquires: Has he then merely disappeared, or does he indeed no longer exist?

For him who has disappeared, says the Buddha, there is no form; that by which they say 'He is' exists for him no more; when all conditions are cut off, all matter for discussion is also cut off.[2]

Or again:

As the fiery sparks from a forge are one by one extinguished,
And no one knows where they have gone, . . .
So it is with those who have attained to complete emancipation,
Who have crossed the flood of desire,
Who have entered upon the calm delight.
Of these no trace remains.

[1] *Majjhima Nikāya*, Sutta 63.

[2] *Sutta-nipāta*, 1073–5.

On this account they are sometimes compared to the birds of the air, whose path is hard to follow, because they leave no trace.[1]

Let us return to the meaning of Nibbāna or Vimutti as it applies to the still living Arahat. The Arahat and the Buddha have alike attained Nibbāna or Vimutti, and are Vimutto; are we to understand that this state is continuously maintained from the moment of enlightenment to the moment of death? If so, what is it that maintains life in the delivered being? This question arises equally in the Vedānta. The usual answer is that the momentum of antecedent *kamma* suffices to carry on the individual life even after the 'Will to Life' has ceased, and this is expressed in the brilliant simile of the potter's wheel, which continues to turn for some time after the hand of the potter is removed. In any case it is evident that the freedom of the Arahat or Jīvan-mukta does not involve an immediate and permanent emancipation from mortality: the Buddha, for example, though he had long since attained Perfect Enlightenment, is recorded to have suffered from severe illness, and to have been aware of it. It is, no doubt, considerations of this sort which determined the distinction which was sometimes drawn between Nibbāna, or 'Dying Out,' and Parinibbāna, 'Complete or Final Dying Out,' coincident with physical death.

The Arahat has, indeed, passed through an experience which illumines all his remaining life: he knows things as they really are, and is saved from fear and grief: he has realized, if but for an instant, the Abyss, wherein all Becoming is not. He is satisfied of the authenticity of the experience by the very fact that the thought 'I am

[1] *Dhammapada*, v. 92.

experiencing, I have experienced' was not present. But the mere fact that he knows that he has had this experience, and may have it again—may even command it at will—proves that he does not continuously realize it.

It is contrary, moreover, to all spiritual experience—and we must protest strongly against the Buddhist claim that the Buddhist experience of salvation is unique—that the highest rapture should be regarded as consciously coexistent with the ordinary activity of the empirical consciousness, even where the daily routine of life is so simple as that of the Buddhist Brother. And in Buddhist scriptures it is frequently indicated that both the Buddha and the Brethren pass into and out from the highest rapture. At other times the empirical consciousness must be awake—and, indeed, this consciousness, being component and mutable, cannot, as such, be 'set free.' Experience therefore suggests that while Nibbāna is most assuredly accessible here and now—as the mystics of all ages have emphatically testified—a continuous realization of salvation is only thinkable after death. And, as the Buddha says, what that realization involves is not thinkable.

Later Buddhism affords another explanation of the fact that we cannot regard Nibbāna or Vimutti in this life as an uninterrupted experience. This explanation, which is akin to the Docetic heresy of Christianity, logically well founded, asserts that the emancipated individual—the case of the Buddha is particularly considered in a system which regards Buddhahood rather than Arahatta as the goal—is once and for all freed: and what remains, the living and speaking man on earth, is merely a mirage, existent in the consciousness of others, but not maintained by any inherent Will to Life—it is once more, the potter's wheel, from which the hand of the potter has been lifted.

There is a certain amount of evidence tending to show that the Nibbāna or Vimutti state affords the franchise of both worlds, the Byss as well as the Abyss. We read, for example, that when a Brother has mastered the Eight Stations of Deliverance "so that he is able to lose himself in, as well as to emerge from, any one of them, whenever he chooses, wherever he chooses, and for as long as he chooses—when too by rooting out the Taints, he enters into and abides in that emancipation of heart, that emancipation of the intellect which he by himself, here in this present world, has come to know and realize—then such a Brother, Ānanda, is called 'Free-in-both-ways.'"[1] Unfortunately we cannot here take "Free-in-both-ways" to mean "free of both worlds" —the conditioned and the unconditioned—for the phrase clearly refers to the dual character of Deliverance as at once psychological and ethical. But it *is*, nevertheless, indicated that the adept Brother is free to pass from one world to the other, from the Byss to the Abyss, and the Abyss to the Byss at will: and we can hardly suppose that physical death involves the loss of this power: or if we do so, we have immediately drawn a distinction between Nibbāna of the living individual, and Nibbāna of the dead—and the latter becomes the more limited, the less free. And that the Vimutta consciousness after the death of the individual—or rather, altogether apart from the birth or death of the individual—really touches both the Byss and the Abyss, as Brāhmanical mysticism plainly asserts, is at any rate not denied by the Buddha. We even find it laid down that "To say of a Brother thus set free by insight—'He knows not, he sees not'—that were absurd!"[2] In other words, it is clear, the

[1] *Maha-Nidāna Sutta*, 36. [2] *Ibid.* 32.

emancipated 'individual,' after death, does not cease 'to know things as they really are': the doors of perception being cleansed, he must continue to see all things as they are, infinite—or to revert to Buddhist phraseology, as void. There is however no individual who 'sees,' for the erstwhile individual is likewise infinite or void: subject and object are unified in the Abyss. Thus once again, we cannot set up a final distinction between the positive and negative phraseology of mysticism. What is in any case certain is that the Buddhist (and Brāhmanical) use of negatives does not imply that the state of freedom involves a loss for those who find it. For Western readers the language of Western mystics should be a sufficient indication of what is meant: Nibbāna is assuredly 'that noble Pearl, which to the World appears *Nothing*, but to the Children of Wisdom is *All Things*.' Precisely what Nibbāna signifies in early Buddhism, and *Nirvāna* in the Mahāyāna, could not be more exactly explained than in the first and second of the following paragraphs of Behmen's *Dialogues*:

"Lastly, whereas I said, *Whosoever finds it finds Nothing and all Things*; that is also certain and true. But how finds he *Nothing*? Why, I will tell thee how He that findeth it findeth a supernatural, supersensual Abyss, which hath no ground or Byss to stand on, and where there is no place to dwell in; and he findeth also nothing is like unto it and therefore it may fitly be compared to *Nothing*, for it is deeper than any *Thing*, and it is as Nothing with respect to All Things, forasmuch as it is not comprehensible by any of them. And because it is Nothing respectively, it is therefore free from All Things, and is that only Good, which a man cannot express or utter what it is, there being Nothing to which it may be compared, to express it by.

"But in that I lastly said: *Whosoever finds it finds All Things*; there is nothing can be more true than this assertion. It hath been the Beginning of All Things; and it ruleth All Things. It is also the End of All Things; and will thence comprehend All Things within its circle. All Things are from it, and in it, and by it. If thou findest it thou comest into that ground from whence All Things are proceeded, and wherein they subsist; and thou art in it a King over all the works of God."

V. ETHICS

"Let not a brother occupy himself with busy works."
Theragāthā, 1072.

In considering the subject of Buddhist morality, we cannot, in the first place, too strongly emphasize the fact that it was no more the purpose of Gautama than of Jesus to establish order in the world.[1] Nothing could have been further from his thoughts than the redress of social injustice, nor could any more inappropriate title be devised for Him-who-has-thus-attained, than that of democrat or social reformer. A wise man, says the *Dhammapada*, should leave the dark state of life in the world and follow the bright state of life as a monk.[2]

[1] *Dhammapada*, v, 412. The Buddhist, like the Tolstoyan Christian, has no faith in government. We read of spiritual lessons for princes, but the 'road of political wisdom' is called 'an unclean path of falseness' (*Jātakamālā*, xix, 27). The point is further illustrated in Gautama's refusal to intervene when the message is brought that Devadatta has usurped the throne of Kapilavatthu (*supra*, p. 32).

[2] *Ibid.* 87, 88.

VII

THE VICTORY OF BUDDHA

ABANINDRO NĀTH TAGORE

Page 126

Gautama's message is addressed to those in whom he perceived the potentiality of final insight already upon the point of ripening: for these he speaks the word of release from which arises the irresistible call to leave the world and to follow—Nibbāna. "To the wise belongeth this Law, and not to the foolish:" for children and those who are like children (as Professor Oldenberg remarks) the arms of Buddha are not opened. It is not even just to Gautama to contrast his Dhamma—the Buddhist Norm—with the Dharmas which are assigned to men of diverse social status in the Brāhmanical social order. In order to view his doctrine without prejudice we must concentrate our attention upon the *Sangha*, the Order, which he founded: we must compare his system, not with other religions, but with other monastic systems, and consider whether or no its mental and moral discipline is calculated to bestow on those who follow it, the salvation which they desired. For Gautama certainly did not believe that salvation could be attained in any other way, nor by Brethren of any other Order: for such as these and for the vast mass of laymen there could be only a question of rebirth in favourable or unfavourable conditions according to the moral value of their deeds.[1]

The early Buddhist ideal is not only far removed from what is immoral, but also, and not less far, from what is moral: it goes beyond these conceptions of good and

[1] Buddhism has much to say of the future state of those who die unsaved, not having cut off the conditions which determine rebirth. As it is expressed by Mrs Rhys Davids, "The mass of good average folk, going, with the patience and courage of all sane mortals, through stage after stage of green immaturity, through the joys and sorrows that have recurred and will recur so infinitely often, heaven and purgatory and earth itself await their future."

evil, for even good deeds, after the judgment of the world, determine rebirth: verily, they have their reward. "And ye, Brethren," says Gautama, "learn by the parable of the raft that ye must put away good conditions, not to speak of bad." The good is but the raft that carries us across the dangerous sea; he that would land upon the farther shore must leave the raft when it touches the strand. To realize this truth however detracts in no way from a realization of the present value of the raft.

This is a 'Religion of Eternity'—the Brāhmanical *nivritti mārga*—and as such could be legitimately spoken of as anti-social, if it were in the least degree likely or had it been contemplated that it should or could be adopted in its entirety by all. Such religions, while they embody the highest truth to which mankind has attained, are only to be criticized as puritanical in so far as their followers seek to impose an ascetic regime (rather than one of temperance) on all alike; in so far as their view of art is exclusively hedonistic; and their view of worship and ritual wholly unsympathetic.

There is much to be said for the Brāhmanical doctrine of the social debt, and for the view that a man should retire from the world only late in life, and only after taking due part in the life of the world. Nevertheless we must affirm the conviction that the renunciation of the world, at any moment, by those who experience the vocation to asceticism, is entirely justifiable, if the vocation be real. It is, further, a positive social and moral advantage to the community that a certain number of its finest minds, leading a life that may be called sheltered, should remain unattached to social activities and unbound by social ties. Too much stress is laid upon 'utility' in communities where neither *religieux* nor women are 'protected.' And notwithstanding that it is not the purpose of the hermit to establish order in the world, let us remember that the onlooker sees most of the game; it is not without reason that it has become an established tradition of the East that the ruler should be guided by the sage. The example of asceticism, moreover, where this asceticism is natural and effortless, provides a useful corrective to luxury; where voluntary poverty is highly respected, some part of the suffering involved in ordinary poverty is taken away. To this day, the Indian Brāhman ideal of plain living and social discipline strongly influences the manners and customs of all other castes; and the same result is attained by Buddhist monasticism in Burma, where it is customary, not merely for life ascetics, for all men of whatever calling, to spend a shorter or longer time within the fold of the Order.

Most likely the root of the objection which many feel for monastic ideals of the Buddhist type is to be found in the 'selfishness' of their aim, or to put the matter in another way, in the laying of stress on Knowledge, rather than Love. But let us remember that most and maybe all of our 'unselfishness' is a delusion.

No one can grow for another—not one.
The gift is to the giver, and comes back most to him—it cannot fail,
And no man understands any greatness or goodness but his own, or the indication of his own.

Let us also remember that *pity no more could be, if all were as happy as ye*: and just this happiness is promised to all who are prepared to relinquish desire, resentment, and sentimentality. We must not forget that it was a recognized duty of the Brethren, and sometimes of the Sisters, to preach the Dhamma; and who will put forward the assertion that man shall live by bread alone? According to the Edict of Asoka, "There is no such almsgiving as is the almsgiving of the Dhamma." This was equally the view of so practical a Western mind as Cromwell's, whose first extant letter (as Mr Vincent Smith has pointed out) supplies a near parallel to the saying of Asoka just quoted: "Building of hospitals," he writes, "provides for men's bodies; to material temples is judged a work of piety; but they that procure spiritual food, they that build up spiritual temples, they are the men truly charitable, truly pious."

It is most likely that the earliest Buddhism had no other moral code than that of the mental and moral discipline appointed for those who renounced the world and entered the Paths. The following Ten Commandments are those which are binding upon the Brethren:

To avoid (1) the destruction of life, (2) theft, (3) unchastity, (4) lying, (5) the use of intoxicating liquors, (6) eating between meals, (7) attending secular entertainments, (8) use of unguents and jewellery, (9) the use of high or luxurious beds, and (10) the handling of money. Those who attached themselves to the teaching of the Brethren, but remained laymen, were required to obey the first five of these injunctions—all of which, it will be noticed, are of a negative character; but in the case of laymen, the third commandment is taken to mean only the avoidance of adultery.

Practically all these rules are taken over from Brāhmanic sources. This is more particularly evident in other passages of the canonical books where lay morality is expounded in greater detail. When matters are referred to Gautama for his decision, or to the Brethren, the decision given evidently accords with current public opinion; marriage and family life are not directly attacked, it is merely pointed out that the secular life does not lead to emancipation from rebirth and suffering.[1] We have indeed in some books a detailed exposition of the mutual duties of children and parents, man and wife, master and servant. These injunctions lay down just those duties which are acknowledged in the Brāhmanical works, and indicate a blameless mode of life, where special stress is laid on not injuring others, support of parents, and the giving of alms to the Brethren. This is the next best condition to that of the Wanderer, who is a member of the Order, and 'homeless.' The duties of laymen are set forth in the *Sigālavādā Sutta* under six heads: parents should restrain their children from vice, train them in virtue, have them taught arts and sciences, provide them with suitable wives or husbands, and give them their inheritance: children should support those who have supported them, perform family duties, guard their parents' property, make themselves worthy to be their heirs, and finally honour their memory. Pupils should honour their teachers by rising in their presence, by ministering to them, by obeying them, by supplying their wants, and by attention to instruction; the teacher should show affection

[1] But the superiority of the homeless life is again and again emphasized, *e.g.* "Full of hindrances is the household life, a path defiled by passion: free as air is the path of him who has renounced all worldly things. How difficult it is for the man who dwells at home to live the higher life in all its fulness, in all its purity, in all its bright perfection! Let me then cut off my hair and beard, let me clothe myself in the orange-coloured robes, and let me go forth from a household life into the homeless state."—*Tevijja Sutta.* "It is easy to obtain righteousness in the forest, but not so for a householder."— *akamālā of Ārya Sūra*, xxxii.

for his pupils by training them in all that is good, teaching them to hold knowledge fast, instructing them in science and lore, speaking well of them, and by guarding them from danger. The husband should treat his wife with respect and kindness, be faithful to her, cause her to be honoured by others, and give her suitable clothes and jewels: she should order the household duly, be hospitable to kinsmen and friends, be chaste and thrifty, and in all matters exhibit skill and diligence. A man should minister to his friends by presents, courteous speech, promote their interests, treat them as equals, and share with them his prosperity; they should watch over him when he is off his guard, protect his property when he is careless, offer him a refuge in danger, adhere to him in misfortune, and show kindness to his family. The master should care for his dependents by apportioning their work according to their strength, giving suitable food and wages, tending them in sickness, sharing with them unusual delicacies, and giving them occasional holidays; they should rise before him, retire later to rest, be content with what is given them, work cheerfully and well, and speak well of him. A layman should minister to Bhikkhus and to Brāhmans by affection in thought, word, and deed, by giving them a ready welcome, and by supplying their temporal needs; and they should dissuade him from vice, exhort him to virtue, feel kindly to him, instruct him in religion, clear up his doubts, and point the way to heaven. "And by thus acting the six airts (N., S., E., W., Zenith, and Nadir) are preserved in peace and free from danger."

We may also remark of the Brethren and Sisters, that though the practice of good works is by no means enjoined, they were constantly engaged with what we should now call moral education, and to a considerable extent, and more so in later times, with education and learning in general. On the whole, it can hardly be controverted that Buddhist monasticism has been a true benefit to every country where it has been introduced, and that in India also Buddhism as a whole contributed valuable and specific elements to the permanent improvement of current standards of social ethics.

It will be a useful commentary on the present section to append the following quotation descriptive of popular morality in Buddhist Ceylon, where the social influence of early Buddhism may fairly be credited with a considerable part of popular culture:

"There is annually a gathering from all parts of the Island at Anurādhapura to visit what are called sacred places. I suppose about 20,000 people come here, remain for a few days, and then leave. There are no houses for their reception, but under the grand umbrage of trees of our park-like environs they erect their little booths and picnic in the open air. As the height of the festival approaches, the place becomes instinct with life; and when there is no room left to camp in, the later comers unceremoniously take possession of the verandas of the public buildings. So orderly is their conduct, however, that no one thinks of disturbing them. The old Kacceri (Government Office) stands, a detached building not far from the bazaar, and about one-eighth of a mile from the Assistant-Agent's house. Till lately the treasure used to be lodged in a little iron box that a few men could easily run away with, guarded by three native treasury watchers. There lay this sum of money, year after year, at the mercy of any six men who chose to run with it into the neighbouring jungle—once in detection was almost impossible—and yet no one ever supposed the attempt would be made. These 20,000 men from all parts of the country come and go annually without a single policeman being here; and, as the Magistrate of the district, I can only say that any to surpass their decorum and sobriety of conduct it is impossible to conceive. Such a thing as a row is unheard of."—Report of the Government Agent, Anurādhapura, Ceylon, 1870.

To this we may add the testimony of Knox, who was a prisoner in the interior of Ceylon late in the seventeenth century. He says that the proverb, *Take a ploughman from the plough, and wash off his dirt, and he is fit to rule a kingdom*, "was spoken of the people of Cande Uda . . . because of the civility, understanding, and gravity of the poorest among them." Their ordinary ploughmen, he adds, and husbandmen, "do speak elegantly, and are full of complement. And there is no difference between the ability and speech of a Countryman and a Courtier."

But perhaps the best idea of the ethical consequences of Buddhist modes of thought will be gathered from the following Japanese criticism of Western Industrialism, originally published in the Japan *Daily Mail* (1890) by Viscount Torio, who was deeply versed in Buddhist philosophy, and also held high rank in the Japanese army: "Order or disorder in a nation does not depend upon something that falls from the sky or rises from the earth. It is determined by the disposition of the people. The pivot on which the public disposition turns is the point where public and private motives separate. If the people be influenced chiefly by public considerations, order is assured; if by private, disorder is inevitable. Public considerations are those that prompt the proper observance of duties. . . . Private considerations are those suggested by selfish motives. . . . To regard our family affairs with all the interest due to our family and our national affairs with all the interest due to the nation, this is to fitly discharge our duty, and to be guided by public considerations. . . . Selfishness is born in every man; to indulge it freely is to become a beast. Therefore it is that Sages preach the principles of duty and propriety, justice and morality, providing restraints for private aims and encouragement for public spirit. . . . What we know of Western civilization is that it struggles on through long centuries in a confused condition, and finally attained a state of some order; but that even this order, not being based upon such principles as those of the natural and immutable relations between sovereign and subject, parent and child, with all their corresponding rights and duties, is liable to constant change, according to the growth of human ambitions and human aims. Admirably suited to persons whose actions are controlled by selfish ambition, the adoption of this system in Japan is naturally sought by a certain class of politicians. From a superficial point of view, the Occidental form of society is very attractive, inasmuch as being the outcome of a free development of human desires from ancient times, it represents the very extreme of luxury and extravagance. Briefly speaking, the state of things obtaining in the West is based upon the free play of human selfishness, and can only be reached by giving full sway to that quality. Social disturbances are little heeded in the Occident; yet they are at once the evidences and the factors of the present evil state of affairs. . . . In the Orient, from ancient times, national government has been based on benevolence, and directed to securing the welfare and happiness of the people. No political creed has ever held that intellectual strength should be cultivated for the purpose of exploiting inferiority and ignorance. . . . Now, to satisfy the needs of one luxurious man, the toil of a thousand is needed. Surely it is monstrous that those who owe to labour the pleasures suggested by their civilization should forget what they owe to the labourer, and treat him as if he were not a fellow being. But civilization, according to the Occident, serves only to satisfy men of large desires. It is of no benefit to the masses, but is simply a system under which ambitions compete to establish their aims. . . . That the Occidental system is gravely disturbing to the order and peace of a country is seen by men who have eyes, and heard by men who have ears. The future of Japan under such a system fills us with anxiety. A system based on the principle that ethics and religion are made to serve human ambition naturally accords with the wishes of selfish individuals; and such theories as those embodied in the modern formula of liberty and equality annihilate the established relations of society, and outrage decorum and propriety. . . . Absolute equality and absolute liberty being unattainable, the limits prescribed by right and duty are supposed to be set. But as each person seeks to have as much right and to be burdened with as little duty as possible, the results are endless disputes and legal contentions. . . . It is plain that if the mutual rights of men and their status are made to depend on degrees of wealth, the majority of the people, being without wealth, must fail to establish their rights; whereas the minority who are wealthy will assert their rights, and, under society's sanction, will exact oppressive duties from the poor, neglecting the dictates of humanity and benevolence. The adoption of these principles of liberty and equality in Japan would vitiate the good and peaceful customs of our country, render the general disposition of the people harsh and unfeeling, and prove finally a source of calamity to the masses. . . . Though at first sight Occidental civilization presents an attractive appearance, adapted as it is to the gratification of selfish desires, yet, since its basis is the hypothesis that men's wishes constitute natural laws, it must ultimately end in disappointment and demoralization. . . . Occidental nations have become what they are after passing through conflicts and vicissitudes of the most serious kind. . . . Perpetual disturbance is their doom. Peaceful equality can never be attained until built up among the ruins of annihilated Western States and the ashes of extinct Western peoples."[1]

VI. CONSCIENCE

It has often been objected as against Buddhism that while its moral code is admirable, it provides no sanction, or no sufficient sanctions, for morality. And we may say at once, that since the 'individual' does not exist, there can be no question of reward or punishment for the individual, and therefore there is no sanction for morality based on reward or punishment affecting the individual in the future. Neither does Buddhism name any God from whom have proceeded Tables of the Law invested with supernatural authority. The true Buddhist, however, does not need to be coerced by hopes of heaven or fears of hell; nor can he imagine a higher sanction than that of reason (Truth).[2]

[1] Lafcadio Hearn, *Japan*, p. 241.

[2] Those who do not admit the sufficiency of reason cannot be called Buddhists; at the same time it cannot be argued by such *a priori*, that

Since Buddhism is essentially a practical system, psychological and ethical, rather than philosophical or religious, it may very justly demand to be judged by its fruits, and it has no need to fear comparisons.

At the same time it will throw some light on Buddhist thought if we inquire what in Buddhism corresponds to 'conscience.' Conscience—to define the English word—is an internal moral judgment upon the motives and actions of the individual, and as such is an undeniable fact of consciousness; it automatically and instantly refers all activities to a moral standard. This moral standard in a theistic system like the old Semitic is formulated in a series of commandments: in an atheistic system of self-assertion such as is implicitly acknowledged in competitive societies (modern Industrialism) there exist similar commandments, but admittedly man-made and recorded in legal codes; he who breaks no laws has there a good conscience. In idealistic systems such as that of Jesus, the moral standard is resumed in the principle, to love one's neighbour as oneself, a position which the monist justifies by adding, for thy neighbour *is* thyself indeed.

Thus in its lowest form, conscience, which is already recognizable in certain of the lower animals, consists in little more than the fear of punishment, which, however,

for true Buddhists, reason may not be a sufficient sanction. As said by C. A. F. Rhys Davids (*Psalms of the Sisters*, p. xxix), "are we sure we have gauged the working of all human hearts and every touch to which they will respond?" It is noteworthy that in the thirty-four edicts of Asoka advocating moral behaviour, there is only one allusion to the word of the Buddha as such; the only sanction, in the sense of motive for morality, is the welfare of the individual and the common welfare. The idea of promoting the welfare of all beings is deeply rooted in Indian sentiment, and an activity devoted to that end would scarcely have seemed to require a further motive, whether to Buddhist or Brāhman.

may soon develop into a sense of 'sin' which does not altogether depend on fear, but is largely a matter of convention. Another and higher aspect of conscience is based on reason, the knowledge of cause and effect—a full realization that evil actions must sooner or later recoil on the doer, and the reflection, on the other hand, that all beings are like-natured, and therefore it must be right to do to others as one would have them do to oneself. A third and still higher form of conscience arises from the intuition (O.E. *inwit*) of identity: a bad conscience then signifies a consciousness of selfish motive equivalent to a denial of the inner relation of unity to which the conscience is witness.

The Buddhist *sati*, mindfulness or recollectiveness, is to be identified with the conscience based on reason. It works not so much through the fear of consequence, as by a sense of the futility of admitting hindrances to spiritual progress. He that is recollected *reminds* himself of natural law, viz. the coming-to-be as the result of a cause, and the passing-away-again, of all phenomena, physical or mental. To act as if this actual fact of Becoming were not a fact, would be foolish, sentimental, wrong. Whoever realizes, "all existences are non-ego," he cannot act from selfish motives, for he knows no self.

To many Western minds it may appear that to be ever mindful of impermanence cannot be a sufficient sanction for morality. Nor can it be pretended that such a sanction would or does suffice for all. Those, for example—perhaps the majority of professing Buddhists—who regard a heaven to be reached after death, perform meritorious actions in order to attain it. But for those who understand the true significance of Nibbāna, ethical behaviour is derived from a categorical inner imperative, "because of

Nibbāna."[1] Since the highest good is a state of mind (the state of mind of the Arahat, who is delivered from desire, resentment, and glamour), every ethical activity must be judged as a means to the attainment of that state. A bad conscience, then, a state of sin, would be described by a Buddhist as a state of mind contrary to Nibbāna.

It may seem that "Because of Nibbāna" is not a sufficient ethical *motif.* In the same way even the true Buddhist might fail to understand the force of the Christian "Thy will be done," "Thy way, not mine, O Lord," or of the resignation signified in 'Islām.' Yet all these refer to one and the same inner experience, of which we are reminded by the Sūfī, when he says: "Whoso hath not surrendered will, no will hath he." Most probably the force of these statements can never be made fully apparent to those who have not yet in their own consciousness experienced at least the beginning of the turning of the personal will from affirmation to denial. But just in so far as a man allows his thoughts and actions to be determined by impersonal motive—Anattā or Nibbāna motive, as a Buddhist might say—so far he begins to taste of a peace that passes understanding. It is this peace which lies at the heart of all religion, and Buddhism may well claim that the principle "Because of Nibbāna" suffices to settle in the affirmative the question whether or not the system of Gautama is properly described as a religion (though this expression suggests rather a Mahāyāna than an early mode of thought).

[1] Shwe Zan Aung, *Buddhist Review,* iii, 2, p. 107. *Cf.* Clive Bell, *Art,* ii, iii, and G. E. Moore, *Principia Ethica.*

Cf. *Shikshasamuccaya* of Shānti Deva, vv. 21, 23: "Make thy merit pure by deeds full of the spirit of tenderness *and the Void.* . . . Increase of enjoyment is from almsgiving full of the spirit of tenderness *and the Void.*"

That aspect of conscience which inhibits wrong activities—it will be remembered that most of the early Buddhist commandments are negative—is, then, sati or recollectedness. There is, however, another side to conscience which impels the individual not merely to refrain from injuring others, but to expend himself to their advantage, in accordance with the principle that *Love can never be idle*: this is spoken of, in Mahāyāna Buddhism, as the *Bodhi-citta*, or Heart of Enlightenment. It differs from sati chiefly in its spontaneity; it does not arise from reflection, but from the harmony of the individual will with the wisdom and activity of the Buddhas. This condition is sometimes spoken of in Western books of edification as a state of grace, or more popularly as the state of 'being in tune with the Infinite.' But a very excellent rendering of 'bodhi-citta' may be found in Feltham's '*shoot of everlastingnesse*':[1] this phrase is the more appropriate, because the awakening of the bodhi-citta is poetically represented in Buddhist literature as the opening of the lotus of the heart.

The two states of mind which in Buddhism correspond to the Western idea of conscience, are then, *recollectedness*, and *love*; and it is from these conditions that there naturally flow all those conceptions of *the good* which are defined at length in the Buddhist passages on ethics.

VII. SPIRITUAL EXERCISES

A regular part of the daily work of the members of the Sangha—whether Brethren or Sisters—consisted in the practice of certain contemplations. These stations of

[1] "The Conscience, the Character of a God stampt in it, and the Apprehension of *Eternity* doe all prove it a *shoot of everlastingnesse*."—Feltham's *Resolves*.

meditation differ only in minor details from those which are regularly practised by Indian ascetics of other orders. With characteristic systematization, these modes of training heart and mind are often spoken of as forty-four in number. How essentially self-educational is the purpose of these stations of meditation appears from the fact that certain ones are appointed for persons of one temperament, and certain others for those of other temperaments. I have spoken of these meditations deliberately as 'work,' because it is important to understand that we do not speak here of any simple matter such as day-dream or reverie, but of a severe system of mental training, founded on an elaborate psychology, and well calculated—now by auto-suggestion, now by close attention—to produce the type of character aimed at.

Training of the Heart

The first meditations are of an ethical character, and in some respects may be compared to prayer. They consist in cherishing the moods (*bhavanas*) of loving-kindness, compassion, sympathy, and impartiality (*mettā*, *karunā*, *muditā*, and *upekkhā*). These are called the Four Illimitable Sublime Moods (*Brahmavihāras*). The meditation on Loving-kindness, for example, consists in the emphasis of this feeling, the active radiation of goodwill in all directions and toward all forms of life: and whoever will practise this one Buddhist exercise daily at a fixed hour, for a fixed time, and with entire attention, though he learn little else of Buddhism, may be judge for himself what is the development of character to which it tends.

Perhaps we can best understand what the Four Sublime Moods really signify by considering their equivalents in the thought of a modern. When Walt Whitman says:

I do not ask you who you are, that is not important to me,
You can do nothing and be nothing but what I will infold you,

and

When I give, I give myself,

that is mettā. When he says:

I do not ask the wounded person how he feels, I myself become the wounded person,
My hurts turn livid upon me as I lean on a cane and observe,

that is karunā. When he says:

I understand the large hearts of heroes,
The courage of present times and all times. . . .
I am the man, I suffered, I was there,

that is muditā. When he says:

Have you outstripped the rest? Are you the President?[1]
It is a trifle, they will more than arrive there every-one, and still pass on,

that is upekkhā.

The purely intellectual character of *upekkhā*, however (which as it were corrects and balances the three other Sublime Moods), is better explained perhaps by the *Bhagavad Gītā* (v. 18): "They that are pandits indeed, regard alike a wise and modest Brāhman, a cow, an elephant, or even a dog or an outcaste." We are reminded

[1] If for 'President,' we read 'Indra' or 'Brahmā'—precisely the *Presidents* of the deva-world and of the whole Universe, holding office only for the time being—we can understand these lines in a thoroughly Buddhist sense.

of the sun that shines alike upon the evil and the good; and Buddhism also knows of special meditations upon the elements, *e.g.* upon the earth, which harbours no resentment, and is the Indian symbol of patience, or upon water, which becomes again transparent and clear, whatever mud or filth is cast into it. The Buddhist would at all costs avoid sentimentality and partiality: Gautama, perhaps, had reflected, like Nietzsche, "Ah, where in the world have there been greater follies than with the pitiful?"

With the Four Meditations just mentioned is associated another (*asubha-bhavana*), on "Foul things." This very different contemplation is appointed for those whose emotional nature is already active enough, but are on the other hand too readily moved by the thought or sight of physical beauty, or feel a pride in their own physical perfection. The object of this meditation is to impress on the mind that every living organism is subject to change and decay; the practice consists in the contemplation of human bones or half-decayed corpses, such as may be seen in an Indian burial-ground.

It would be difficult to secure for this discipline the sympathy of modern minds. Nor does the method appear quite calculated to secure the desired end; may it not rather enhance the value of the fleeting moment to reflect—

> *Such is the beauty of a maid—*
> *Like autumn leaves they fall and fade?*

Not all the analytic lore of the physiologist makes him any the less susceptible to love. If we neglect, however, this purely monastic aspect of a rather futile endeavour to induce disgust by artificial means, and remember how

Buddhist thought is always on guard to avoid sentimentality, we may understand such a meditation as a corrective to the temperament which falls in love with all that is new and fair, and admires only such art as represents the charms of youth and beauty. But it seems to be overlooked that physical beauty is in itself and so far *a good.* He that would go further must renounce indulgence, not because that indulgence is bad, but because he has other and stronger desires. The true ascetic is not he who is such by a species of mental violence,[1] but he who is thinking of other things than passing goods.

With regard to the purpose of these meditations: we may observe that they are not intended for ascetics only, but equally for laymen, and must have resulted in active deeds of compassion. Buddhist thought, however, is more concerned with states of mind than with direct injunctions to labour for others; and the true purpose of the Four Sublime Moods is to correct the disposition of those who are ill-tempered and uncharitable. To overcome resentment is essential to all further progress; but the Sublime Moods by themselves lead only to rebirth in the Brahmā Heavens of Form. In the subsequent development toward Nibbāna the Sublime Moods are overpast, since they are directed toward other persons, while the thought of the most advanced is directed only to Nibbāna. For the realization of Nibbāna there must be put away not only *bad* states of mind, but also good ones. The former lead to rebirth under painful conditions, the latter to rebirth under favourable conditions; but neither constitutes the saving knowledge which gives emancipation. Buddha is made,

[1] The saying of the poet, that "Desires suppressed breed pestilence," is confirmed by the researches of the psycho-analyst.

in the *Buddha-carita* of Asvaghosha (vii, 25), to speak of these efforts as follows:

"It is not the effort itself which I blame, which flinging aside the base pursues a high path of its own; but the wise, by all this common toil, ought to attain that state in which nothing needs ever to be done again."

Jhāna

A further group of meditations consists of the Jhānas or Dhyānas strictly so-called; these, too, are disciplines of attention and abstraction almost identical with those which are better known as belonging to Yoga.

"Blessed art thou, therefore," says Behmen, "if thou canst stand still from self-thinking and self-willing, and canst stop the wheel of thy imagination and thy senses; forasmuch as hereby thou mayst arrive at length to see the great Salvation of God, being made capable of all manner of divine sensations and heavenly communications. Since it is nought indeed but thine own hearing and willing that do hinder thee." Just as the mystic seeks to be abstracted from mental activity, in order the better to know the One Reality, in just the same way the Buddhist makes a practice of abstraction that he may be delivered from self-thinking and may come to know things as they really are. If we omit the two words 'of God' in the above quotation, or remember that God is No-thing, it will exactly explain the character and ultimate purpose of the Buddhist Jhānas.

One series of these consists in meditation upon certain set objects—for example, a circle of smooth earth—in such a way as to separate oneself from all appetite or impulse in connexion with them. This exercise recalls the disinterestedness of æsthetic contemplation, where the

PLATE K

THE BUDDHA IN SAMĀDHI

Colossal image at Anurādhapura, Ceylon, *ca.* 2nd century A.D

spectator "is from himself set free"; the Buddhist Jhāna aims to attain the same result in a more mechanical way. This contemplation prepares the way for higher things, and by itself leads to favourable rebirth in the Heaven of Ideal Form (*rūpaloka*). The resulting trance is divided into four or five phases.

A further series, which secure rebirth in the Heaven of No-form (*arūpaloka*), consists in the successive realization of the stations of the Infinity of Space, of the Infinity of Intellection, of Emptiness, and of Neither-consciousness-nor-unconsciousness. In these exercises the aspirant experiences, as it were, a foretaste of the worlds of re-becoming to which his character will lead after death; for the moment, indeed, he already enters those worlds.

These exercises, however, do not lead directly and immediately to Nibbāna, but only to re-becoming in the more ideal conditions of those higher other-worlds. Beyond these stations there remained the cultivation of 'thought engaged upon the world beyond' (*lokuttaram cittam*). The method hardly differs from what has been last described, but is *without* thought or desire of any other world, whether of form or formless, and is pursued solely with the view to achieving perfection of insight here and now. For this reason, notwithstanding the similarity of method, the Buddhist authors draw a sharp distinction between the Jhāna which leads to Nibbāna directly, and those Jhānas which merely lead to rebirth in the Brahmā Heavens of Form or No-form.

The term *Samādhi* must also be mentioned, originally indicating any profound pious meditation or concentration —"'*citt'ekaggatā*,' the one-pointed state of the mind, is a synonym for samādhi . . . this samādhi, which is called self-collectedness, has as its characteristic mark the absence of wandering, of distraction . . . and as its concomitants, calmness, or wisdom . . . and ease."[1] Samādhi is also divided under many separate classes, *e.g.* the Empty (suññata), the Signless (animitta), and the Aimless (appanihita), corresponding to the three phases of Vimutti similarly characterized.

VIII. CONSOLATION

Nothing is more characteristic of Gautama's thought than the form of the consolation which it offers to the suffering individual. There is no promise of future compensation, as of a reunion in heaven, but there is reference to the universality of suffering; the individual is led to regard his sorrow, not as 'his own,' but as world sorrow, *welt-schmerz*, inseparable from life itself; all sorrow is self-inflicted, inherent in the conceit of an I. Consolation is to be found in the 'knowledge of things as they really are.'

"The pilgrimage of beings (Samsāra), my disciples," says Gautama, "has its beginning in eternity. No opening (first cause) can be discovered, whence proceeding, creatures fettered by a thirst for being, stray and wander. What think ye, disciples, whether is more, the water which is in the four great oceans, or the tears which have flowed from you and have been shed by you, while ye strayed and wandered on this long pilgrimage, and sorrowed and wept, because that was your portion which ye abhorred and that which ye loved was not your portion?"[2] Not only has each in himself this long inheritance of suffering, but all have experienced and still experience the same. It is related that there came a mother, Gotamī the Slender, to

[1] Commentary on the *Dhamma-Sanganī.*

[2] *Samyutta Nikāya*, iii, 149.

Gautama, having lost her only son, while yet a child. Bewildered by her grief, she set the child's dead body on her hip and went from door to door crying, "Give me medicine for my child!" When she came to Gautama, he answered, "Go into the town, bring me a little mustard-seed from any house where no man hath yet died." She went; but there was no family where death had never entered. At last, going from house to house in vain, she came to herself, and thought, "This will be the same throughout the city . . . it is the Law, that all things pass away." So saying, she returned to the master; and when he asked for the seed, she said, "Wrought is the work, lord, of the little mustard. Give thou me confirmation." At that time she entered the First Path, and it was not long before she attained to Arahatta.

In another place, the Buddhist nun Patācārā is represented as consoling many bereaved mothers of the city in the following words:

> *Weep not, for such is here the life of man.*
> *Unasked he came, unbidden went he hence.*
> *Lo! ask thyself again whence came thy son*
> *To bide on earth this little breathing space?*
> *By one way come and by another gone, . . .*
> *So hither and so hence—why should ye weep?* [1]

And these mothers also, it is recorded, were moved to leave the world; and practising as sisters the mental and moral discipline of the Order, they shortly attained to Arahatta and the ending of grief.

[1] C. A. F. Rhys Davids, *Psalms of the Sisters*, p. 78. Observe that Patācārā's consolation differs little from that of Srī Krishna in the *Bhagavad Gitā* (ii, 27): "For to the born, sure is death, to the dead, sure is birth: so for an issue that may not be escaped thou dost not well to sorrow."

Very significant also is the consolation which the Buddha offers to his disciples at the time of his own death.[1]

"Enough, Ānanda! do not let yourself be troubled; do not weep! Have I not already, on former occasions, told you that it is in the very nature of all things most near and dear unto us that we must divide ourselves from them? How, then, Ānanda, can this be possible—whereas anything whatever born, brought into being, and organized, contains within itself the inherent necessity of dissolution—how, then, can this be possible, that such a being should not be dissolved? No such condition can exist!"

It will be remembered that Ānanda, though in a measure the favourite disciple of Buddha, was also spiritually the youngest, the most backward, and did not attain to Arahatta until after the death of the Buddha. And so when that death takes place, he is represented as overcome by grief, and exclaiming:

Then was the terror!
Then stood the hair on end!
When he endowed with every grace—
The supreme Buddha—died!

and "of those of the Brethren who were not yet free from the passions, some stretched their arms and wept, and some fell headlong on the ground, rolling to and fro in anguish at the thought: 'Too soon has the Exalted One died! Too soon has the Happy One passed away! Too soon has the Light gone out in the world!' But those of the Brethren who were free from the passions bore their grief collected and composed at the thought: 'Impermanent are all component things! How is it possible that (they

[1] Compare with this the death-bed consolation of King Dutthagāmani, quoted p. 300, below, from the *Mahāvamsa*.

VIII

BUDDHA AS MENDICANT

Abanindro Nāth Tagore

Page 150

should not be dissolved)?'" The venerable Anuruddha, one who had already attained, and was an Arahat, does not feel the personal and passionate grief which distresses Ānanda, and he says:

> *When he who from all craving want was free*
> *Who to Nirvana's tranquil state had reached*
> *When the great sage finished his span of life*
> *No gasping struggle vexed that steadfast heart!*
> *All resolute, and with unshaken mind*
> *He calmly triumphed o'er the pain of death.*
> *E'en as a bright flame dies away, so was*
> *The last emancipation of his heart.*

While Sakka, the king of the gods of heaven, under Brahmā, utters the famous lines:

> *They're transient all, each being's parts and powers,*
> *Growth is their very nature, and decay,*
> *They are produced, they are dissolved again:*
> *To bring them all into subjection—that is bliss.*

IX. THE ORDER

The central institution of Hīnayāna Buddhism is the *Sangha*, the 'Company' of Brethren, the men, and in smaller number the women, who left the world to walk on the Path that leads to Arahatta, the attainment of Nibbāna. Gautama himself, together with his disciples, belonged to the class of *religieux*, then well-known as 'Wanderers' (*Paribbājakas*), who are to be distinguished from the forest-dwelling hermits (*Vānaprasthas*). The Wanderers travelled about singly or in bands, or took up their residence for a time in the groves or buildings set apart for their use by good laymen. Thus we hear of the wandering mendicant Potthapāda, who on a certain occasion "was dwelling at the hall put up in Queen Mallikā's Park for the discussion of systems of opinion the hall set round with a row of Tinduka trees, and known by the name of 'The Hall.' And there was with him a great following of mendicants; to wit, three hundred mendicants."[1]

Such mendicants, or *Bhikkhus* (a term afterward coming to have a distinctively Buddhist significance) were often associated in companies, under the teaching of some leader, such as the Potthapāda above mentioned; and we hear amongst others of the following orders with members of which Gautama at one time or another enters into argument: the Niganthas (or Jainas), led by Mahāvīra; the Ājīvikas; the Gotamakas, followers most likely of Devadatta, the Buddha's schismatic and ill-minded cousin; various Brāhmanical groups, and many others of whose views we know little. The first of these groups developed like Buddhism into an Order and a religion, and has survived in India to the present day with an extensive literature and over a million adherents. The Rule adopted by one or the other group of Wanderers varied in detail, but always embraced a certain degree of asceticism (always including celibacy), combined with voluntary poverty.

[1] T. W. Rhys Davids, *Dialogues of the Buddha*, i, 224. Professor Rhys Davids adds the following note: "The very fact of the erection of such a place is another proof of the freedom of thought prevalent in the Eastern valley of the Ganges in the sixth century B.C. Buddhaghosha tells us that after 'The Hall' had been established, others near it had been built in honour of various famous teachers; but the group of buildings continued to be known as 'The Hall.' There Brāhmans, Niganthas, Achelas, Paribbājakas, and other teachers met and expounded, or discussed, their views."

PLATE L

152

BUDDHIST MONK (*bhikkhu*)

Chinese, school of Long-men (8th century)

Collection of Mr Victor Golonbew

We can now examine in greater detail the special Rule which was adopted in the Order founded by Gautama, and organized under his immediate guidance. We have already mentioned the Ten Commandments, or rather, Prohibitions, which must be observed by every member of the Order. The Brethren are also required to wear a monastic costume of yellow or orange cloth, made of torn pieces, sewn together so as to have no commercial value: to seek their daily food as alms; to abstain from food between meals at the appointed hours: and generally, to maintain a decorous behaviour. But they are not required to take any vow of life-long adhesion—on the contrary, those who find they have no true vocation are encouraged to return to the world, where, if they cannot attain Arahatta in this life, they may yet aspire to a favourable rebirth. Nor are the Brethren required to take any vow of obedience to superiors: all are equal, with due allowance for seniority, and degree of spiritual advancement: even in large monasteries, the head is merely *primus inter pares*. The Order constitutes thus a self-contained democracy, analogous to a guild or occupational caste. Discipline is maintained formally by the Order as a whole, acting upon the confession or proved fault of the erring Brother, and appointing, in bi-monthly convocation, a suitable penance; the heaviest punishment, appointed for infringement of either of the Four Cardinal Sins (breach of the vow of chastity, theft, killing, and laying claim to miraculous powers), is expulsion from the Order; mention is also made in Asoka's edicts of expulsion or unfrocking of heretics or schismatics. An external check is also provided by public opinion, which neither in the days of Gautama, nor in modern Burma or Ceylon, would tolerate the mere pretence of a holy life. Thus, says Mr Fielding

Hall, in modern Burma "the supervision exercised by the people over their monks is most stringent. As long as the monks act as monks should, they are held in great honour, they are addressed by titles of great respect, they are supplied with all they want within the rules of the Wini (*Vinaya*), they are the glory of the village. . . . Directly he breaks his laws, his holiness is gone. The villagers will have none such as he. They will hunt him out of the village, they will refuse him food, they will make him a byword, a scorn."

The monastery is also in many cases the village school;[1] and in Burma it is the custom for almost every young man to take the monastic vows for a short time, and to reside for that period within the monastery walls. This possibility of using the Order as a 'Retreat' also explains how it was possible for Asoka to assume the monastic robes without finally relinquishing his throne.

It is above all important to realize that the Buddhist Brother, Monk, Religious mendicant (Bhikkhu, the word in most general use), Wanderer, or however we speak of him, is not a priest. He does not belong to an apostolic succession, nor has he any power to save or condemn, to forgive sins or to administer sacraments; he has no other

[1] "All monasteries are schools."—Fielding Hall, *The Soul of a People.* Of course, teaching is not an essential duty of the Brother, but a task voluntarily undertaken. Similar conditions prevailed, until recently, in Ceylon: "Besides the relation in which the priests stand to their tenants as landlords, and the religious influence of their possession, they have other holds on the possession of the people. Their *pansalas* (monasteries) are the schools for village children, and the sons of even the superior headmen are very generally educated at them. They have also frequently some knowledge of medicine, and when this is the case they generally give the benefit of their advice gratuitously . . . their influence among the people is, in a social point of view, usefully employed."—Ceylon, *Service Tenures Commission Report*, 1872.

A. MONASTERY OF CHIEH-T'AI-SSŬ, NEAR PEKING

PLATE M

B. COURTYARD OF THE PI-YÜN TEMPLE, NEAR PEKING

Photographs by B. F. Johnston

sanctity than attaches to his own good living. The care of a Buddhist temple is no essential part of his duties, though in most cases a temple is attached to every monastery, and is under the care of the Brethren, while village shrines have their incumbents whose livelihood is provided by the produce of lands dedicated to it. But this care of sacred places has no likeness to priestcraft, nor does the temple contain any sanctum which may not be approached as well by laymen as by Brethren.

Each monk is permitted eight possessions only: the three robes, a waist cloth, an alms bowl, a razor, a needle, and a water-strainer. The modern Bhikkhu generally possesses in addition an umbrella and a few books,[1] but the handling of money is carefully avoided. Nevertheless the hardship of voluntary poverty is largely mitigated by the fact that the Order as such is permitted to receive gifts and endowments from laymen, a practice begun even in the time of the Buddha; later Buddhist monasteries became extremely wealthy and are well furnished with residences for the Brethren. Even under these conditions the mode of life is extremely simple, and no one could accuse the monks of luxury.

X. TOLERANCE

India is the land of religious tolerance. There can be no doubt that Gautama and his disciples extended to those of other persuasions the same courtesy which he received. This is indicated not only by the general procedure adopted in the case of argument with opponents, but also in several amiable anecdotes. We read, for example, that Gautama converted at Vaisali a Licchavi nobleman, who had been

[1] Writing was known, but books were not in general use when the order was founded: the basis of learning was what a man remembered.

a follower of Mahāvīra: but he advised him as follows: "For a long time, Sīha, your house has been a place of refuge for the Niganthas (followers of Mahāvīra, *i.e.* Jainas). Therefore you should consider it becoming that alms should still be given to them when they come to you."[1] Primitive Buddhism included eighteen various schools of thought, sometimes spoken of as sects or denominations; according to another classification the number is twelve. Concerning these schools which would arise after his death, Gautama is said to have made the following pronouncement: "These schools will be the repositories of the twelve diversified fruits of my scriptures without priority or inferiority—just as the taste of sea-water is everywhere the same—or as the twelve sons of one man, all honest and true, so will be the exposition of my doctrine advocated by these schools."[2] If these are not the actual words of the Buddha, they testify at least to what the Buddhists at a later period considered that he might very well have said; and this sympathetic position is also well illustrated in practice, for Hiouen Tsang in the sixth century found representatives of all the eighteen sects living side by side in a single monastery without dissension. The traditional tolerance of Indian kings, who extend their support to all sects alike, is also well seen in the case of Asoka, who patronized even the Ājīvikas, whose doctrines are so often denounced by Gautama as definitely false. Certain passages in the Edicts treat of tolerance as follows:

"His Sacred and Gracious Majesty the King does reverence to men of all sects, whether ascetics or householders, by gifts and various forms of reverence.

"His Sacred Majesty, however, cares not so much for gifts or external reverence as that there should be a

[1] *Mahāvagga*, vi, 31. [2] Beal, *Ind. Ant.*, ix, 1880, p. 300.

A. SUMMIT OF ADAM'S PEAK

Shrine of the Sacred Foot-print, with two Bhikkhus

B. LANKĀTILAKA, NR. KANDY

growth of the essence of the matter in all sects. The growth of the essence of the matter assumes various forms, but the root of it is restraint of speech, to wit, a man must not do reverence to his own sect or disparage that of another man without reason. Depreciation should be for specific reasons only, because the sects of other people all deserve reverence for one reason or another . . . he who does reverence to his own sect while disparaging the sects of others wholly from attachment to his own, with intent to enhance the splendour of his own sect, in reality by such conduct inflicts the severest injury on his own sect.[1] Concord, therefore, is meritorious, to wit, hearkening and hearkening willingly to the Law of Piety as accepted by other people. For this is the desire of His Sacred Majesty that all sects should hear much teaching and hold sound doctrine."

[1] He, in the words of Schopenhauer, who "labours carefully to prove that the dogmas of the foreign belief do not agree with those of his own, to explain that not only they do not say the same, but certainly do not mean the same as his." With that he fancies in his simplicity that he has proved the falsity of the doctrines of the alien belief. It really never occurs to him to ask the question which of the two is right. I was once acquainted with an ardent English supporter of foreign missions who informed me that a Hindu was a Buddhist who worshipped Muhammad. Asoka's view of tolerance is that which has always prevailed in India. Compare "Let every man, so far as in him lieth, help the reading of the scriptures, whether those of his own church or those of another" (*Bhakta-kalpadruma* of Pratapa Simha, 1866). The only true missionary is he who brings to the support of the scriptures of others, that which he finds in his own books. The more one knows of various beliefs, the more impossible it becomes to distinguish one from another; and indeed no religion could be true which did not imply the same which every other religion implies. "These are really the thoughts of all men in all ages and lands, they are not original with me. If they are not yours as much as mine, they are nothing, or next to nothing."—Walt Whitman.

It must not, however, be supposed that early Buddhists extended the idea of tolerance so far as to believe that it was possible to attain salvation otherwise than through the Doctrine and Discipline expressly taught by Gautama. Heresy, on the contrary, is regarded as a damnable sin, to be expiated in the purgatories. The Ājīvikas are regarded as particularly impious, and Gautama being asked whether any such can attain to heaven after death—to say nothing of Nibbāna—replies: "In the ninety-one æons, O Vātsya, which I recall, I remember but one single Ājīvika who attained to heaven and he acknowledged the truth of kamma and the efficacy of works."[1]

"Void are the systems of other teachers," says Gautama, —"void of true saints,"[2] a view that is echoed by Brother Nāgita as follows:

> *Outside our Order many others be, who teach*
> *A path, never, like this one, to Nibbāna leading.*[3]

Nor was free thinking actually tolerated within the order. The whole object of the Buddhist Councils, as well as of the final writing down of the Pāli canon, was to fix the true doctrine and eradicate the false. Heretical brethren were excommunicated; the best evidence of this appears in certain of the Edicts of Asoka, who lays down that the Way of the Church must not be departed from, and that those who break the unity of the Church shall be unfrocked, and must dwell apart from the Brethren.[4] It is quite

[1] *Anguttara Nikāya*, ii, p. 227.

[2] *Mahāparnibbāna Sutta* (*Dialogues of the Buddha*, ii, 152). *Cf.* also, "For all beings salvation is only to be found in Buddha, Dhamma, and Sangha."—*Khuddakapatha*.

[3] *Psalms of the Brethren*, No. lxxxvi (Nāgita).

[4] Mr. R. F. Johnston is therefore not quite correct in saying that expulsion from monkhood is never inflicted for free thought or infidelity.—*Buddhist China*, p. 308.

clear that the early Buddhists claimed not merely to possess the truth, but to possess a monopoly of truth. The Mahāyāna is more Catholic. The fundamental doctrine of Convenient Means (*upāya*) of itself implies the necessary variety of external form and formula which intuition or revelation must assume. We therefore read characteristically that—

"Perceiving an incarnation of the Dharmakāya in every spiritual leader regardless of his nationality and professed creed, Mahayanists recognize a Buddha in Socrates, Mohammad, Jesus, Francis of Assisi, Confucius, Laotze, and many others."[1]

The Mahāyāna is indeed in principle as eclectic as Hinduism, and could easily assimilate to itself any foreign religious system as a new sect. For "the Conquerors are masters of various and manifold means whereby the Tathāgata reveals the supreme light to the world of gods and men,—means adapted to their temperament and prejudices."[2] All past and all future Buddhas teach the same saving knowledge in the manner best suited to the time and place of their appearance.

XI. WOMEN

"Reverend Sir, have you seen a woman pass this way?" And the elder said:

> "Was it a woman, or a man
> That passed this way? I cannot tell.
> But this I know, a set of bones
> Is travelling upon this road."
>
> *Visuddhi Magga*, ch. 1.

A good number of the Jātakas or Birth-stories of Gautama are designed to point the moral of feminine iniquity.

[1] Suzuki, *Outlines of Mahāyāna Buddhism*, p. 63.

[2] *Saddharmapundarīka Sūtra*, ii, 36 and 73.

"Unfathomably deep, like a fish's course in the water," they say, "is the character of women, robbers with many artifices, with whom truth is hard to find, to whom a lie is like the truth and the truth is like a lie. . . . No heed should be paid either to their likes or to their dislikes."

The doctrine of Gautama is monastic, as his temperament is unemotional. In the words of Oldenberg, "Was it possible for a mind like Buddha, who in the severe determination of renunciation had torn himself away from all that is attractive and lovely in this world, was he given the faculty, to understand and to value woman's nature?"

We must understand that the Early Buddhist want of sympathy with woman is not an unique phenomenon, but rather one that is typical of monastic sentiment all the world over. It is based on fear. For of all the snares of the senses which Ignorance sets before the unwary, the most insidious, the most dangerous, the most attractive, is woman.

"Master," says Ānanda, "how shall we behave before women?"—"You should shun their gaze, Ānanda."—"But if we see them, master, what then are we to do?"—"Not speak to them, Ānanda."—"But if we do speak to them, what then?"—"Then you must watch over yourselves, Ānanda." To fall in love is a form of *Moha*, infatuation: and just as the monastic view of art takes note only of its sensuous elements, so the monastic view of woman and the love of woman takes into account none but the physical factors. To compare Nibbāna—as the *Brihadāranyaka Upanishad* compares the bliss of Ātman-intuition — to the self-forgetting happiness of earthly lovers, locked in each other's arms, would be for Buddhist thought a bitter mockery. No less remote from Buddhist sentiment is the view of Western chivalry which sees in woman a guiding star, or that of Vaishnava or Platonic idealism which finds in the adoration of the individual an education to the love of all.

We need not deny that the position of Gautama is from a certain point of view just. It is scarcely to be gainsaid that woman is nearer to the world than man; and sexual differentiation is one of those things which are 'not so, not so' in Nirvāna. We have only to recognize that Gautama had no conception of a moral duty to provide for the continuance of the race, such as is implied in the later Brāhmanical doctrine of the debt to the ancestors. He called on men and women alike to root up the infernal grove, to abandon the sexual nature, and to put on spiritual manhood; for those not yet prepared for this change, he felt such compassion as a gentle spirit may feel for those who suffer and whose suffering is the result of their own infatuation.

Gautama's favourite and spiritually youngest disciple Ānanda is frequently represented as advocating the cause of woman. When the question of the admission of women to the Order—in effect a claim to the rights of women not altogether unlike that of the moderns—was raised, Ānanda, already three times refused, finally asks:

"Are women competent, Reverend Sir, if they retire from the household life to the houseless one, under the doctrine and discipline announced by the Tathāgata, to attain to the fruit of conversion, to attain to the fruit of once-returning, to attain to the fruit of never-returning, to attain to Arahatta?"

Gautama cannot deny their competence; in response to Ānanda's further pleas he admits women to the Order, subject to eighty weighty regulations, beginning with one to the effect that even the eldest ordained Sister must stand before and behave with extreme humility toward a Brother, if even only ordained a single day. But he adds: "If, Ānanda, women had not retired from household life to the houseless one, under the doctrine and discipline announced by the Tathāgata, religion, Ānanda, would long endure; a thousand years would the good doctrine abide. But since, Ānanda, women have now retired from the household life to the houseless one, under the doctrine and discipline announced by the Tathāgata, not long, Ānanda, will religion endure; but five hundred years, Ānanda, will the good doctrine abide."

Elsewhere, in reply to another question propounded by Ānanda, Gautama replies:

"Women are soon angered, Ānanda; women are full of passion, Ānanda; women are envious, Ānanda; women are stupid, Ānanda. That is the reason, Ānanda, that the cause, why women have no place in public assemblies, do not carry on a business, and do not earn their living by any profession."

Highly characteristic is the story of thirty charitable men, led by the Bodhisatta when existing in the form of the young Brāhman, Magha: these men, upon a certain occasion were setting up a rest-house at the cross-roads by way of charity. "But as they no longer took delight in womankind, they allowed no woman to share in the good work." It is pleasing to reflect that a lady of the name of Piety succeeded in bribing one of these painfully good men to agree to a stratagem by which she was enabled to share in the meritorious work, and that she thereby earned for herself a palace in the heaven of Sakka.[1]

[1] *Kulāvaka Jātaka.*

On the other hand we find that Gautama did not disdain to accept the hospitality and the gifts of devout laywomen.[1] Such a one is represented to us in the honourable matron Visākhā, "a rich citizen commoner at Savatthi, the chief town of Kosala, the mother of many blooming children, the grandmother of countless grandchildren." This lady makes provision on a liberal scale for the Buddha and his disciples while they reside at Sāvatthi. One day she approaches Gautama and makes eight requests, and these are, that she may be allowed to furnish the brethren with clothes for the rainy season, food to the brethren who reach Sāvatthi, or pass through Sāvatthi, or who are sick, or who reside there, medicine for the sick, and bathing-dresses to the sisters. She sets forth the desirability of such alms in detail. The Buddha replies with words of approval, and is pleased to grant the eight favours. It should be remarked, that in accordance with the Indian view of charity, these are so many favours bestowed upon Visākhā,—not, as Western readers might think, upon the Order; for the religious mendicant, by accepting gifts, confers upon the giver the opportunity of a meritorious deed. Accordingly the Holy One praised Visākhā as one who walks the shining, commendable path, and will joyfully reap for a long period the reward of her charity, in heaven above.

It is justly remarked by Professor Oldenberg: "Pictures like this of Visākhā, benefactresses of the Church, with their inexhaustible religious zeal, and their not less inexhaustible resources of money, are certainly, if anything

[1] The seven most illustrious women of Early Buddhism are: Khemā, Uppalavannā, Patācārā, Bhaddā, Kisā Gotamī, Dhammadinnā, and Visākhā. For the full story of Visākhā see Warren, *Buddhism in Translations*, p. 451 *f.*; for Kisā Gotamī see pp. 23, 148, 270; for Visākhā see p. 52; for Khemā see p. 223.

ever was, drawn from the life of India in those days: they cannot be left out of sight, if we desire to get an idea of the actors who made the oldest Buddhist community what it was."

Gautama, however, did not merely accept the offerings of the respectable, but also those of 'sinners.' It is recorded that upon a certain occasion he accepted for himself and his followers an invitation to dinner[1] from the courtesan Ambapālī, and refused the alternative invitation of the Licchavi princes, to their great annoyance.[2] He also for some time took up his residence in her mango pleasaunce, of which, moreover, she made a gift to the Order. The Sutta says:

"The Exalted One accepted the gift; and after instructing, and rousing, and inciting, and gladdening her with religious discourse, he rose from his seat and departed thence."

It is worthy of note that neither Visākhā nor Ambapālī is represented to have left the world as an immediate result of his teaching, or even to have changed her mode of life; their gifts were accepted by Gautama simply as those of pious laywomen. Each would receive in some heaven the immediate reward of her generosity, and in some future life the fruit of perfect enlightenment.

Buddhist thought gives honour to woman to this extent, that it never doubts the possibility of her putting off her woman's nature, and even in this life becoming, as it were, a man. The case is given of the lady Gopikā who, "having abandoned a woman's thoughts and cultivated the thoughts of a man" was reborn as a son of Sakka in heaven. There was also, and more conspicuous, the

[1] This does not involve sitting down to eat at the same table or at the same time.

[2] See above, pp. 74, 75.

great body of the Sisters—initiated, though under protest, with the consent of Gautama himself—of whom many attained to Arahatta, to Nibbāna; and of these last, the beautiful songs of triumph are preserved in the *Psalms of the Sisters.* And although these Sisters were technically appointed juniors in perpetuity to the Brethren, "it is equally clear that, by intellectual and moral eminence, a Therī might claim equality with the highest of the fraternity." [1]

The woman who left the world and adopted the Sister's rule not only escaped from the restrictions and drudgery of domesticity, but—like the Hindu widow of the type of Lilāvatī, or like the modern woman thinker who meets her masculine colleagues on equal terms—obtained from her brethren recognition as a rational being, a human being rather than a woman; she shared the intellectual communion of the religious aristocracy of the Ariyas. Her point of view in this regard is clearly expressed in the Psalms:

> *Am I a woman in such matters, or*
> *Am I a man? or what am I then?*

and

> *How should the woman's nature hinder Us?*

while all that is essentially feminine is left behind

> *Speak not to me of delighting in aught of sensuous pleasures!*
> *Verily all such vanities now no more may delight me.*

This position is very closely paralleled by that which is put forward by Schopenhauer, and by Weininger. The latter sums up his argument by saying: "Man can only

[1] C. A. F. Rhys Davids, *Psalms of the Sisters*, p. xxvi.

respect woman when she herself ceases to be object and material for man. . . . A woman who had really given up her sexual self, who wished to be at peace, would be no longer 'woman.' She would have ceased to be 'woman,' she would have received the inward and spiritual sign as well as the outward form of regeneration." He asks, "Is it (then) possible for woman really to wish to realize the problem of existence, the conception of guilt (dukkha)? Can she really desire freedom? This can happen only by her being penetrated by an ideal, brought to the guiding star. . . . In that way only can there be an emancipation (Nibbāna) of woman."[1] To these questions the Buddhist experience replies that it *is* possible for woman to really desire freedom, and that no small number of women amongst the Buddhist Sisters attained it.

It may be left to the advocates of woman's 'emancipation' on the one hand, and to feminine idealists on the other, to debate how far these views involve the honour or the dishonour of 'woman.'

XII. EARLY BUDDHISM AND NATURE

> Here, O Bhikkus, are the roots of trees, here are empty places: meditate.—*Majjhima Nikāya*, i, 118.

That deep understanding of Nature which characterizes the later developments of Buddhism in China and Japan we must not regard as entirely alien to the early Buddhists, still less as essentially Far Eastern rather than Indian. In spite of themselves the early Buddhist hermits were lovers of Nature, and even in Hīnayāna literature the poet now and again overcomes the monk. That delight in flowers and forests which is characteristic of

[1] Weininger, *Sex and Character* (1906), pp. 347–9.

the Brāhmanical epics, especially the Rāmāyana, and of the Indian love-song throughout, was also felt by some of the Buddhist Brethren and Sisters. Almost exactly that sentiment which finds expression in Whitman's exclamation

I think I could turn and live with the animals, they are so placid and self-contain'd,
I stand and look at them long and long.
They do not sweat and whine about their condition. . . .
Not one is dissatisfied, not one is demented with the mania of owning things,

is to be recognized in the customary Indian, and therefore also Buddhist, comparison of the ideal man, be he Rāma or Buddha, to a lion or an elephant, or sometimes to a mountain that may not be shaken:

Like elephant superb is he
On wooded heights in Himalay . . .
The Nāga's trunk is confidence;
His white tusks equanimity. . . .
Detachment is the tail of him. . . .
From store laid up he doth refrain.[1]

or, again, the hermit

Shineth glorious in a patchwork robe
As lion in the sombre mountain cave.[1]

or is likened to the mountain's self:

Sure-based, a Brother with illusions gone,
Like to that mountain stands unwavering.[1]

[1] *Psalms of the Brethren* (*Theragāthā*), trans. T. W. and C. A. F. Rhys Davids. The eight quotations next following are from the same source.

Elsewhere the Buddha, or one like Buddha is compared to the flower of the lotus:

So is the Buddha in this world,
Born in the world and dwelling there,
But by the world nowise defiled
E'en as the lily by the lake.

The way of the Buddhist freeman, the Ariyas who have escaped the fetters of the world, is likened to the flight of the white cranes against the cloudy sky.

We find also among the Psalms of the Brethren veritable nature poems:

Those rocky heights with hue of dark blue clouds,
Where lies embosomed many a shining tarn
Of crystal-clear, cool waters, and whose slopes
The 'herds of Indra' cover and bedeck . . .
Fair uplands rain-refreshed, and resonant
With crested creatures cries antiphonal,
Lone heights where silent Rishis oft resort . . .
Free from the crowds of citizens below,
But thronged with flocks of many winged things,
The home of herding creatures of the wild . . .
Haunted by black-faced apes and timid deer,
Where 'neath bright blossoms run the silver streams:
Such are the braes wherein my soul delights.

Another of the poet monks is credited with nine gāthās, of which one runs:

When in the lowering sky thunders the storm-cloud's drum,
And all the pathways of the birds are thick with rain,
The brother sits within the hollow of the hills
Alone, rapt in thought's ecstasy. No higher bliss
Is given to men than this.

While yet another writes:

Whene'er I see the crane, her clear pale wings
Outstretched in fear to flee the black storm-cloud,
A shelter seeking, to safe shelter borne,
Then doth the river Ajakaranī
Give joy to me.
Who doth not love to see on either bank
Clustered rose-apple trees in fair array,
Beyond the great cave of the hermitage,
Or hear the soft croak of the frogs? . . .

No less characteristic are the rain-songs:

God rains as 'twere a melody most sweet,
Snug is my little hut, sheltered, well-roofed.
The heart of me is steadfast and at peace.
Now, an it pleaseth thee to rain, god, rain!

But these are the utterances of individual monks; we cannot frankly credit early Buddhism—the teaching of Buddha—with the kinship of the wild. The love of lonely places is most often for their very loneliness, and because there is the most convenient refuge from the bustle and temptations of the world, from intercourse with worldly men and with women. The lines thus quoted ending, 'Such are the braes wherein my soul delights,' are followed immediately by the edifying justification sounding almost like an excuse:

For that which brings me exquisite delight
Is not the strains of string and pipe and drum,
But when with intellect well-poised, intent,
I gain the perfect vision of the Norm.

While he that notes how "all the pathways of the birds are thick with rain" claims to be absorbed in the ecstasy of thought. As Mrs Rhys Davids says, the ecstasy is here scarcely the product of religious pleasure alone. Is not then the 'gentle paganism' which allows the individual poet anchorite to feel this positive pleasure in the scenes and sights of the forests, regarded from the standpoint of the Norm, a spiritual weakness? To such as yielded thereto, a city life might very well have been appointed by way of penance.

More truly in accord with the monastic will to entire aloofness is the coldness of the monk Citta Gutta, of whom the *Visuddhi Magga* relates that he dwelt for sixty years in a painted cave, before which grew a beautiful rose-chestnut: yet not only had he never observed the paintings on the roof of the cave, but he only knew when the tree flowered every year, through seeing the fallen pollen and the petals on the ground. In the *Mahā-Parinibbāna Sutta*, too, the Buddha holds up to highest admiration the man (himself) who, "being conscious and awake, neither sees, nor hears the sound thereof when the falling rain is beating and splashing, and the lightnings are flashing forth, and the thunderbolts are crashing."

It is true that Early Buddhist literature abounds with many comparisons of the ideal man to an elephant or a rhinoceros. The heart of the comparison, to the Buddhist, lay in the particularization of the elephant as a solitary elephant, and the fact that the rhinoceros is by nature solitary. In this way the Buddhists called on higher men to leave the market-place, knowing that

> "*Great things are done when men and mountains meet*
> *They are not done by jostling in the street.*"

But we cannot credit the Buddhist authors who use these metaphors with any special understanding of Nature, any more than we should the early Christian writers who speak of the lamb and the dove. The comparison very soon, indeed, becomes ridiculous. "Cultivating kindness, equanimity, compassion, deliverance and sympathy, unobstructed by the whole world, let him wander alone like a rhinoceros," is the constant theme of the *Khaggavisāna Sutta*. But this is a false and sentimental view, or at least nothing better than the twisting of natural fact to edifying ends, for the rhinoceros is a surly beast, and the solitary elephant a 'rogue.' Still more is it false, and not "regarding things as they really are" to pretend for the animals—who are not in fact at all emancipate from passion, and who do not think about their sins, or practise *Asubha* meditations—the temperament of an ascetic human. The pagan innocence of animals and children is in truth very far indeed from the Ideal of Early Buddhist monasticism. What these metaphors show us is a phase of the common Oriental tendency to find in natural objects the symbols of general ideas. But they do not yet imply any such sense of the unity of life as finds expression in Matsunaga's poem on the morning glory,[1] or Whitman's passionate confession of belief "in those winged purposes." Even the epithets *migabhutena cetasā*, 'having a heart like the wild deer,' and *araññā-saññino*, 'having the forest sense of things'—for all their beauty—may not always mean all that they seem to say. At least we cannot but doubt if those who used these terms realized all that they implied. In Zen Buddhism, on the contrary, phrases of this sort have a real and deep meaning, for in animals and children the inner and outer life are at one, the duality of flesh and spirit which afflicts us with the sense of sin is not yet felt; the Zen Buddhist does in truth aspire to

[1] See below, p. 256.

recover that unity of consciousness which is asked for in the beautiful prayer of Socrates—to make at one the inner and outer man—and he knows that to recover the kingdom of heaven, the state of Buddhahood, he must become again as a little child, he must possess the heart of the wild deer; notwithstanding he must also overcome the ignorance of which they are not yet aware. But it was not in this sense that the early Buddhist ascetics yearned for the 'forest sense of things;' or if for some it was so, then these individual singers are no longer typical exponents of primitive Buddhism, but forerunners of the Mahāyāna and Zen, taught by their forest masters to understand the unity of life, hearing already the Sermon of the Woods, already breaking through the spiritual isolation of the Arahat and Pacceka Buddha.

That the early Buddhist culture is still far from a true intimacy with the Suchness of the world appears in its lack of sympathy with human nature. It is impossible to claim for a monastic rule which includes as an essential practice the Meditation on the Foulness of Things, a real sympathy with Nature: it is inconsistent to delight in the ways of the wild creatures of the woods, and to turn with loathing from the nobility and innocence of men. It is a strange view of Nature that regards the human body as "impure, malodorous, full of foul matter," an "offensive shape," and a "carrion thing," and strives to promote a disgust for the healthy flesh by a contemplation of decaying corpses. "This body vile," says Sister Vijaya, "doth touch me only with distress and shame."[1]

[1] The morbid aspects of this hot-house cultivation of indifference and purity are indicated in *Psalms of the Brethren*, vv. 316, 1055, and almost equally so in vv. 567 *ff*. See also *Visuddhi Magga*, ch. vi, Warren, *Buddhism in Translations*, p. 298.

No one will wish to deny that the truths of early Buddhism are true, or that the stress that was laid on Anicca (transcience) and Anattā (no eternal soul), and the thought of salvation here and now, constituted a permanent contribution to our realization of 'things as they really are;' and we can hardly be too grateful for the condemnation of sentimentality as a cardinal sin. But the early Buddhists, like so many other enthusiasts, used their share of truth for the denial of others: they were so convinced of the sorrows of the world that they could not sympathize with its joys. In saying this, I do not forget the Sublime Mood of Muditā; but I remember that early Buddhist literature as a whole is filled with a contempt of the world which inevitably precludes a sympathy with its hopes and fears. Early Buddhism does not associate itself with the hopes and fears of this life: it seeks only to point out the haven of refuge from both hope and fear, and its sympathy is with the struggles of those who are caught in the toils of either. The early Buddhist could not possibly grasp the thought that 'The soul of sweet delight can never be defiled.' We must not, on the other hand, allow ourselves to carry too far this criticism of early Buddhist deficiencies. Let us once more remember that this is not a religion for laymen, but a rule for monks, and as such, though severe, it is reasonable and sane, and well designed to cultivate the noble type of character desired. We must also remember that Gautama did not stand alone in his Puritanism; this was the intellectual bias of his age, and is reflected as much in Brāhmanical and Jaina as in Buddhist texts, and it survives as a tendency in Indian thought to the present day, though only as one among others more powerful. The general (not only Buddhist) æsthetic of Gautama's age, moreover, was wholly hedonistic; it was not imagined that music or plastic art considered as secular could have any other than a sensuous appeal, or considered as religious could subserve a more spiritual aim than that of pleasing the gods or fulfilling the purposes of the magician. It was also an age of highly developed material civilization and, at least for those classes where the intellectual movements of Ātmanism and Buddhism originated, of great, if simple, luxury. It was, then, the first natural reaction of the thinking mind to escape from the bondage of the senses by asceticism, cutting off as it were the hand, and plucking out the eye. Amongst many who felt this impulse, Gautama was distinguished by moderation.

This Indian age of asceticism, moreover, we ought to regard as the useful *brahmācārya*, the severe and spartan early education of the future householder, accomplished according to the discipline of the final truths Anattā and *neti, neti.* As one of the most severe critics of early Buddhism has remarked: "Asceticism and Puritanism are almost indispensable means of educating and ennobling a race which seeks to rise above its hereditary baseness and work itself upward to future supremacy."[1] In later centuries the race[2] that had thus by self-knowledge and self-control attained to spiritual manhood, could permit to itself a relaxation of the monastic discipline, proportionate to its growing power to achieve the union of renunciation with sweet delight, and to find in work, no-work. The future civilization of India, above all its wonderful social ideal, was based on the intellectual *tapas* of the Forest-dwellers and the Wanderers of the age of

[1] Nietzsche, *Beyond Good and Evil*, p. 81.

[2] By 'race' I mean no more than the succession of individuals sharing the Indo-Aryan culture.

the Upanishads and of Gautama, and it would ill-become us to depreciate that without which the future could not have been.

The early Buddhist ideal considered as such needs no justification; it is only as against those who seek to establish it as the one and only mode of saving truth, and in particular those who speak of the Mahāyāna and of Hinduism as a falling away into superstition and ignorance, that we have to point out very unmistakably, that the Theravāda ideal, if not positively narrow, is at least definitely limited. No one pretends that with change there did not come both loss and gain; but no religion has ever yet persisted for even a single century unchanged, the possibility of such a thing is even contrary to Anicca, and the Buddhist Dhamma could no more defend itself from growth than any other living seed. Those who would cast away the stem and the branches, whether to 'return to the vedas' of Brāhmanism, or to return to the Theravāda Dhamma of Gautama may be compared to a man who is old in years and experience, and in honourable achievement, and yet, remembering the greatness of the sainted teachers of his youth, would fain never have departed from their feet to deal with good and evil in the world of living men. Let us on the contrary recognize that there exists no breach of continuity between the old and the new laws, and that the Mahāyāna and the later expansion of Hinduism are the very fruit of the earlier discipline. From this point of view it becomes of the utmost interest to seek out and recognize in early Buddhist thought the unmistakable germs which are afterward fully developed in the Mahāyāna, especially the Mahāyāna of the Zen type, and which in alliance with Taoist philosophy effected a reconciliation of religion with the world. Amongst the sources of this wider culture, not the least important are those traces of the love of nature, and that tendency to lyrical and ballad-form expression which we observe so well marked in the Psalms of the Brethren and Sisters, and in the Jātakas.

XIII. BUDDHIST PESSIMISM

It has often been said, and not altogether without reason, that (early) Buddhism is a pessimistic faith. It is to Buddha and such as Buddha that Nietzsche refers when he exclaims:

"They meet an invalid, or an old man, or a corpse—and immediately they say 'Life is refuted.'"

Can we agree that Buddhism is pessimistic? The answer is both Yes and No. Human life is of supreme value to the Buddhist as the only condition from which the highest good can be reached; hence suicide (the real proof of the conviction that life is not worth living) is explicitly and constantly condemned by Buddhist scripture as waste of opportunity. But we have to recognize that the quality of life is very varied, and Buddhism is far from optimistic about any and every sort of life, the mere fact of existence. Gautama ridicules the mere will to life as much as Nietzsche himself despises sensual men; even the desire for rebirth in the highest heavens is spoken of by Buddhists as 'low.' The common life of the world, according to Gautama, is not worth living—it is no life for an Ariya, a gentleman. But on the other hand he puts forward a mode of life for higher men which he regards as well worth living, and claims that by this life the highest good is attainable, and in this conviction that 'Paradise is still upon earth' he is anything but pessimistic. It is true that he refuses to regard life as an end in itself; but so do Nietzsche and Whitman. We do not call the latter pessimistic when he praises death more than life.

Through me shall the words be said to make death exhilarating . . .
Nor will I allow you any more to balk me with what I was calling life,
For now it is conveyed to me that you are the purports essential,
That you hide in these shifting forms of life. . . .
That you will one day perhaps take control of all.

In precisely the same way using 'Death' for Nibbāna, the artist disparages 'life':

"For, looking too long upon life, may one not find all this to be not the beautiful, nor the mysterious, nor the tragic, but the dull, the melodramatic, and the silly: the conspiracy against vitality—against both red and white heat? And from such things which lack the sun of life it is not possible to draw inspiration. But from that mysterious, joyous, and superbly complete life which is called Death . . . which seems a kind of spring, a blossoming from this land and from this idea can come so vast an inspiration, that with unhesitating exultation I leap forward to it; and behold, in an instant, I find my arms full of flowers."[1]

The first of the Four Ariyan Truths then—which affirms the existence of suffering, Dukkha, as the symptom and constitutional sickness of individuality, cannot be called pessimistic, because it merely states the obvious: we know that a conditioned life of eternal happiness is a contradiction in terms.

Moreover, the early Buddhists were very far from miserable; they rejoiced as those who were healthy amongst the

[1] Gordon Craig, *The Art of the Theatre.*

ailing, and had found a remedy for every possible recurrence of illness.

We read, for example, in the *Dhammapada*:

"In perfect joy we live, without enemy in this world of enmity . . . among sick men we dwell without sickness . . . among toiling men we dwell without toil. . . . The monk who dwells in an empty abode, whose soul is full of peace, enjoys superhuman felicity, gazing solely on the truth."

It is to be observed, however, and must be admitted, that the Buddhist view of ordinary life is lacking in courage. The very emphasis laid on Dukkha is false: for it is not Dukkha only, but an exactly equal measure of Dukkha and Sukha alike, Pain and Pleasure, which is the mark of this life. There are indeed many reasons why we cannot place the zenith of our being in this world of Pain and Pleasure; but the predominance of Pain over Pleasure cannot be one of these.

Another mark of genuine pessimism—by which I mean only 'looking on the dark side of things'—is the characteristic Early Buddhist distrust of pleasure. We cannot nobly find a ruling principle of life either in seeking to avoid pain, or in courting pleasure; but much rather in the thought: "I strive not after my happiness, I strive after my work."

The highest state must be without desire, because desire implies a lack, and in this sense the superman, the Arahat, is by definition passionless. Now this is a state which we may best conceive in the manner of Chuang Tzu: "By a man without passions I mean one who does not permit good and evil to disturb his internal economy, but rather falls in with whatever happens, as a matter of course, and does not add to the sum of his mortality."

But the Buddhist is very much disturbed by good and evil—he fears pleasure, and he would avoid pain, and the whole of the Dhamma is designed to achieve the latter end. It is true that saving knowledge must at last release the individual from the possibility of pain: "But Buddhism was the first to transform that which was a mere consequence into a motive, and by conceiving emancipation as an escape from the sufferings of existence, to make selfishness the mainspring of existence."[1] This is probably the most severe criticism that has anywhere been passed on Early Buddhism, and though I think it is unfairly comprehensive, it contains some elements of truth. It is, of course, otherwise with the Bodhisatta ideal, where the individual for an end beyond himself takes upon his own shoulders the burden of the world's ignorance, and freely spends himself in countless lives of supernatural generosity. The Bodhisatta ideal is practically identical with that of the Nietzschean Superman, with his 'Bestowing Virtue.'

But while in certain aspects Early Buddhism has a pessimistic character, we must protest against either of the assumptions: (1) that the view that ordinary life, a mere existence, is relatively worthless, is properly to be described as pessimistic, or (2) that Indian religious pessimism, real or fancied, has any connexion whatever with the supposed unhappy circumstances of Indian life or the enervating consequences of the Indian climate.

As regards the first assumption, it may suffice to indicate that the 'optimistic' Nietzsche pours more scorn on 'mere existence' than is to be found anywhere in Buddhism. And as regards the second, it may be pointed out—to select but one of many arguments—that

[1] Deussen, *The Philosophy of the Upanishads*, p. 341.

the so-called pessimistic beliefs have always proceeded from the higher classes, who enjoyed the good things of this life to the full: if there is a contrast between the childish 'optimism' of the early Vedic hymns, with their prayers for many cattle and long life, and the 'pessimism' of the Vedānta or of Buddhism, this is a result not of a decline in material civilization, but of the accumulation of experience. For the Indian view is the correct one, that it is not deprivation of the good things of this world that leads the wise at last to turn to higher thoughts, but rather long experience of their ultimate monotony. Desires suppressed breed pestilence: but the road of excess leads to the palace of wisdom. Emancipation seeks to avoid a future heaven no less than a future hell—had it been prompted by a mere reaction for the misery of physical existence, this must have created a religion similar to certain aspects of Christianity where *compensation* for the sorrows of this life is expected in a heaven of endless delight.

XIV. A BUDDHIST EMPEROR

A characteristic story is related in the later legendary history of Gautama. It is said that when he was seated beneath the Bodhi tree, and near to attain Nibbāna, the Evil One, failing to shake his purpose in other ways, appeared in the guise of a messenger with letters bearing the false report that Devadatta—Gautama's cousin and constant enemy—had usurped the throne of Kapilavastu, and had taken the wives and the goods of Gautama to himself and imprisoned his father; the letters urged him to return to restore peace and order. But Gautama reflected that Devadatta's action resulted from his malice and lust, while the Sākyas, in not defending their king had shown a cowardly and despicable disposition. Contemplating these follies and weaknesses of the natural man, his own resolution to attain to something higher and better was confirmed in him.[1]

This legend aptly expresses the indifference of Buddhism to the order of the world. It is in full accord with this point of view that Buddhism has never formulated the ideal of a social order of this or that type: its ethic is purely individualistic, and places no reliance whatever on external regulation. Mere good government cannot lead to the Dying Out (Nibbāna) of Craving, Resentment, and Infatuation: and since the Gospel of Gautama has solely to do with the way to that Dying Out, it is not concerned with government at all. This position is practically identical with that of Jesus, who repudiated any alliance of the Kingdom of God with temporal power. In agreement with this view, both the father and mother of Gautama, and his wife and son, and a host of Sākya princes resigned their worldly status and became homeless followers of Him-who-has-thus-attained.

If, however, every ruler who accepted the Buddhist Gospel had immediately adopted the homeless life, it would be impossible to speak of Buddhist emperors or kings. We find, on the contrary, that ruling princes, Buddhist by education or conversion, constantly retained their temporal power, and used this power for the propagation of the Dhamma, for the support of the Brethren, and for the maintenance of social order conformable to Buddhist ethic. History preserves for us the names of many such Buddhist kings, who, notwithstanding that Buddhism is a Gospel of self-mastery alone, sought to improve the order of the world by ruling others. It is in this way that the doctrine which was

[1] Beal, *Romantic History of Buddha*, p. 207: *supra*, p. 32.

originally, not perhaps altogether anti-social, but at least non-social, has come to have an influence upon the social order.

We shall gain a good idea of the social influence of Buddhism by devoting attention to Asoka Maurya, the most famous of the Buddhist rulers of India. Asoka succeeded to the throne of Magadha about 270 B.C. and received a more formal coronation four years later. The first great event in his reign took place eight years later; this was the conquest of Kalinga, a considerable territory bordering the east coast, south of the modern Orissa; with this addition, his territory embraced the whole of India except the extreme south. This conquest involved the slaughter of 100,000 persons, while half as many again were carried into captivity, and many more perished from famine and pestilence. Perhaps the spectacle of so much suffering predisposed the Emperor to consider with special attention that system of which the sole aim was to point out the way of salvation from Suffering, Dukkha.[1] At any rate Asoka himself records his adhesion to the Buddhist Dhamma in the following terms:

"Directly after the annexation of the Kalingas, began his Sacred Majesty's zealous protection of the Dhamma, his love of that Dhamma, and his giving instruction therein. Thus arose His Sacred Majesty's remorse for having conquered the Kalingas, because the conquest of a country

[1] "Victory," says the *Dhammapada*, v. 201, "breeds hatred, for the conquered is unhappy." It is worth notice that it has been suggested that the study of Buddhism is likely to receive a great impetus in the immediate future, because of "its power to restrain its adherents from those sanguinary outbreaks of international butchery which occur about once in every generation in the West."—*Cambridge Magazine*, April 24, 1915.

previously unconquered involves the slaughter, death, and carrying away captive of the people. That is a matter of profound sorrow and regret to His Sacred Majesty," and thus connecting his conversion with the change of attitude toward others, he continues:

"Thus of all the people who were then slain, done to death, or carried away captive in the Kalingas, if the hundredth or the thousandth part were to suffer the same fate, it would now be matter of regret to His Sacred Majesty. Moreover, should any one do him wrong that too must be borne with by His Sacred Majesty, if it can possibly be borne with. . . . His Sacred Majesty desires that all animate beings should have security, self-control, peace of mind, and joyousness. . . . And for this purpose has this pious edict been written in order that my sons and grandsons, who may be, should not regard it as their duty to conquer a new conquest. If, perchance, they become engaged in a conquest by arms, they should take pleasure in patience and gentleness, and regard as (the only true) conquest the conquest won by piety. That avails for both this world and the next. Let all joy be in effort, because that avails for both this world and the next."

In many other edicts, which were engraved on stone and are still extant, Asoka proclaims his Dhamma in great detail. This Dhamma is distinctively Buddhist, but it differs from the teaching of Gautama in omitting all references to the analytic aspect and dwelling exclusively on ethics: Nibbāna is not even mentioned, and the reward of well-doing is to be the Imperial favour in this world and well-being in the next, 'the beyond'—not the avoidance of rebirth. The mention of former Buddhas together with other details, shows already some development of Mahāyānist doctrines. It is thus possible that

Asoka made the determination to attain Buddhahood in some future life, but more likely he looked forward only to a future attainment of Arahatta.

The edicts are essentially concerned with ethical behaviour; they imply a considerable amount of interference with personal liberty, such as we should now call 'making people good by Act of Parliament.' Asoka desires to be a father to his subjects, and speaks with parental authority. He lays the greatest stress on religious tolerance and on the duty of reverence to those whose age or station deserves it; and strongly inculcates the sanctity of animal life. On the other hand there is no attempt to abolish capital punishment. Reverence, compassion, truthfulness and sympathy are the cardinal virtues.

The most remarkable, far-reaching and permanent effects of Asoka's activities are those which resulted from his Foreign Missions. This phrase is to be understood in the modern evangelical, and not in a political, sense: for we find that not content with preaching the Dhamma to his own subjects, Asoka dispatched imperial missionaries to all other parts of India, to Ceylon, and then to Syria, Egypt, Cyrene, Macedonia, and Epirus, and these missionarises together with the Buddhist Dhamma were also charged to diffuse a knowledge of useful medicines. It is due more to Asoka than to any other individual that Buddhism became and long remained the predominant religion of India, and indeed of Asia, and up to the present day counts more adherents than any other faith.

The conversion of Ceylon is recorded in the Chronicles of Ceylon with a wealth of picturesque detail which is partly confirmed by archæological discoveries in Northern India, but cannot be regarded as historical *in toto*. In

PLATE O

SĀNCHĪ STŪPA AND GATEWAY
3rd and 2nd century B.C.

particular, it is related that Asoka's chief missionary to Ceylon was a son named Mahendra, who converted the King of Ceylon and 40,000 of his subjects. In order that the Princess Anula and other women might also be ordained, a return mission was sent to request the dispatch of Asoka's daughter Sanghamitta, with a branch of the sacred Bodhi tree to be planted in Ceylon. It is claimed that the sacred Bo-tree still preserved at Anurādhapura in Ceylon, is that same branch, which has become the oldest historical tree in the world. The Princess was duly ordained by Sanghamitta and became an Arahat. In point of fact the conversion of Ceylon must have been more gradual than is here indicated, but there is no doubt that embassies were exchanged and converts made. The Sinhalese—not, of course, the Tamils who occupy a good part of the north of the island—have remained Buddhists to this day, and for the most part, though not exclusively, of the orthodox Hīnayāna persuasion.

We must also think of Asoka as a great administrator and a great builder. His Empire embraced almost the whole of India and Afghanistan, of which the administration was already highly organized alike for record and executive action. With tireless energy Asoka attempted the impossible task of personally supervising all the affairs of government: "I am never fully satisfied," he says, "with my efforts and my dispatch of business."

The essential character of his rule was a paternal despotism. That he successfully ruled so large an Empire for forty years is proof of his ability, as the words of his edicts are of his strong individuality—which has been likened to that of Cromwell and Constantine—and practical piety.

We have already mentioned that the Edicts were engraved

on stone, and that many survive. Some of these are recorded on monolithic pillars; by far the finest of these is the pillar recently discovered at Sārnāth, among the monasteries on the site of the old deer-park at Benares, where Gautama preached his first sermon. The pillar was surmounted by a lion capital (Plate P), with a string course bearing a horse, lion, bull, and elephant in relief, and the Wheel of the Law, above a bell-shaped base of Persian character, such as appears elsewhere in contemporary architecture. The whole is of extraordinarily perfect workmanship only paralleled in finish by the accurate fitting of some of the Asokan masonry, and the burnished surfaces of some of the rock-cells dedicated by Asoka for the use of the Ājīvikas: and we must not forget the engineering skill implied in the transport and erection, often hundreds of miles from the present quarries, of monolithic pillars weighing as much as fifty tons.

Asoka's own capital at Pātaliputra,[1] modern Patna, is described as follows by the Chinese pilgrim Fa Hien, eight centuries later:

"The royal palace and halls in the midst of the city, which exist now as of old, were all made by spirits which he employed, and which piled up the stones, reared the walls and gates, and executed the elegant carving and inlaid sculpture work in a way which no human hands of this world could accomplish."

[1] Excavations on this site are now in progress.

PLATE P

CAPITAL OF ASOKA COLUMN

Sārnāth, 3rd century B.C.

PART III : CONTEMPORARY SYSTEMS

I. THE VEDĀNTA

THE system of philosophy which is above all the philosophy of India is the Vedānta, the 'completion' or 'goal' of the Vedas: and by this term Vedānta is to be understood the interpretation of the Upanishads, and of the Vedānta Sūtras, according to Sankarācārya in the ninth century A.D. and by Rāmānūja in the eleventh. It will be seen that these synthetic interpretations are long post-Buddhist; but that is not the case with the most important of the actual Upanishads, viz. the Brihadāranyaka and the Chāndogya, which are undoubtedly pre-Buddhist. These are likewise the most important of the Vedānta scriptures, and they must be the more referred to here because some writers have considered that "it is the ideas of the Upanishads which by a kind of degeneration have developed into Buddhism on one side and the Sāmkhya system on the other."

Just as the Old Testament is superseded by the New, so the Upanishads declare the insufficiency of ritual and its reward, and substitute for these a religion of the spirit. All the Upanishads alike treat of one subject, the doctrine of the Brahman or Ātman. Very often these are treated as synonymous. If or where a distinction is made, then the Brahman is the Absolute, and the Ātman is that Absolute as realized in the individual consciousness; we can then express the fundamental thought of the Upanishads by the simple equation

Brahman = Ātman.

If we should seek a simile for this identity we may

find it in the identity of Infinite Space with the space in any closed vessel—shatter the bounding walls of the vessel, that is to say, the ignorance that maintains our seeming individuality, and the identity of space with space is patent. "That art Thou"—this is the form the equation takes: in the actual language of the Brihadāranyaka, *Tat tvam asi.* That Absolute is one and the same with whatever in ourselves we must consider as our true Self, the unchangeable essence of our being, our spirit. What then is the spirit of man? What am I? That is a question to which, as the Vedānta recognizes, there may be many answers. Even the most idealistic Upanishads do not start by denying, as Gautama denies, the existence of an I, a knowing, perduring subject; it is only by a process of elimination that the thought is reached that the Subject is No-thing. Thus, some identify the ego with the body, as we still do in everyday parlance, when for example, we say 'I am cold,' meaning 'The body is cold.' But seeing that the body visibly changes and decays how are we to identify our overwhelming consciousness of the eternity and freedom of our being with the mortal flesh? Another answer postulates an 'Eternal Soul,' a dweller in the body passing from body to body: this is the well-known Indian theory of transmigration of an individual—for which, in Buddhism, is substituted the transmigration of character. Such a soul, if imagined to be freed from corporeal fetters, may be likened to the dream consciousness, where the bonds of time and space are loosely drawn. Analogous to this view is the Christian doctrine of an Eternal Soul which passes from Earth to an Eternal Heaven or Hell, and it is against such conceptions of the Ātman that the Anattā theory of Buddhism is directed. A third view is idealistic, recognizing only one supreme soul, wherein there is no duality, "neither shadow of turning" nor consciousness of subject and object. This view, subject to slight differences of interpretation, forms the common philosophic basis of a great part of Eastern and Western mysticism. Here the state of the self is likened to Deep Sleep. It is this universal Self, one without any other, which the individual seeker pressing inward to the centre finds in his own consciousness, when nothing of himself is left in him. Philosophically, as we have said, it is reached by a process of elimination—the superposition of attributes,[1] and the successive denial of each in turn, as each is found to contradict our consciousness of timeless being and utter freedom: and thus we reach the great Vedāntic formula, descriptive of the Ātman or Brahman as 'Not so, not so.' The 'soul' is, then, void, No thing, it does not pass from birth to death, it has no parts, it is not subject to becoming nor to time, but is that timeless Abyss which is now as it was in the beginning and ever shall be. To these three stations of the soul the later Upanishads add a fourth, which is simply so called, The Fourth.

We have, then, four stations. First is the *Waking Consciousness* of everyday experience:

[1] The full list of these attributes, called *Upādhis* or individualizing determinations, includes (1) all things and relations of the outer world, (2) the body, consisting of the gross elements, (3) the *Indriyas*, viz., the five organs of sense and the corresponding five organs of action, (4) the *Manas* (mind) or *Antahkarana* (inner organ) which covers the understanding and conscious will, the unified or seemingly unified principle of conscious life, the 'soul' in a popular sense, and (5) the *mukhya prāna*, vital airs, the similarly unified or seemingly unified principle of unconscious life. All these are cut away by him who finds the Self, which is the Brahman, 'not so, not so.'

When the soul is blinded by glamour (māyā)
It inhabits the body and accomplishes actions ;
By women, food, drink, and many enjoyments,
It obtains satisfaction in a waking condition.[1]

In the second station, of Dream-sleep:

In the dream-state he moves up and down,
And fashions for himself as god many forms.[2]

In the third station of Deep Sleep there is no empirical consciousness, but an identification with the Brahman. This condition corresponds to the 'Eternal Rest' of Western mysticism. This state of liberation is described in a beautiful passage of the Brihadāranyaka Upanishad, which we transcribe here as an example of the pre-Buddhist Vedāntic literature:

" But like as in yon space a falcon or an eagle, after he has hovered, wearily folds his pinions and sinks to rest, thus also hastens the Spirit to that condition in which, sunk to sleep, he feels no more desire, nor beholds any more dreams. That is his (true) form of being, wherein he is raised above longing, free from evil and from fear. For, like as one whom a beloved woman embraces, has no consciousness of what is without or what is within, so also the Spirit, embraced by the Self of Knowledge (the Brahman), has no consciousness of what is without or what is within. That is his form of being, wherein his longing is stilled, himself is his longing, he is without longing, and freed from grief. Then the father is not

[1] *Kaivalya Upanishad* (12). This is living on the surface, empirical experience.

[2] *Brihadāranyaka Upanishad* 4, 3. Compare the state of the creative artist or personal god.

father, nor the mother mother, nor the worlds worlds, nor the gods gods, nor the Vedas Vedas . . . then is he unmoved by good, unmoved by evil, then has he vanquished all the torments of the heart. . . . Yet is he a knower, even though he does not know; since for the knower there is no interruption of knowing; because he is imperishable. . . . He stands in the tumultuous ocean as beholder, alone and without a second, he whose world is the Brahman. This is his highest goal, this is his highest joy, this is his highest world, this is his highest bliss."

He who is *not* thus liberated, but is still subject to desire,

After he has received reward
For all that he has here performed,
He comes back from that other world
Into the world of deeds below.

But "he who is without desire, free from desire, whose desire is stilled, who is himself his desire, his vital spirits do not depart; but Brahman is he and into Brahman he resolves himself":

When every passion utterly is gone,
That lurks and nestles in the heart of man,
Then finds this mortal immortality,
Then has he reached the Brahman, the Supreme.

Of this liberation, the natural fruit in this life is asceticism, and thus—

"This knew those of old, when they longed not for descendants, and said: 'Why should we wish indeed for descendants, we whose self is the universe?' And they ceased from the longing after children, from the longing after possessions and from the longing after the world, and wandered forth as beggars. For longing for children is longing for possessions, and longing for possessions, is longing for the world; for one like the other is merely longing. But He, the Ātman, is *Not thus, not thus.*"

There is another station, called the Fourth, transcending alike Non-being and Being. This station is indicated in the 'Om' logion, and corresponds to the Western conception of Eternal Rest and Eternal Work as simultaneous aspects of the Unity. Precisely how this station differs from Deep Sleep will be apparent from the verses of Gaudapāda:

> *Dreams and sleep belong to the two first,*
> *A dreamless sleep is the possession of the third,*
> *Neither dreams nor sleep does he who knows it*
> *Ascribe to the fourth.*
>
> *The dreamer's knowledge is false,*
> *The sleeper knows nothing at all.*
> *Both go astray; where all this vanishes*
> *There the fourth state is reached.*
>
> *It is in the beginningless illusion of the world*
> *That the soul (indeed) sleeps: when it (in sooth) awakes,*
> *Then there awakes in it the eternal,*
> *Timeless and free from dreams and sleep alike.*[1]

These lines are post-Buddhist, but represent a perfectly logical development of the conception of the Brahman indicated as eternal knower, without object, in the phrase just quoted, "Yet is he a knower, even though he does not know; since for the knower there is no interruption

[1] Here the usage of the symbols of waking and sleeping is reversed—the true awakening is a sleeping to the world.

of knowing, because he is imperishable." This phrase, it may be noticed, vividly recalls the saying of the Buddha regarding the after-death state of him who has attained Nibbāna: "But to say of a Brother who has been so set free by insight: 'He knows not, he sees not,' that were absurd!"[1]

The object of the Upanishad teaching, then, is to remove our ignorance, for ignorance lies at the root of desire, and desire, implying lack, is a mark of imperfection, and cannot characterize the highest state. The knowledge which is opposed to ignorance, as light to darkness, consists in the realization of the unity of the one which is not so, not so. This knowledge is not the means of liberation, it is liberation itself.

He who attains to the realization 'I am the Brahman'—not, of course, who merely makes the verbal statement—knowing himself to be the totality of all that is, has nothing to desire or fear, for there is nought else to fear or to desire, nor will he injure any being, for no one injures himself by himself. He who has reached this understanding continues to exist, for the consequences of his former deeds are still valid in the empirical world of causality; but life can no longer deceive him. His former works are burnt away in the fire of knowledge. He knows that his body is not 'his' body nor his works 'his' works; and when he dies, his Self goes nowhere where it is not already, nor may he ever again be subject to the limitations of individual existence.

As rivers run and in the deep
Lose name and form and disappear,
So goes, from name and form released,
The wise man to the deity.

[1] cf. *supra*, p. 124.

Here the Buddhist thinker must ever bear in mind that 'the deity,' in passages like this, refers to the Brahman which is 'not so,' and not to any personal god: precisely as the Buddhist himself is constrained by the necessity of language to symbolize Nibbāna as 'Bliss' and the like. Of Brāhman and Buddhist it may well be said, as it may be said of all religions in the deepest application—

Thou goest thine, and I go mine—
Many ways we wend;
Many days and, many ways,
Ending in one end.

Many a wrong, and its curing song:
Many a word, and many an inn:
Room to roam, but only one home
For all the world to win.

II. SĀMKHYA

There exists another system, the Sāmkhya, not, like the Upanishads, the creation of a school, but known to us as formulated by one sage, of the name of Kapila; from whom most likely the name of Kapilavatthu, the city of Buddha's birth and youth, is derived. It is not without significance in this connexion that Buddhism "seems to have arisen in a quarter where Sāmkhya ideas were dominant, and to have borrowed very considerably from them;" and the fact that the Sāmkhya is really the chief source of Buddhist modes of thought, gives to this system considerable importance for our study. By contrast with the monistic idealism of the Upanishads, which define the *Ātman* or *Purusha* (spirit) as the sole reality, the Sāmkhya is an explicit dualism, postulating the eternal reality of *Purusha* and *Prakriti*, spirit and nature; the Sāmkhya moreover speaks of a plurality of *Purushas* or spirits, whereas the *Purusha* of Vedāntic thought is one and indivisible. Nature is the naturally undifferentiated equilibrium of the three qualities *sattva*, *rajas*, and *tamas*, 'goodness, passion, and inertia';[1] evolution results from the proximity of spirit. The first product of differentiation is *buddhi*, 'reason'; then *ahamkāra*, 'the conceit of individuality'; and from this on the one hand the five subtle and five gross elements, and on the other *manas*, 'mind' or 'heart,' and the outer and inner organs of sense. These, together with soul constitute the twenty-five categories of the Sāmkhya. That which migrates from body to body is not the spirit, for this is unconditioned, but the characteristic body, the individual 'soul,' consisting of buddhi, ahamkāra, manas and the inner and outer organs of sense, bearing the impressions (*samskāras*, *vāsanās*) of its previous deeds, and obtaining a new physical body in precise accordance with their moral worth.

The individual Purusha—the *jīva*—is unaffected, even in its state of bondage; even its apparent consciousness of subject and object is a delusion. It is the 'inner man,' the 'soul'—*antahkarana*, viz. buddhi, ahamkāra and manas—moved by the attached spirit shining all unconsciously upon it, which falsely imagines itself to be an ego; in this complex 'soul' arise conceptions of pleasure and pain, love and hate; these it projects upon the Spirit or Self, which it thus knows only through a glass, darkly. Such a vicious circle of life is perpetuated for ever, only temporarily interrupted by the cosmic rhythm of involution and evolution, evolution and involution, in successive æons (*kalpas*). But some few there are who, after many births, attain to saving knowledge: with the

[1] More strictly, the extremes and the mean.

axe of reason is felled the tree of the egoism of the 'soul,' and the axe too being cast away, the bond of Spirit and Matter is severed—the Spirit is evermore single (*kaivalya*) no more involved in the wheel of birth and death (samsāra). Whoever fully understands this point of view, will be prepared to understand the cardinal doctrines of Buddhism, which differ chiefly from those of the Sāmkhya in their tacit denial of Purusha, or perhaps we should rather say, in their refusal to discuss aught but the nature of the 'soul' and the practical means of deliverance; Buddhism and the Sāmkhya, with the Vedānta no less, are agreed that pleasure and pain are alike suffering—for the impermanence of any pleasure constitutes an eternal skeleton at the feast.

III. YOGA

> Cease but from thine own activity, steadfastly fixing thine Eye upon *one* point.—*Behmen*

A third system, which was well known, though not yet expounded in full detail before the time of Buddha, is that of Yoga, or Union. This is a discipline designed to secure the deliverance contemplated in the Sāmkhya. It has a practical aspect, which is partly ethical and partly physiological; and a 'kingly' part, consisting of the three phases of meditation, *dharana*, *dhyāna*, and *samādhi*, in which by concentration of thought the distinction of subject and object is overreached, and the soul becomes aware of its eternal separateness from reason (buddhi) and its conformations (samskāras), and becomes for ever single (kaivalya). The system differs from the Sāmkhya and from early Buddhism in that it is not atheistic—that is to say, it recognizes an Overlord (Īsvara), who is a particular and exalted purusha, or individual soul, by whom the devotee may be aided on the way of emancipation; but this Īsvara is by no means essential to the system, and is but one of the many objects of meditation which are suggested to the student. The spiritual exercises of the Buddhist contemplative are taken over almost unchanged from Brāhmanical sources, and for this reason it is not necessary to repeat here what has already been said on this subject; but it may be useful to illustrate from a quite distinct source what is the significance of accomplished Yoga, in the following passage from Schelling's *Philosophical Letters upon Dogmatism and Criticism*:

"In all of us there dwells a secret marvellous power of freeing ourselves from the changes of time, of withdrawing to our secret selves away from external things, and of so discovering to ourselves the eternal in us in the form of unchangeability. This presentation of ourselves to ourselves is the most truly personal experience, upon which depends everything that we know of the suprasensual world. This presentation shows us for the first time what real existence is, whilst all else only appears to be. It differs from every presentation of the sense in its perfect freedom, whilst all other presentations are bound, being overweighted by the burden of the object. . . . This intellectual presentation occurs when we cease to be our own object, when, withdrawing into ourselves, the perceiving image merges in the self-perceived. At that moment we annihilate time and duration of time: we are no longer in time, but time, or rather eternity itself (the timeless is in us. The external world is no longer an object for us, but is lost in us."

IV. BUDDHISM AND BRĀHMANISM

All writers upon Buddhism are faced with the difficulty to explain in what respect the teaching of Gautama differs from the higher phases of Brāhman thought. It is true that the distinction appeared clear enough to Gautama and his successors; but this was largely because the Brāhmanism against which they maintained their polemic was after all merely the popular aspect of Brāhmanism. From a study of the Buddha's dialogues it would appear that he never encountered a capable exponent of the highest Vedāntic idealism, such a one as Yājnavalkhya or Janaka; or if Ālāra is to be considered such, Gautama took exception to the Ātmanistic terminology rather than its ultimate significance. It appeared to Gautama and to his followers then and now that the highest truths—especially the truth embodied by Buddhists in the phrase *An-attā*, no-soul—lay rather without than within the Brāhmanical circle.

Many times in the history of religions has the Protestant, having thus easily carried the outer defences of an Orthodox faith, believed that there remained no other citadel. It may be, on the other hand, that Gautama knew of the existence of such a Brāhman citadel—where the truth was held, that the Ātman is 'not so, not so'—but regarded the surrounding city as so hopelessly habituated to errors of thought and action, as to determine him rather to build upon a new site than to join hands with the beleaguered garrison. Perhaps he did not take into account that all such garrisons must be small, and did not foresee their final victory. However this may be, it is at least certain that at this period there existed no fundamental doctrinal opposition of Brāhmanism and Buddhism; but Gautama, and some other Kshattriyas, and some Brāhmans were alike engaged in one and the same task.

At first sight nothing can appear more definite than the opposition of the Buddhist An-attā, 'no-Ātman,' and the Brāhman Ātman, the sole reality. But in using the same term, Attā or Ātman, Buddhist and Brāhman are talking of different things, and when this is realized, it will be seen that the Buddhist disputations on this point lose nearly all their value. It is frankly admitted by Professor Rhys Davids that

"The neuter Brahman is, so far as I am aware, entirely unknown in the Nikāyas, and of course the Buddha's idea of Brahmā, in the masculine, really differs widely from that of the Upanishads." [1]

There is nothing, then, to show that the Buddhists ever really understood the pure doctrine of the Ātman, which is 'not so, not so.' The attack which they led upon the idea of soul or self is directed against the conception of the eternity in time of an unchanging individuality; of the timeless spirit they do not speak, and yet they claim to have disposed of the theory of the Ātman! In reality both sides were in agreement that the soul or ego (manas, ahamkāra, vijñāna, etc.) is complex and phenomenal, while of that which is 'not so' we know nothing.

Buddhist dialectic, by the simile of the chariot, and so

1 *Dialogues of the Buddha*, i, p. 298: C. A. F. Rhys Davids, *Buddhism*, p. 57—and yet in the latter place it is claimed that "it is the Ātmanist position against which the Buddhist argument is drawn up." It is just this position which Gautama does *not* refer to. The parting of Gautama and Ālāra represents, perhaps, the greatest tragedy recorded in religious history. It has been remarked with perfect justice by A. Worsley: "It is possible that had Gautama chanced to meet, in his earliest wanderings, two teachers of the highest truth, the whole history of the Old World might have been changed."—*Concepts of Monism*, p. 197.

forth, is directed to show that things are 'Empty'; when their component elements are recognized there is no remainder, but only the 'Void'; he who realizes this, attains Nibbāna and is freed. But we cannot distinguish this 'Void' or 'Abyss' from that Brahman which is 'No thing.'

It is true that the Vedānta speaks of many Ātmans, three or even five, and also that the *jīvātman* or 'unconditioned Self in the individual' is sometimes confused with the individual ego or discriminating subject[1] (ahamkāra or vijñāna—as if we should attribute individuality to a portion of space enclosed in a jar, forgetting that space is 'traceless' and the jar alone has 'marks'); but the strictly non-animistic view is maintained in many other and more important passages.[2] Either Gautama was only acquainted with popular Brāhmanism, or he chose to ignore its higher aspects. At any rate, those whom he defeats in controversy so easily are mere puppets who never put forward the doctrine of the unconditioned Self at all. Gautama meets no foeman worthy of his steel, and for this reason the greater part of Buddhist polemic is unavoidably occupied in beating the air. This criticism applies as much to modern as to ancient exposition.

We are told, for example, that Buddhism differs from Brāhmanism in its refutation of the "then current pessimistic idea that salvation could not be reached on earth, and must therefore be sought for in rebirth in heaven."[3] But if this idea was 'current' as a motif of the sacrificial ritual, it certainly was not maintained by the Brāhman idealists. 'That *art* thou' denotes a present condition,

[1] *Chāndogya*, 7, and *Brihadāranyaka*, 4, 3, 7 *f.*, etc.

[2] *Chāndogya*, 8, 7–12, and *Taittirīya*, 2.

[3] T. W. Rhys Davids, *Early Buddhism*, p. 55.

and not a state to be reached after death. "*To-day* also," says the *Brihadāranyaka* (1, 4, 10), "he who knows this—I am Brahman—becomes this universe; and even the gods have no power to prevent his so becoming; for he *is* its Ātman." In the face of utterances such as these we cannot admit the suggestion that the doctrine of salvation here and now was "never clearly or openly expressed in pre-Buddhist thought."[1]

We also hear that "in *all* Indian thought except the Buddhist, souls, and the gods who are made in imitation of souls, are considered as exceptions," and that "to these spirits is attributed a Being without Becoming, an individuality without change, a beginning without an end."[2] It is difficult to understand how anyone acquainted with Indian thought 'except the Buddhist' can make a statement of this kind. For it is clearly stated by Sankara that the word 'Indra' means "not an individual, but a certain position (*sthāna-visesha*), something like the word 'General'; whoever occupies the position bears the name."[3] This view is taken for granted in popular Hindu literature; it is commonly held, for example, that Hanuman is to be "the Brahmā" of the next æon. Moreover in the pre-Buddhist Upanishads the position of the personal gods is no more privileged than it is in Buddhism; precisely as in Buddhism they are represented as standing in need of, and capable of receiving, saving knowledge, and in this respect they have no advantage over men.[4] Would it be possible to point to any Hindu text claiming for any personal deity as such a beginning without an end? And

[1] T. W. Rhys Davids, *Early Buddhism*, p. 74.

[2] *Ibid.* p. 55 (italics mine).

[3] Deussen, *System of the Vedānta*, p. 69.

[4] *Chāndogya*, 8, 7 *f.*

if such texts could be discovered, could they be regarded as representing the Vedānta? Most likely, in making the statements above quoted, modern exponents of Buddhism have confused the position of the Vedic deities (*devas*) in the Vedānta with the theism which is a subsequent development—analogous to the theistic developments in Buddhism itself—where individual gods (*Īshvaras*) appear as symbolical representatives of the Ātman, taking the forms that are imagined by their worshippers.

Buddhists lay considerable stress upon the refusal of Gautama to allow speculation on the after-death state of those who attain Nibbāna, a refusal based on grounds of expediency. But there is nothing peculiar to Buddhism in the refusal to speculate, only in the Vedānta it is not based on 'practical' grounds, but on the ground of the evident futility of any such inquiry, for, as the Sūfīs say, "this is too high for our limited and contingent being." Sankara, for example, preserves an old story, to the effect that a man of the name of Bahva was questioned by Vashkali on the nature of the Brahman, and that he kept silence. Being questioned a second and a third time, at last he replied: 'I teach you, indeed, but you do not understand; this Brahman is silence.' For that Ātman of which it is said 'That art thou' is neither the body nor the individual 'soul'; it is not an object of knowledge, but like the future state of the Arahat it lies on the other side of experience, invisible, unutterable, and unfathomable. That the Brahman cannot be known is again and again affirmed in the Upanishads:

That to which no eye penetrates, nor speech, nor thought,
Which remains unknown, and we see it not, how can instruction therein be given to us?[1]

[1] *Kena Upanishad*, 3.

Buddhism & Brāhmanism

Not by speech, not by thought, not by sight is he comprehended,
He is! by this word is he comprehended, and in no other way.[1]

Much confusion still exists amongst exponents of Buddhism as to what the doctrine of the Ātman really signifies. The formula of identity, 'Thou art thou,' is hopelessly distorted by Mrs Rhys Davids when she writes:

"The *anti-attā* argument of Buddhism is mainly and consistently directed against the notion of a soul, which was not only a persistent, unchanging, blissful, transmigrating, superphenomenal being, but was also a being wherein the supreme Ātman or world soul was immanent, one with it in essence, and as a bodily or mental factor issuing its fiat." [2]

This confusion does not belong to the Vedānta as understood by the Vedāntins. Buddhists have perhaps always made the mistake of underrating the intelligence of their opponents. We can only say that the high intrinsic value of Buddhist thought does not demand a spurious exaltation achieved by such comparison with merely popular or inconsistent forms of Brāhmanism. The best must be compared with the best if the best is to be known.

Buddhists very likely would point to passages such as

[1] *Kathaka Upanishad*, 6, 12, 13.

[2] C. A. F. Rhys Davids, *Buddhist Psychology*, 1915, p. 31. The Ātman is precisely that which does *not* transmigrate. The 'fiat' seems to refer to the conception of the Brahman as inner guide (*antaryāmin*) and of the universe as the result of his command (*prasāsanam*), *e.g.* in *Brihadāranyaka*, 3, 8, 9. But the language is in this case misunderstood. The 'inner guide' is the categorical imperative, the highest form of conscience, and with this we may compare the Buddhist sanction 'because of Nibbāna'; while the 'command' is that suchness (*tattva*) whereby everything becomes as it becomes.

Bhagavad Gītā, ii, 22—"As a man lays aside outworn garments and takes others that are new, so the Body-Dweller puts away unborn bodies and goes to others that are new"—as animistic, notwithstanding that it is constantly asserted throughout the same chapter that *That* "is never born and never dies." But Buddhists also are compelled to make use of current phraseology, and even though they do not mean to speak of the transmigration of a soul, they cannot avoid saying that when some one dies, 'he' is reborn in a new life, and in the Pitakas "we seem to see a belief in transmigration of a passing soul, just as much as we see it in the books of animistic creeds."[1] Buddhaghosha comments on this: "It would be more correct not to use popular modes of stating the case," and "we must just guard ourselves" from supposing that these modes express fact. The difficulties of language were the same for Buddhists and Brāhmans; and the same allowance must be made for both.

We are told again that those Upanishads which are ranked as the oldest "show a *naïf* animism: those ranked later reveal thought attained to relative maturity."[2] This is a complete inversion. It is true, indeed, that there are still many animistic passages in the old Upanishads; but the formulas 'Not so, not so,' and 'That art thou,' taken together, represent the highest attainment of Indian thought; and the later Upanishads show, not an advance due to the absorption of Buddhist ideas, but a reaction in favour of ritual and realistic thought[3]—a sort of High Church development not without parallels in Buddhism itself.

[1] C. A. F. Rhys Davids, *Buddhism*, p. 137.

[2] Rhys Davids, *Dialogues of the Buddha*, vol. ii, p. 48.

[3] Deussen, *Philosophy of the Upanishads*, pp. 64, 65, 171 172.

Professor Rhys Davids says again "the highest teaching current before the Buddha, and still preserved in the pre-Buddhist Upanishads, was precisely about union with Brahmā"; we do not know how this statement is to be reconciled with the admission already cited that "the Buddha's idea of Brahmā, in the masculine, really differs widely from that of the Upaṅishads."[1]

The 'further shore' is a symbol of salvation used by both parties; in the *Tevijja Sutta* Gautama suggests that it is employed by the Brāhmans to mean union with Brahmā (in the masculine), whereas he himself means Arahatta. If he really understood the heart of the Ātmanist position in this manner, it proves that he spoke without knowledge; if he assumed that this was the Brāhman view for purposes of argument, he was guilty of deliberate dishonesty.

The latter view should not be entertained. But it is undeniable that Gautama's dialogue is largely determined by controversial necessity.[2] The compilers of the Dialogues had to represent the Buddha as victorious in argument, and they succeed by setting up a dummy which it is easy to demolish, while the object of nominal attack, the *Ātman* theory, is never attached. Gautamá constantly accuses others of eel-wriggling, but in the Dialogues he adopts the same method himself. The neuter Brahman is 'quietly ignored,' and words are interpreted in new senses. In particular, the word *attā* (Ātman) is used in a different sense from that of the Brāhman ātmanists, and thus an easy victory is secured by 'thinking of something else.' The coining of the term An-attā to imply the absence of a perduring individuality

[1] *Dialogues of the Buddha*, vol. ii, p. 298.

[2] As indicated also by Mrs Rhys Davids, *J.R.A.S.* (1903), p. 591.

is a triumph of ingenuity, but it should not blind us to the fact that the perduring Ātman of the Brāhmans was not an individuality at all.

It may readily be granted that Buddhist thought is far more consistent than the thought of the Upanishads. The Upanishads are the work of many hands and extend over many centuries; amongst their authors are both poets and philosophers. The Buddhist Dhamma claims to be the pronouncement of a single rationalist, and to have but one flavour. Gautama propounds a creed and a system, and it is largely to this fact that the success of his missionary activities was due. The Upanishads do not formulate a creed, though they constantly revert to the thought of unity; it is with Sankara, or Rāmānūja, and not with the authors of the Upanishads that we must compare Gautama, if we would see a contrast of consistency with consistency.

No one will assert that the Upanishads exhibit a consistent creed. But the explanation of their inconsistencies is historical and leaves the truth of their ultimate conclusions quite untouched. Gautama's Dhamma purports to be the considered work of a single individual, and it would be strange indeed if it failed to attain consistency; the Upanishads are the work of many minds, and a compendium of many thoughts. In other words, the literature of Indian thought, apart from Buddhism as interpreted by Buddhists, exhibits a continuous development, and knows no acute crises; or rather, the real crises—such as the identification of all gods as one, and the development of the doctrines of emancipation and transmigration—are not determined by names and dates, they were not announced as the Dharma of any one teacher, and they are only recognized in retrospection. Here there is a gradual process of 'thinking aloud,' wherein by stripping the self of veil after veil of contingency there is nothing left but the Abyss which is 'not so, not so,' the 'Ground' of unity. From animism to idealism there is direct development, and it is for this reason that we meet with primitive terminologies invested with a new significance; moreover the old strata persist beneath the newest layers, and thus it is not only primitive terms, but also primitive thoughts which persist in the great complex that we speak of as Brāhmanism. But this does not mean that the highest of these thoughts is primitive, it means only that the historical continuity of thought is preserved in the final system, and that system remains adapted to the intelligence of various minds. Sankara, writing long afterward, and looking back on this development as it had so far proceeded, very clearly perceived this complexity of thought in the Upanishads, and explained their inconsistencies and contradictions by the brilliant generalization in which the scriptural teachings are divided into absolute or esoteric truth (*parā vidyā*), and relative or exoteric truths (*aparā vidyā*). With this clue in our hands we are able to regard the whole Aupanishadic literature as a process of thought, culminating in certain well-defined formulæ, and we can distinguish the poetic and symbolic nature of many other passages which do not the less refer to truth because they speak in parables. The necessities of controversy may have prevented the Early Buddhists from taking any such extended view of their 'opponent's' teachings; or it may be that with the best will, it would have been impossible so early and so close to the actual development to synthesize the whole body of Indian speculation. However this may be, we find in point of fact that the essential thought of the Upanishads is never grasped by the Early Buddhists, and is sometimes but obscurely apprehended by modern exponents.

In Buddhism great stress is laid on the doctrine of the Mean, both from the standpoint of ethics and of truth. In the latter case it is, as usual, the phenomenal world alone which comes under discussion: Gautama repudiates the two extreme views, that everything is, and that everything is not, and substitutes the thought that there exists only a Becoming.[1] It is due to Gautama to say that the abstract concept of causality as the fundamental principle of the phenomenal world is by him far more firmly grasped and more clearly emphasized than we find it in the early Upanishads; nevertheless the thought and the word 'Becoming' are common to both, and both are in agreement that this Becoming is the order of the world, the mark of organic existence, from which Nibbāna, or the Brahman (according to their respective phraseology) alone is free.

Where a difference of outlook appears is in the fact that the Buddha is content with this conclusion, and condemns all further speculation as undefying; and thus, like Sankara, he excludes for ever a reconciliation of eternity and time, of religion with the world.

The same result is reached in another way by those Vedāntists of the school of Sankara who developed the doctrine of *Māyā* in an absolute sense[2] to mean the absolute nonentity of the phenomenal world, contrasted with the only reality of the Brahman which alone is. This is one of the two extreme views rightly repudiated by Gautama, but there is agreement to this extent that both Gautama and the Māyāvādins reject the unreal world of Becoming,

[1] *Samyutta Nikāya*, xxii, 90, 16.

[2] *Svetasvatara Upanishad*, 4, 9–10.

either because it is inseparable from Evil, or simply because it is unreal.

But the interpretation of the term Māyā to signify the absolute nonentity of the phenomenal world, if it belongs to the Vedānta at all,[1] is comparatively late; and even in the *Rig Veda* we find another thought expressed, in which the whole universe is identified with the 'Eternal Male,'[2] afterward a recognized symbol of the Ātman. The same idea finds many expressions in the Upanishads, notably in the saying, 'That art thou.' Here in place of, or side by side with the thought, 'Not so, not so,' we have the equally true consideration of totalistic philosophy, that there is No thing which That Brahman is not: That Brahman, which is No thing, is at the same time All things. To dismiss the world of Becoming as a simple nonentity, is a false extreme, as rightly pointed out alike by Gautama, and in *Isa Upanishad*, 12. It is quite true that things have no self-existence as such, for Becoming never stops; but the process of Becoming cannot be denied, and as it cannot have a beginning, so it cannot have an end.

There is thus asserted from two points of view an irreconcilable opposition of Becoming and Being, *Samsāra* and *Nirvāna*, This and That. Over against these extremes there appears another doctrine of the Mean, entirely distinct from that of Gautama which merely asserts that Becoming, and not either Being nor non-

[1] Which is to be doubted. The conception of the absolute nonentity of the phenomenal world is entirely contrary to many passages in *Brihadāranyaka* and *Chāndogya*, as well as to the *Brahma Sūtra*, 1, 2, which asserts that 'Everything is Brahman.' It is not the 'world,' but the extension of the world in time and space—the contraction and identification into variety—which constitutes *Māyā*. This is the Vedānta according to *Rāmānuja*.

[2] *Rig Veda*, x, 90–2.

Being is the mark of *this* world. This other Mean asserts that the Sole Reality, the Brahman, subsists, not merely as not-Becoming, but also as Becoming: not merely as the unregistrable, but also as that of which our registration is and must be imperfect and incomplete.

In truth, there are two forms of Brahman, that is to say—

> "*The formed and the unformed, the mortal and the immortal,*
> *The abiding and the fleeting, the being and the beyond.*"[1]

The Brahman is not merely *nirguna*, in no wise, but also *sarvaguna*, 'in all wise;' and he is saved—attains Nirvāna—knows the Brahman—who sees that these are one and the same, that the two worlds are one.

Empirical truth (aparā vidyā) is then not absolutely untrue, but merely relatively true, while the absolutely true (parā vidyā) embraces and resumes all relative truth; seen from the standpoint of our empirical consciousness it is veritably the Real that is reflected through the doorways of our five or six senses, and takes the forms of our imagination. Here the phenomenal world is not without significance, but has just so much significance as the degree of our enlightenment allows us to discover in it. "If the doors of perception were cleansed everything would appear to man as it is, infinite."

From this point of view the doctrine of *Avidyā* or *Māyā*, ignorance or glamour, does not and should not assert the absolute nonentity and insignificance of the world, but merely that as we see it empirically, extended in the order of space, time and causality, it has no static

[1] *Brihadāranyaka Upanishad*, 2, 3, 1.

existence as a thing in itself: our partial vision is false in so far, and *only in so far*, as it is partial.

This position is obscured in Buddhism, and likewise in the system of Sankara, by the emphasis which is laid on Becoming as a *state to be avoided;* and this hedonistic outlook which finds logical expression in monasticism and puritanism has occupied the too exclusive attention of modern students. Too exclusive, for it is not this one-sided view of life, but the doctrine of the identity of this world and that, which can and does afford the key to the historical development of the Indian culture, the most remarkable characteristic of which appears in a general apprehension of the indivisibility of the sensuous and the spiritual.

Another, and *ethical* Mean is put forward by Gautama as the Middle Path between extremes of self-mortification and self-indulgence. But here again it must be recognized that this is not really a middle path, and that it remains, in contrasting the bright state of the Wanderer with the dark state of the Householder, if not at all morbidly ascetic,· nevertheless unmistakably a rule of abstention, rather than moderation. Certain actions and certain environments are condemned as bad in themselves. Gautama hardly contemplates the possibility that freedom may also be attained by those who are still engaged in worldly activities, nor that this freedom must depend on absence of motif rather than absence of activity; the *Jñānā Mārga* is for him the only way.[1]

It is justly pointed out by Oldenberg that "there was

[1] Not only does he not perceive that the wish to avoid Dukkha is in itself a desire, and as such a hindrance, but still less does he see that the fear of pleasure—even as it may come unsought—is a still more subtle bondage.

nothing in Buddha's attitude generally which could be regarded by his contemporaries as unusual, he had not to introduce anything fundamentally new; on the contrary, it would have been an innovation if he had undertaken to preach a way of salvation which did not proceed on a basis of monastic observances."[1]

The first systematic expression of such an 'innovation,' of which the source and sanction are to be found in the already old doctrine of the identity of This and That, Becoming and not-Becoming, is in the *Bhagavad Gītā*. This is variously dated as between 400 B.C. and A.D. 200, but whatever remodelling it may have undergone it can hardly be doubted that its essential thought is the recognition of *Karma Yoga* and *Bhakti Yoga* side by side with *Jñāna Yoga* as 'means' of salvation:

"It was with works that Janaka and others came into adeptship; thou too shouldst do them, considering the order of the world . . . as do the unwise, attached to works, so should the wise do, but without attachment, seeking to establish order in the world."

"He who beholds in Work No-work, and in No-Work Work, is the man of understanding amongst mortals; he is in the rule, a doer of perfect work. . . . Free from attachment to the fruit of works, everlastingly contented, unconfined, even though he be engaged in Work he does not Work at all."

"Casting off all thy Works upon Me with thy mind on the One over Self, be thou without craving and without

[1] *Buddha*, English translation, ed. 2 (1904), p. 119. It is true that the layman Arahat is not altogether unknown to Early Buddhism (twenty-one are mentioned in the *Anguttara Nikāya*, iii, 451, and Suddhodana, Gautama's father is also specially mentioned), but the fulfilment of worldly duties, however selflessly, was never preached as a way of salvation.

thought of a Mine, and with thy fever calmed, engage in battle."

Thus it is that even laymen may attain to perfect freedom, in a life obedient to vocation, if only the activity be void of motive and self-reference. The degree of bondage implied in various environments depends entirely on the outlook of the individual, and not on any good or bad quality intrinsic in any thing or any status. Bondage and deliverance are alike to be found in the home and in the forest, and not more nor less in one than the other; everything alike is Holy (in terms of Buddhism, 'Void'), and men and women are not less so than mountains or forests. Above all, this reconciliation of religion with the world is practically manifested in selfless obedience to vocation (*sva-dharma*); for notwithstanding this world is but a Becoming, it has a meaning which cannot be fathomed by those who turn their backs upon it in order to escape from its pains and elude its pleasures.

Precisely the same crisis that we here speak of as distinguishing Buddhism from Brāhmanism, is passed through in the history of Brāhmanism itself, and must, perhaps, be passed over in the history of every school of thought that attains to its full development. It had been held amongst Brāhmans, as it had been also for a time assumed by Gautama, that salvation must be sought in penance (*tapas*) and in the life of the hermit. Gautama introduced no radical change[1] in merely insisting on the futility of carrying such disciplines to a morbid extreme. But in

[1] Perhaps we ought to say no change at all, for it would be difficult to point to any early or important Brāhmanical text advocating a mental and moral discipline more severe than that of the Buddhist Brethren; on the contrary, the Upanishads constantly insist that salvation is won by knowledge alone, and that all else is merely preliminary.

Brāhman circles, that wide movement of thought, of which Gautama reveals but a single phase and a single stage, culminates in a very different theory of tapas, which is expressed as follows in the *Mānava Dharma-sāstra*:

"The tapas of the Brāhmana is concentrated study; of the Kshattriya, protection of the weak; of the Vaishya, trade and agriculture; of the Sūdra, service of others. . . . For the Brāhman, tapas and vidyā, self-denial and wisdom, are the only means to the final goal, etc."

This is merely another version of the doctrine of vocation already referred to.

It is perfectly true that the more deeply we penetrate Buddhist and Brāhmanical thought, the less is it possible to divide them. If, for example, we imagine the question propounded to a teacher of either persuasion, 'What shall I do to be saved?'—the same answer would be made, that salvation veritably consists in overcoming the illusion that any such ego—'I'—exists, and the way to this salvation would be described as the overcoming of craving. These are indeed the answers of Christ and of all other great Masters: He that loses his life shall save it; Thy will, not mine. It is when we proceed to formulate a discipline that distinctions arise, and here that the idiosyncrasy of the individual teacher becomes most evident. Gautama's scheme of the Ariyan Eightfold Path, as a complete scheme, is universal only in the sense that in all lands and in all ages there are to be found individuals of rationalist and ascetic temperament kindred

The fruit of asceticism as such, as of all other deeds, must be finite in itself: "Of a truth, O Gargi," says Yājnavalkhya, himself a hermit, "he who does not know this imperishable One, though in this world he should distribute alms and practise penance (*tapas tapyate*) for many a thousand years, thereby wins but finite good."—*Brihad-āranyaka Upanishad*, 3, 8, 10.

with his own. If we liken Early Buddhism to a 'Lesser Raft,' then we may justly speak of Brāhmanism, as of the 'Mahāyāna,' as a Greater Vessel; each conveys the traveller to his desired haven, but the larger vessel serves the needs of a greater variety of men. Here is to be sought the explanation of that final 'victory' of Hinduism and of the Mahāyāna, which the exponents of Early Buddhism, and of the 'pure religions of the Vedas' have agreed to regard as a descent into superstition and priestcraft.

It had been, and always remained to a certain extent a principle of Brāhmanism to impart the highest teachings only in pupillary succession to those who show themselves qualified to receive it. The fact of Gautama's ignorance of the Ātmanist position may be taken to prove that in his day the doctrine of the Ātman was still an esoteric truth known only to the few. Gautama, on the other hand, while he refused to answer insoluble problems of eschatology and metaphysics, expressly says that he does not reserve an esoteric doctrine; all his sermons were preached in public, and accessible to laymen and to women. He did not reserve to twice-born castes the right to enter the spiritual order, and it has been estimated that some ten per cent. of the Brethren were 'low-born'; for him, the only true Brāhman is the man who excels in wisdom and goodness.

On these grounds it is sometimes assumed that Gautama was a successful social reformer who broke the chains of caste and won for the poor and humble a place in the kingdom of the spirit. But this view of the mission of Gautama, whose kingdom, like that of Jesus, was not of this world, is unhistorical. Had Gautama been of those who seek to improve the world by good government, and to secure their just rights for the poor and despised, he would not have left his kingdom to become a homeless wanderer, he would not have preferred the status of a teacher to that of a powerful prince; there need have been no 'Great Renunciation,' but history would have recorded another Asoka, fulfilling the ideal of an earthly Dharmarājā such as Rāma. But Gautama, when he saw the sick and the dying did not think of suffering as due to external causes, or to be alleviated by the bettering of the social order; he saw that suffering was bound up with the ego-asserting nature of man, and therefore he taught nothing but a mental and moral discipline designed to root out the conceit of an I. It is made abundantly clear that Gautama regards the state of the world as hopeless and irremediable, and while the truth of this is in one sense undeniable, and the Brāhmans were equally aware of it,[1] and of the relativity of all ethics, nevertheless it is they, and not Gautama, who have seen a profound significance in the maintenance of the order of the world, considering it a school where ignorance may be gradually dispelled. It is they who occupied themselves with the development of an ideal society, which they anticipated in the Utopias of Vālmīki, Vyāsa, and Manu. Had any Buddhist pointed out to a Brāhman philosopher the impossibility of establishing a millennium, the latter would have replied that he found significance in the task itself, and not in its achievement.

There is too a fallacy in the very suggestion that Gautama could have broken the chains of caste; for notwithstanding that those skilful craftsmen, the Brāhman Utopists referred to, were already at work, the so-called chains were not

[1] For example, *ato 'nyad artam*, 'What is distinct from Him (the Brahman), that is full of suffering.'—*Brihadāranyaka*, 3, 4, 2, etc.

yet forged. The caste system as it now exists is a sort of 'Guild Socialism' supported by theocratic sanctions and associated with eugenics; each caste being self-governing, internally democratic, and having its own norm (*sva-dharma*). We need not discuss the merit or demerit of this system here; but it must be realized that in the time of Gautama the system had not yet crystallized. What already existed was a classification of men according to complexion, in the 'Four Varnas' or colours; each of these included many groups which afterward crystallized as separate castes. Moreover at this time the position of the Brāhmans as leaders of society was not yet secure; we cannot regard the indications of the Brāhman Utopists as historical, and it would appear that the status of Brāhmans in the age of Gautama was somewhat lower than that of Kshattriyas. At any rate in Magadha the intellectual rank of the latter is sufficiently indicated by their achievements, such as the formulation of the Ātman doctrine, the institution of wandering friars, the An-attā doctrine of Gautama, the teachings of Mahāvīra, and so forth. Nevertheless it is clear that the Brāhmans claimed intellectual and ethical superiority; and no one acquainted with Indian history can doubt that Indian Brāhmans-born have to a large extent deserved by character and achievement the respect in which they have always been held; it is easy to criticize, as did Gautama, the empirical method of determining Brāhmanhood by birth, but this was the most practical method that could be devised, and the world has yet to discover a better way to secure in all its affairs the guidance of the wisest. Gautama does not offer any alternative to the doctrine of Brāhmanhood by birth, regarded as the solution to a social problem—the means of preserving a given type of high culture. He was able to ignore this problem, only because he wished that all higher men should 'wander alone.'

At the same time it is not only Gautama who sought to use the term Brāhman in a purely ethical sense; the same usage is found in the pre-Buddhist *Brihadāranyaka Upanishad* (iii, 5, 1) and elsewhere. Even where, as in Manu, the doctrine of Brāhmanhood by birth is taken for granted, we find it said that the Brāhman is born for dharma alone and not for wealth or pleasure; while the (later) *Mārkandeya Purāna* lays down that nothing is permitted to be done by the Brāhman "for the sake of enjoyment." And with regard to the remaining point, the right of the lowest classes to share in the kingdom of the spirit: this was by no means first or only asserted by Gautama; it is, for example, taken for granted in the *Samañña-phala Sutta* that religious orders already existing in the time of Gautama and not founded by him admitted even slaves to their ranks, and in many others of the Buddhist Suttas there are mentioned Sūdras who became Wanderers, as if it were a common occurrence and well recognized. And if the Brāhmans were careful to exclude the uncultivated classes from hearing the Vedas repeated and taught, this applied almost entirely to the older Vedic literature, in its priestly and magical aspects; although the doctrine of the Ātman may have been known to few in the days of Gautama (and it is in the nature of things that such doctrines must long remain in the hands of the few) nevertheless the Brāhmanical objection to Sūdra initiation does not extend to the Upanishads, which constitute that part of the Veda which alone in itself suffices for salvation. Moreover, we have to know that the Brāhmans themselves, by means of the Epics (and especially the *Bhagavad Gītā*) and the Purānas, deliberately undertook and accomplished that education of the whole Indian people, women included, which has made them, from the standpoint of character and courtesy, if not of technical literacy, the most educated race in the world. In comparing Buddhism (the teaching of Gautama, that is) with Brāhmanism, we have then to understand and take into account the difference of the problem sought to be solved. Gautama is concerned with salvation and nothing but salvation: the Brāhmans likewise see in that *summum bonum* the ultimate significance of all existence, but they also take into account the things of relative importance; theirs is a religion both of Eternity and Time, while Gautama looks upon Eternity alone. It is not really fair to Gautama or to the Brāhmans to contrast their *Dharma*; for they do not seek to cover the same ground. We must compare the Buddhist ethical ideal with the (identical) standard of Brāhmanhood expected of the Brāhman born; we must contrast the Buddhist monastic system with the Brāhmanical orders; the doctrine of Anattā with the doctrine of the Ātman, and here we shall find identity. But if the exponents of Buddhism insist on confining the significance of Buddhism to what is taught by Gautama, we must point out at the same time that it stands for a restricted ideal, which contrasts with Brāhmanism as a part contrasts with a whole; Buddhism might well have been accounted by Vijñāna Bhikshu as a 'seventh *darsana*.'

Just as with the history of the various Brāhmanical darsanas, so with Buddhism as a sect there remains much to be accomplished in historical elucidation and in exegesis and interpretation. But a more important task has hardly been envisaged: the connected historical study of Indian thought as an organic entirety. Just as we now see clearly that Indian architecture cannot be divided into styles on a sectarian basis, but is always primarily Indian, so also with the philosophic and religious thought. There is no true opposition of Buddhism and Brāhmanism, but from the beginning one general movement, or many closely related movements. The integrity of Indian thought, moreover, would not be broken if every specifically Buddhist element were omitted; we should only have to say that certain details had been less adequately elaborated or less emphasized. To some Buddhists may be recommended the words of Asoka:

"He who does reverence to his own sect while disparaging the sects of others wholly from attachment to his own, with intent to enhance the splendour of his own sect, in reality by such conduct inflicts the severest injury on his own sect. Concord, therefore, is meritorious, to wit, hearkening and hearkening willingly to the Dharma accepted by others."

To sum up: Gautama does not enunciate the conception of Freedom as a state independent of environment and vocation; the unity of his system, like that of Haeckel's, is only achieved by leaving out of account the Unregistrable; in a majority of fundamentals he does not differ from the Ātmanists, although he gives a far clearer statement of the law of causality as the essential mark of the world of Becoming. The greater part of his polemic, however, is wasted in a misunderstanding. Implicit in Brāhman thought from an early period, on the other hand, and forming the most marked features of later Indian mysticism—achieved also in the Mahāyāna, but with greater difficulty—is the conviction that ignorance is maintained only by attachment, and not by such actions as are void of purpose and self-reference; and the thought that This and That world, Becoming and Being, are seen to be *one* by those in whom ignorance is destroyed. In this identification there is effected a reconciliation of religion with the world, which remained beyond the grasp of Theravāda Buddhists. The distinctions between early Buddhism and Brāhmanism, however practically important, are thus merely temperamental; fundamentally there is absolute agreement that bondage consists in the thought of I and Mine, and that this bondage may be broken only for those in whom all craving is extinct.[1] In all essentials Buddhism and Brāhmanism form a single system.

[1] Those who claim that Buddha did not teach the extinction of desire do him less than justice. Even Nietzsche teaches a *nishkāma dharma* when he says: 'Do I then strive after happiness? I strive after my work!'

PART IV : THE MAHĀYĀNA

I. BEGINNINGS OF THE MAHĀYĀNA

A FIRST Buddhist council was summoned in the reign of Asoka—about 240 B.C.—with a view to the settlement of sectarian disputes. It is clear that heresies had already arisen, for certain of Asoka's edicts are concerned with the unfrocking of schismatics; and, indeed, we know that heresies were promulgated even during the life of the Buddha himself. In course of time we find that a large number of sects developed, all equally claiming to be followers of the true doctrine, just as has been the case with Christianity and every other great faith. The Buddhist sects are divided into two main groups: those of the Hīnayāna ('The Little Raft') and the Mahāyāna ('The Great Raft'). The former, whose scriptures are preserved in Pāli, claim to represent the pure original teaching of Gautama, and do in the main preserve its rationalistic, monastic and puritanical features to a marked extent: the latter, whose scriptures are in Sanskrit, interpret the doctrine in another way, with a development that is mystical, theological and devotional. The Hīnayāna has maintained its supremacy mainly in the South, particularly in Ceylon and Burma; the Mahāyāna mainly in the North, in Nepal and China. But it is misleading to speak of the two schools as definitely Northern and Southern.

Let us recall that according to the orthodox Hīnayāna, Gautama was originally a man like other men, and differed from others only in his intuitive penetration of the secret of life and sorrow, in his perception of things as they really are, as an eternal Becoming; with that knowledge he attained Nibbāna, and for him the causes of birth were extinguished. Other men, to whom the Way has been revealed by the Buddha or his disciples, can attain to Arahatta and Nibbāna, but are not regarded as Buddhas, nor is it suggested that every creature may ultimately reach the condition of Buddhahood. Speculation is forbidden as to whether the Buddha and the Arahats exist or do not exist after the death of the body.

If now we survey the canonical scriptures as a whole—written down in Pāli about 80 B.C.—we shall find that they include certain elements which are more or less inconsistent with this pure intellectual doctrine which appears to have formed the very consistent Dhamma of Gautama himself. In the dialogue of Pasenadi, king of Kosala, with the nun Khemā, regarding the state of the Buddha after death, we find: "Released, O great king, is the Perfect One from this, that his being should be gauged by the measure of the corporeal world: he is deep, immeasurable, unfathomable as the great ocean."[1] Here is at least the suggestion that the undetermined, the unregistrable, that which is other than Becoming, yet *is*, though beyond our ken or understanding. In another place, answering the question: What kind of being is a Buddha? Gautama himself is made to reply that he is neither a Deva, nor a Gandharva, nor a Yakkha nor a man, but is a Buddha. It may be intended only that a Buddha must not be regarded as an ordinary man; nevertheless there is clearly to be seen here an opening for the later Mahāyāna doctrine of the Body of Transformation.

We find, again (in the *Udnāa*, viii, 3), the following passage, which sounds more like a Brāhmanical than a Buddhist saying:

"There is, O Bhikkhus, an unborn, unoriginated, un-

[1] *Avyākala Samyutta*, I.

created, unformed. Were there not, O Bhikkhus, this unborn, unoriginated, uncreated, unformed, there would be no escape from the world of the born, originated, created, formed."

It may also be remarked that the most definite and universal verbal profession of the Buddhist or convert runs: 'I take refuge in the Buddha, the Dhamma, and the Sangha' (collectively, the 'Three Jewels').[1] No doubt this formula was first used in the lifetime of Gautama, whose own person may well have seemed to the world-weary a haven of refuge, no less than the Gospel and the Order. But after his death, what can the words, 'I take refuge in the Buddha,' have meant to a layman, or any but the most critical of the Brethren? It did not mean the Buddha's gospel, for that is separately mentioned. Those women and others whom we see in the sculptured reliefs of Sānchī and Amarāvatī, kneeling with passionate devotion and with offerings of flowers before an altar, where the Buddha is represented by the symbols of the footprints or the wisdom-tree (Plate Q)—what did it mean to them to take refuge in the Buddha?

This phrase alone must have operated with the subtle power of hypnotic suggestion to convince the worshipper—and the majority of men are worshippers rather than thinkers by nature—that the Buddha still was, and that some relation, however vaguely imagined, could be established between the worshipper and Him-who-had-thus-attained. It was, almost certainly, the growth of this conviction which determined the development of Buddhist

[1] The doctrine of devotion also occurs in another form, where almost in the words of the *Bhagavad Gītā*, Gautama is made to say that those who have not yet even entered the Paths "are sure of heaven if they have love and faith towards Me."—*Majjhima Nikāya*, 22.

Plate Q

LAY-WORSHIPPERS AT A BUDDHA SHRINE

The Buddha is represented by Footprints. Amarāvatī, 2nd century A.D.

iconolatry and all the mystical theology of the Mahāyāna. It is the element of worship which changed the monastic system of Gautama into a world-religion.

In the earliest Buddhist literature the word 'Buddha' has not yet come to be used in a technical sense: Gautama never speaks of himself as "the Buddha," and when others do so the term means simply the Enlightened One, the Awakened. The Buddha is but the wisest and greatest of the Arahats. In course of time the term became more specialized to mean a particular kind of being; while the term Bodhisatta, or Wisdom-Being, first used of Gautama between the Going-forth and the attainment of Nibbāna, came to mean a Buddha-designate—any being destined to become a Buddha in this or some future life. This doctrine of the Bodhisatta is extensively developed in the book of the 550 Jātakas, or Birth Stories, which recount the edifying histories of Gautama's previous existence as man, animal, or fairy. When the Brāhman Sumedha rejects the thought of crossing alone the sea of Becoming and registers the vow to attain omniscience, in order that he may also convey other men, and gods, across that sea, he speaks already in the sense of the Mahāyāna. Associated with the doctrine of the Bodhisatta is that of previous Buddhas, who are duly named in the *Mahāpadāna Sutta*, and the details of their lives set forth according to a set formula; their number is three or seven or, according to a later account, twenty-four. Of future Buddhas, only the Bodhisatta Metteya, the personification of Loving-kindness, is mentioned, and that in the *Milinda Panha*, which is a little later than the canonical scriptures.

It is possible that the three former Buddhas who are said to have appeared in the present age, but very long ago, represent a memory of actual teachers before Buddha: in

P

any case, the theory that all Buddhas teach the same doctrine is of considerable interest, and it corresponds to the Brāhman view of the eternity of the Vedas, which are heard rather than invented by successive teachers. This belief in the timeless unity of truth, which is shared by Indians of divers persuasions, is of much significance.

Without referring in greater detail to the mythological and magical elements which enter into even the earliest Buddha literature, it will suffice to point out that this literature already includes, as partly indicated above, the germs of most of those doctrines which are elaborated to a far greater extent in the dogmas of the 'Great Raft.' The development of that religion from the basis of early Buddhist psychology is nearly parallel to the development of mediæval Hinduism on the basis of the pure idealism of the Upanishads.

II. SYSTEM OF THE MAHĀYĀNA

Le plus saint, c'est le plus amant.—RUYSBROECK

The Mahāyāna or Great Vessel is so-called by its adherents, in contradistinction to the Hīnayāna or little Vessel of primitive Buddhism, because the former offers to all beings in all worlds salvation by faith and love as well as by knowledge, while the latter only avails to convey over the rough sea of Becoming to the farther shore of Nibbāna those few strong souls who require no external spiritual aid nor the consolation of Worship. The Hīnayāna, like the 'unshown way' of those who seek the '*nirguna Brahman*,' is exceeding hard;[1] whereas the burden of the

[1] In the words of Behmen (*Supersensual Life*, Dialogue 2): *But, alas, how hard it is for the Will to sink into nothing, to attract nothing, to imagine nothing.*

Mahāyāna is light, and does not require that a man should immediately renounce the world and all the affections of humanity. The manifestation of the Body of the Law, says the Mahāyāna, is adapted to the various needs of the children of the Buddha; whereas the Hīnayāna is only of avail to those who have left their spiritual childhood far behind them. The Hīnayāna emphasizes the necessity of saving knowledge, and aims at the salvation of the individual, and refuses to develop the mystery of Nibbāna in a positive sense; the Mahāyāna lays as much or greater stress on love, and aims at the salvation of every sentient being, and finds in Nirvāna the One Reality, which is 'Void' only in the sense that it is free from the limitations of every phase of the limited or contingent experience of which we have empirical knowledge. The Buddhists of the primitive school, on the other hand, naturally do not accept the name of the 'Lesser Vessel,' and as true Protestants they raise objection to the theological and æsthetic accommodation of the true doctrine to the necessities of human nature.

Opinions thus differ as to whether we may regard the Mahāyāna as a development or a degeneration. Even the professed exponents of the Hīnayāna have their doubts. Thus in one place Professor Rhys Davids speaks of the Bodhisattva doctrine as the *bīrana*-weed which "drove out the doctrine of the Ariyan path," and the weed "is not attractive:" [1] while in another, Mrs Rhys Davids writes of the cool detachment of the Arahat, that perhaps "a yet more saintly Sāriputta would have aspired yet further, even to an infinite series of rebirths, wherein he might, with ever-growing power and self-devotion, work for the furtherance of the religious evolution of his fellows," adding that

[1] *Dialogues of the Buddha*, ii, p. 1.

"social and religious ideals evolve out of, yea, and even beyond the finished work and time-straitened vision of the Arahants of old."[1] Perhaps we need not determine the relative value of either school: the way of knowledge will ever appeal to some, and the way of love and action to others, and the latter the majority. Those who are saved by knowledge stand apart from the world and its hopes and fears, offering to the world only that knowledge which shall enable others to stand aside in the same way: those others who are moved by their love and wisdom to perpetual activity—in whom the will to life is dead, but the will to power yet survives in its noblest and most impersonal forms—attain at last the same goal, and in the meanwhile effect a reconciliation of religion with the world, and the union of renunciation with action.

The development of the Mahāyāna is in fact the over-flowing of Buddhism from the limits of the Order into the life of the world; into whatever devious channels Buddhism may have ultimately descended, are we to say that that identification with the life of the world, with all its consequences in ethic and æsthetic, was a misfortune? Few who are acquainted with the history of Asiatic culture would maintain any such thesis.

Mahāyānists do not hesitate to describe the Hīnayāna ideal as selfish; and we have indicated in several places to what extent it must in any case be called narrow. But the Mahāyānists—not to speak of Christian critics of the Hīnayāna—do not sufficiently realize that a selfish being could not possibly become an Arahat, who must be free from even the conception of an ego, and still more from every form of ego-assertion. The selfishness of the would-be Arahat is more apparent than real. The ideal of self-

[1] *Psalms of the Brethren*, p. xlviii.

culture is not opposed to that of self-sacrifice: in any perfectly harmonious development these seemingly opposite tendencies are reconciled. To achieve this reconciliation, to combine renunciation with growth, knowledge with love, stillness with activity, is the problem of all ethics. Curiously enough, though its solution has often been attempted by oriental religions, it has never been so clearly enunciated in the west as by the 'irreligious' Nietzsche—the latest of the mystics—whose ideal of the Superman combines the Will to Power (*cf. pranidhāna*) with the Bestowing Virtue (*cf. karunā*).

If the ideal of the Private Buddha seems to be a selfish one, we may reply that the Great Man can render to his fellows no higher service than to realize the highest possible state of his being. From the Unity of life we cannot but deduce the identity of (true) self-interest with the (true) interest of others. While therefore the Mahāyānists may justly claim that their system is indeed a greater vessel of salvation in the sense of greater convenience, or better adaptation to the needs of a majority of voyagers, they cannot on the other hand justly accuse the captain and the crew of the smaller ship of selfishness. Those who seek to the farther shore may select the means best suited to their own needs: the final goal is one and the same.

The most essential part of the Mahāyāna is its emphasis on the Bodhisattva ideal, which replaces that of Arahatta, or ranks before it. Whereas the Arahat strives most earnestly for Nirvāna, the Bodhisattva as firmly refuses to accept the final release. "Forasmuch as there is the will that all sentient beings should be altogether made free, I will not forsake my fellow creatures." [1]

[1] *Avatamsaka Sūtra.*

The Bodhisattva is he in whom the Bodhicitta or heart of wisdom is fully expanded. In a sense, we are all Bodhisattvas, and indeed all Buddhas, only that in us by reason of ignorance and imperfection in love the glory of the Bodhi-heart is not yet made manifest. But those are specially called Bodhisattvas who with specific determination dedicate all the activities of their future and present lives to the task of saving the world. They do not merely contemplate, but feel, all the sorrow of the world, and because of their love they cannot be idle, but expend their virtue with supernatural generosity. It is said of Gautama Buddha, for example, that there is no spot on earth where he has not in some past life sacrificed his life for the sake of others, while the whole story of his last incarnation related in the *Vessantara Jātaka* relates the same unstinting generosity, which does not shrink even from the giving away of wife and children. But Buddhahood once attained, according to the old school, it remains for others to work out their salvation alone: "Be ye lamps unto yourselves," in the last words of Gautama. According to the Mahāyāna, however, even the attainment of Buddhahood does not involve indifference to the sorrow of the world; the work of salvation is perpetually carried on by the Bodhisattva emanations of the supreme Buddhas, just as the work of the Father is done by Jesus.

The Bodhisattvas are specially distinguished from the Srāvakas (Arahats) and Pacceka-Buddhas or 'Private Buddhas,' who have become followers of the Buddha 'for the sake of their own complete Nirvāna':[1] for the

[1] Hindus would express this by saying that Srāvakas and Pacceka-Buddhas choose the path of Immediate Salvation: Bodhisattvas, that of Ultimate Salvation. 'The deferred path of Liberation is the path of all Bhaktas. It is the path of compassion or service.'—P. N. Sinha, *Commentary on the Bhāgavata Purāna*, p. 359.

PLATE R 230

AVALOKITESVARA (*Bodhisattva*)

Nepalese copper gilt, 9th–10th century A.D.

Author's Collection

Bodhisattvas enter upon their course "out of compassion to the world, for the benefit, weal, and happiness of the world at large, both gods and men, for the sake of the complete Nirvāna of all beings. . . . Therefore they are called Bodhisattva Mahāsattva."[1]

A doctrine specially associated with the Bodhisattva ideal is that of the *parivarta* or turning over of ethical merit to the advantage of others, which amounts very nearly to the doctrine of vicarious atonement. Whereas in early Buddhism it is emphasized that each life is entirely separate from every other (also a Jaina doctrine, and no doubt derived from the Sāmkhya conception of a plurality of Purushas), the Mahāyāna insists on the interdependence and even the identity of all life; and this position affords a logical basis for the view that the merit acquired by one may be devoted to the good of others. This is a peculiarly amiable feature in late Buddhism; we find, for example, that whoever accomplishes a good deed, such as a work of charity or a pilgrimage, adds the prayer that the merit may be shared by all sentient beings.

It will be seen that the doctrine of vicarious merit involves the interpretation of karma in the first and more general sense referred to on page 108. No man lives to himself alone, but we may regard the whole creation (which groaneth and travailleth together) as one life and therefore as sharing a common karma, to which every individual contributes for good or ill. Notwithstanding from the individualist standpoint it may appear both false and dangerous to limit the doctrine of purely individual responsibility, it is not so in fact; the good or evil of the individual also affects others, and rather increases his

[1] *Saddharmapundarīka Sūtra.*

responsibility than lightens it. There is no mystery in karma; it is simply a phase of the law of cause and effect, and it holds as much for groups and communities as for individuals, if indeed, individuals are not also communities. Let us take a very simple example: if a single wise statesman by a generous treatment of a conquered race secures their loyalty at some future time of stress, that karma accrues not merely to himself but to the state for ever; and other members of the community, even those who would have dealt ungenerously in the first instance, benefit undeniably from the vicarious merit of a single man. Just in this sense it is possible for hero-souls to bear or to share the burden of the karma of humanity. By this conception of the taking on of sin, or rather, the passing on of merit, the Mahāyāna has definitely emerged from the formula of psychic isolation which the Hīnayāna inherits from the Sāmkhya.

In other words, the great difficulty of imagining a particular karma passing from individual to individual, without the persistence even of a subtle body, is avoided by the conception of human beings, or indeed of the whole universe, as constituting one life or self. Thus it is from our ancestors that we receive our karma, and not merely from 'our own' past existences; and whatsoever karma we create will be inherited by humanity for ever.

The following account of karma is given by a modern Mahāyānist:

"The aggregate actions of all sentient beings give birth to the varieties of mountains, rivers, countries, etc. They are caused by aggregate actions, and so are called aggregate fruits. Our present life is the reflection of past actions. Men consider these reflections as their real selves. Their eyes, noses, ears, tongues, and bodies—as well as their gardens, woods, farms, residences, servants, and maids—men imagine to be their own possessions; but, in fact, they are only results endlessly produced by innumerable actions. In tracing everything back to the ultimate limits of the past, we cannot find a beginning: hence it is said that death and birth have no beginning. Again, when seeking the ultimate limit of the future, we cannot find the end." [1]

It may be pointed out here just how far the doctrine of karma is and is not fatalistic. It is fatalistic in the sense that the present is always determined by the past; but the future remains free. Every action we make depends on what we have come to be at the time. But what we are coming to be at any time depends on the direction of the will. The karmic law merely asserts that this direction cannot be altered suddenly by the forgiveness of sins, but must be changed by our own efforts. If ever the turning of the will appears to take place suddenly, that can only be due to the fruition of long accumulated latent tendencies (we constantly read that Gautama preached the Law to such and such a one, forasmuch as he saw that his or her intelligence was 'fully ripe,' and in these cases conversion immediately results). Thus, if we are not directly responsible for our present actions, we are always responsible for our character, on which future actions depend. On this account the object of Buddhist moral discipline is always the accumulation of merit (*punya*), that is to say the heaping up of grace, or simply the constant improvement of character. The Mahāyānist doctors recognize ten stations in the spiritual evolution of the Bodhisattva, beginning with

[1] S. Kuroda, *Outlines of the Mahāyāna Philosophy.*

the first awakening of the Wisdom-heart (Bodhicitta) in the warmth of compassion (karunā) and the light of divine knowledge (prajñā). These stations are those of 'joy,' 'purity,' 'effulgence,' 'burning,' 'hard to achieve,' 'showing the face,' 'going afar off,' 'not moving to and fro,' 'good intelligence,' and 'dharma-cloud.' It is in the first station that the Bodhisattva makes those pregnant resolutions (pranidhāna) which determine the course of his future lives. An example of such a vow is the resolution of Avalokitesvara not to accept salvation until the least particle of dust shall have attained to Buddahood before him.

It may be mentioned that the course (*cariyā*) of the Bodhisattva has this advantage, that he never comes to birth in any purgatory, nor in any unfavourable condition on earth. Nor is the Bodhisattva required to cultivate a disgust for the conditions of life; he does not practise a meditation on Foul Things, like the aspirant for Arahatta. The Bodhisattva simply recognizes that the conditions of life have come to be what they are, that it is in the nature (*tattva*, *bhutathā*, suchness) of things to be so, and he takes them accordingly for what they are worth. This position is nowhere more tersely summed up than in the well-known Japanese verselet—

Granted this dewdrop world be but a dewdrop world,
This granted, yet . . .

Thus the new Buddhist law was in no way puritanical, and did not inculcate an absolute detachment. Pleasure indeed is not to be sought as an end in itself, but it need not be rejected as it arises incidentally. The Bodhisattva shares in the life of the world; for example, he has a wife, that his supernatural generosity may be seen in the gift of wife and children, and for the same reason he may be the possessor of power and wealth. If by reason of attachment and this association with the world some venial sins are unavoidably committed, that is of little consequence, and such sins are wiped away in the love of others: the cardinal sins of hatred and self-thinking cannot be imagined in him in whom the heart of wisdom has been awakened. It must not, however, be supposed that the Mahāyāna in any way relaxes the rule of the Order; and even in the matter of the remission of sins of the laity it is only minor and inevitable shortcomings that are considered, and not deliberate deeds of evil. And if the Mahāyāna doctors preach the futility of remorse and discouragement, on the other hand they are by no means quietists, but advocate a mysticism fully as practical as that of Ruysbroeck.

The idea of the Bodhisattva corresponds to that of the Hero, the Superman, the Saviour and the Avatār of other systems. In this connexion it is interesting to note that legitimate pride—the will to power, conjoined with the bestowing virtue—is by no means alien to the Bodhisattva character, but on the contrary, "In respect of three things may pride be borne—man's works, his temptations, and his power," and the exposition follows: "The pride of works lies in the thought 'for me alone is the task.'[1] This world, enslaved by passion, is powerless to accomplish its own weal; then must I do it for them, for I am not impotent like them. Shall another do a lowly task while I am standing by? If I in my pride will not do it, better it is that my pride perish. . . .

[1] *Cf.* Blake:

> But when Jesus was crucified,
> Then was perfected His galling pride.

Then with firm spirit I will undo the occasions of undoing; if I should be conquered by them, my ambition to conquer the threefold world would be a jest. I will conquer all; none shall conquer me. This is the pride that I will bear, for I am the son of the Conqueror Lions![1] . . . Surrounded by the troop of the passions man should become a thousand times prouder, and be as unconquerable to their hordes as a lion to flocks of deer . . . so, into whatever straits he may come, he will not fall into the power of the Passions. He will utterly give himself over to whatever task arrives, greedy for the work . . . how can he whose happiness is work itself be happy in doing no work? He will hold himself in readiness, so that even before a task comes to him he is prepared to turn to every course. As the seed of the cotton-tree is swayed at the coming and going of the wind, so will he be obedient to his resolution; and thus divine power is gained."[2]

We may remark here an important distinction between the Mahāyāna and the Hīnayāna lies in the fact that the former is essentially mythical and unhistorical; the believer is, indeed, warned—precisely as the worshipper of Krishna is warned in the Vaishnava scriptures that the Krishna Līlā is not a history, but a process for ever unfolded in the heart of man—that matters of historical fact are without religious significance. On this account, notwithstanding its more popular form, the Mahāyāna has been justly called 'more philosophical' than the

[1] Buddha is often spoken of as Conqueror (Jina—a term more familiar in connexion with the followers of Mahāvīra, the 'Jainas') and as Lion (Sākyasinha, the lion of the Sākya race).

[2] From the *Bodhicaryāvatāra* of Shānti Deva, translated by L. D. Barnett, 1902.

PLATE S 236

MAITREYA (*Bodhisattva*)

Ceylonese bronze, 6th century A.D. or later

Colombo Museum

Hīnayāna, "because under the forms of religious or mystical imagery it expresses the universal, whereas the Hīnayāna cannot set itself free from the domination of the historical fact."[1]

An important dogmatic distinction, the meaning of which will be made clear as we proceed, is also found in the new interpretation of the Three Refuges. In the Hīnayāna these are the Buddha, the Dhamma, and the Sangha; in the Mahāyāna they are the Buddhas, the Sons of the Buddhas (Bodhisattvas both in the special and in the wider sense), and the Dharmakāya.

Mahāyāna Theology

The Mahāyāna is thus distinguished by its mystical Buddha theology. This must not be confused with the popular and quite realistic theology of Sakka and Brahmā recognized in early Buddhism. The Mahāyāna Buddha theology, as remarked by Rhys Davids, "is the greatest possible contradiction to the Agnostic Atheism," which is the characteristic of Gautama's system of philosophy. But this opposition is simply the inevitable contrast of religion and philosophy, relative and absolute truth, and those who are interested in the science of theology, or are touched by art, will not be likely to agree in denouncing the Buddha gods as the inventions "of a sickly scholasticism, hollow abstractions without life or reality":[2] in this contingent world we live every day by

[1] R. F. Johnston, *Buddhist China*, p. 114. Most likely Christianity also in the near future will succeed in breaking the 'entangling alliance' of religion and history, from which the mystics have already long emerged. There cannot be an absolute truth which is not accessible to direct experience.

[2] T. W. Rhys Davids, *Buddhism* (S.P.C.K., an early edition, pp. 206, 207).

relative truths, and for all those who do not wish to avoid the world of Becoming at the earliest possible moment these relative truths are far from lacking in life or reality. The Mahāyāna as a theistic faith is so only to the same extent as the Vedānta, that is to say it has an esoteric aspect which speaks in negative terms of a Suchness and a Void which cannot be known, while on the other it has an exoteric and more elaborate part in which the Absolute is seen through the glass of time and space, contracted and identified into variety. This development appears in the doctrine of the Trikāya, the Three Bodies of Buddha. These three are (1) the *Dharmakāya*, or Essence-body; (2) its heavenly manifestation in the *Sambhogakāya*, or Body of Bliss; and (3) the emanation, transformation, or projection thereof, called *Nirmānakāya*, apparent as the visible individual Buddha on earth. This is a system which hardly differs from what is implied in the Christian doctrine of Incarnation, and it is not unlikely that both Christianity and the Mahāyāna are inheritors from common Gnostic sources.

Thus the Dharmakāya may be compared to the Father; the Sambhogakāya to the figure of Christ in glory; the Nirmānakāya to the visible Jesus who announces in human speech that 'I and my Father are One.' Or again with the Vedānta: the Dharmakāya is the Brahman, timeless and unconditioned; the Sambhogakāya is realized in the forms of Īsvara; the Nirmānakaya in every avatār. The essence of all things, the one reality of which their fleeting shapes remind us, is the Dharmakāya. The Dharmakāya is not a personal being who reveals himself to us in a single incarnation, but it is the all-pervading and traceless ground of the soul, which does not in fact suffer any modification but appears to us to assume a variety of forms: we read that though the Buddha (a term which we must here understand as impersonal) does not depart from his seat in the tower (state of Dharmakāya), yet he may assume all and every form, whether of a Brahmā, a god, or a monk, or a physician, or a tradesman, or an artist; he may reveal himself in every form of art and industry, in cities or in villages: from the highest heaven to the lowest hell, there is the Dharmakāya, in which all sentient beings are one. The Dharmakāya is the impersonal ground of Buddhahood from which the personal will, thought and love of innumerable Buddhas and Bodhisattvas ever proceed in response to the needs of those in whom the perfect nature is not yet realized. In some of the later phases of the Mahāyāna, however, the Dharmakāya is personified as Ādi-Buddha (sometimes Vairocana) who is then to be regarded as the Supreme Being, above all other Buddhas, and whose sakti is Prajñāpāramitā.

Dharmakāya is commonly translated 'Body of the Law,' but it must not be interpreted merely as equivalent to the sum of the scriptures. The fathomless being of Buddhahood, according to the Mahāyāna, is something more than the immortality of the individual in his doctrine; we must understand Dharma here as the *Om* or *Logos*. To understand the meaning of Dharmakāya more fully we must take into account also its synonyms, for example, *Svabhāvakāya*, or 'own-nature body' (like the Brāhmanical *svarūpa*, 'own-form'), *Tattva*, or 'suchness,' *Sunya*, 'the void' or 'abyss,' *Nirvāna*, 'the eternal liberty,' *Samādhikāya*, 'rapture-body,' *Bodhi*, 'wisdom,' *Prajñā*, 'divine knowledge,' *Tathāgata-garbha*, 'womb of those who attain.'

Some of these terms must be further considered. The

'Void,' for example, is not by any means 'naught,' but simply the absence of characteristics; the Dharmakāya is 'void' just as the Brahman is 'not so, not so,' and as Duns Scotus says that God 'is not improperly called Nothing.' It is precisely from the undetermined that evolution is imaginable; where there is nothing there is room for everything. The voidness of things is the non-existence of things-in-themselves, on which so much stress is rightly laid in early Buddhism. The phrase 'Own-nature body' emphasizes the thought 'I am that I am.' Bodhi is the 'wisdom-heart' which awakens with the determination to become a Buddha. 'Suchness' may be taken to mean inevitability, or spontaneity, that the highest cause of everything must needs be in the thing itself.

A special meaning attaches to the name Prajñā or Prajñāpāramitā, viz. Supreme Knowledge, Reason, Understanding, Sophia; for the name Prajñāpāramitā is applied to the chief of the Mahāyāna scriptures, or a group of scriptures, signifying the divine knowledge which they embody, and she is also personified as a feminine divinity. As one with the Dharmakāya she is the knowledge of the Abyss, the Buddhahood in which the individual Bodhisattva passes away. But as Reason or Understanding she is Tathāgata-garbha, the Womb or Mother of the Buddhas, and the source from which issues the variety of things, both mental and physical.[1] In Hindu phraseology, she is the Sakti of the Supreme, the power of manifestation inseparable from that which Manifests: she is Devī, *Māyā*, or *Prakriti*, the One who is also the many. "In the

[1] Precisely as the Zero may be regarded as a Womb, being the sum and source of an infinite series of plus and of minus quantities, such as the Extremes or Pairs of opposites of the relative world.

root she is all-Brahman; in the stem she is all-illusion; in the flower she is all-world; and in the fruit all-liberation" —(*Tantra Tattva*).[1]

Nirvāna

The Mahāyāna doctrine of Nirvāna requires somewhat lengthier consideration. We have seen that in earlier Buddhism Nibbāna meant the dying out of the fires of passion, resentment, and infatuation, and the dissolution of the individual personality, but what more or less than this it meant metaphysically, Gautama would not say, and he plainly condemns speculation as unedifying. Mahāyānists however do not hesitate to develop a far-reaching idealism, similar to that of the Vedānta, and logically develop the early Buddhism phenomenalism into a complete nihilism which, as we have seen, declares

[1] "Nature ariseth," says Behmen, "in the outflown word of the divine perception and knowledge." "The wisdom is the great Mystery of the divine nature; for in her the powers, colours and virtues are made manifest; in her is the variation of the power and the virtue, viz. the understanding: she is the divine understanding—that is, the divine vision, wherein the Unity is manifest . . . in which the images of angels and souls have been seen from eternity . . . therein have lain all things in one only ground, as an image lieth hid in a piece of wood before the artificer doth carve it out and fashion it" (*The Clavis*).
"At the time of creation Brahmā, Vishnu, Mahesvara and other devas are born of the body of that beginningless and eternal Kālikā, and at the time of dissolution they again disappear in Her" (*Nirvāna Tantra*). Kālikā is one of the many names of Devī, Sakti, Prakriti, Pārvatī, Kālī, etc: she is as Umā, the "wisdom that hath eaten up my mind and rid me of the sense of I and my" (Tāyumānavar): "who with the absolute inseparably is blended as flower with scent, as sun and ray, as life and body . . . her children, all living things with ceaseless bliss ambrosial nourishing" (Chidambara Swāmi). It is not without significance that the traditional name of Gautama's earthly mother is Māyā.

that the whole world of becoming is truly void and unreal.

This 'nihilism' is carried to its farthest extreme in works such as the *Prajñāpāramitās*[1] and the *Vajracchedika Sūtra*: we read, for example, in the latter work:

"And again, O Subhuti, a gift should not be given by a Bodhisattva, while he still believes in the reality of objects; a gift should not be given by him while he yet believes in anything; a gift should not be given by him while he still believes in form; a gift should not be given by him while he still believes in the special qualities of sound, smell, taste, and touch. . . . And why? Because that Bodhisattva, O Subhuti, who gives a gift, without believing in anything, the measure of his stock of merit is not easy to learn!"

And this denial of entity is carried to the logical extreme of denying the existence of scripture:

"'Then what do you think, O Subhuti, is there any doctrine that was preached by the Tathāgata?' Subhuti said: 'Not so, indeed, O Worshipful, There is not anything that was preached by the Tathāgata.'"

Even more striking is the famous 'Middle Path of Eight Noes' of Nāgārjuna:

"There is no production (*utpāda*), no destruction (*uccheda*), no annihilation (*nirodha*), no persistence (*sāsvata*), no unity (*ekārtha*), no plurality (*nānārtha*), no coming in (*āgamana*), and no going forth (*nirgama*)."

This view, however, is not properly to be understood as mere nihilism; it is constantly emphasized that things of

[1] So called because they treat at length of the Six Perfections (*Pāramitās*) of a Bodhisattva, and the last of these in particular. The Six Perfections are *dāna*, charity; *sīla*, morality; *khsānti*, meekness; *vīrya*, energy; *dhyāna*, meditation; and *prajñā*, wisdom.

all kinds neither exist nor do not exist. We may understand this 'middle view' in either of two ways: as the doctrine that of that which is other than phenomenal there cannot be any predication of existence or non-existence; or as the doctrine that from the standpoint of the Absolute, things have no existence, while from the standpoint of the Relative, they have a relative being.

Nāgārjuna

The latter view is distinctly maintained by Nāgārjuna, who, like Asvaghosa, must have been originally a Brāhman, and lived about the end of the second century A.D. The Middle View just mentioned is set forth by him in the *Mādhyamika sūtras.* And here Nāgārjuna gives a very clear answer to the objection that, if all be 'Void,' then the Four Ariyan Truths, the Order of Brethren, and Buddha himself must be considered to be and have been unreal: he meets the difficulty precisely as Sankarācārya meets the inconsistencies of the Upanishads, by saying that the Buddha speaks of two truths, the one Truth in the highest sense, absolute, the other a conventional and relative truth; he who does not comprehend the distinction of these cannot understand the deeper import of the teaching of the Buddha.[1]

[1] The Western student will of course meet with similar contradictions in the Christian gospels. When Christ says 'I and my Father are One,' that is absolute truth; when He speaks upon the cross as if 'forsaken' by the Father, that is a relative truth only. When He says that Mary has chosen the good part that shall not be taken away from her, that is absolute; but when He commands us to render unto Caesar the things that are Caesar's, He recognizes again the realm of relativity. Here also it may be said that he who does not recognize the distinction of relative and absolute truth, cannot be said to understand the gospel of Christ.

The Mahāyāna is thus far from affirming that Nirvāna is non-existence pure and simple; it does not hesitate to say that to lose our life is to save it. Nirvāna is positive, or positively is; even for the individual it cannot be said to come to be, or to be entered into; it merely comes to be realized, so soon as that ignorance is overcome which obscures the knowledge of our real freedom, which nothing has ever infringed, or ever can infringe. Nirvāna is that which is not lacking, is not acquired, is not intermittent, is not non-intermittent, is not subject to destruction, and is not created, whose sign is the absence of signs, which transcends alike non-Being and Being. The Mahāyāna Nirvāna cannot be better explained than in the words of the great Sūfī Al-Hujwīrī—"When a man becomes annihilated from his attributes he attains to perfect subsistence, he is neither near nor far, neither stranger nor intimate, neither sober nor intoxicated, neither separated nor united; he has no name, or sign, or brand or mark" (*Kashf al-Mahjūb*). It is the realization of the infinite love and infinite wisdom, where knowledge and love alike proclaim identity, that constitute this Nirvāna. He in whom the Heart of Wisdom awakes, however, does not shrink from future rebirths, "but plunges himself into the ever rushing current of Samsāra and sacrifices himself to save his fellow creatures from being eternally drowned in it." He does not shrink from experience, for "just as the lotus-flowers do not grow on the dry land, but spring from the dark and watery mud, so is it with the Heart of Wisdom, it is by virtue of passion and sin that the seeds and sprouts of Buddhahood are able to grow, and not from inaction and eternal annihilation" (*Vimala-kīrti Stūra*).

Mahāyāna non-duality culminates in the magnificent paradox of the identity of Nirvāna with the Samsāra, the non-distinction of the unshown and the shown—"this our worldly life is an activity of Nirvāna itself, not the slightest distinction exists between them"—(Nāgārjuna, *Mādhyamika Sāstra*). This view is expressed with dramatic force in the aphorism, '*Yas klesas so bodhi, yas samsāras tat nirvānam*,' That which is sin is also Wisdom, the realm of Becoming is also Nirvāna.[1] One and the same is the heart of Suchness and the Heart of Birth-and-Death—'what is immortal and what is mortal are harmoniously blended, for they are not one, nor are they separate'—(Asvaghosha). If the truth is not to be found in our everyday experience, it will not be found by searching elsewhere.

Mahāyāna mysticism

It scarcely needs to be pointed out, though it is important to realize, that this is the ultimate position to which the mystics of every age and inheritance have ultimately returned. It is that of Blake when he says that the notion that a man has a body distinct from his soul must be expunged, and that it is only because the doors of perception are closed—by ignorance—that we do not see all things as they are, infinite. It is that of Kabīr when he says—"in the home is reality; the home helps to attain Him who is real—I behold His beauty everywhere"; and when he asks, "What is the difference between the river and its waves; because it has been named as wave, shall

[1] Mahāyāna monism is thus totalistic: it affirms the unreality of phenomena as such, but equally affirms their significance. This life is a dream, but not without meaning. There is no sanction for this doctrine in early Buddhism, and in one place it is also condemned by Asvaghosha as born of the devil (*The Awakening of Faith*, trans. T. Suzuki, page 137); perhaps it was sometimes misunderstood in the sense of 'Let us eat, drink and be merry, for to-morrow we die.'

it no longer be considered water?" It is that of Behmen when he says the Enochian life "is in this world, yet as it were swallowed up in the Mystery; but it is not altered in itself, it is only withdrawn from our sight and our sense; for if our eyes were opened, we should see it":[1] Paradise is still upon earth, and only because of our self-thinking and self-willing we do not see and hear God.[2] It is that of Whitman, when he says there "will never be any more perfection than there is now, nor any more of heaven or hell than there is now," and inquires, "Why should I wish to see God better than this day?"

Strange and hard that paradox true I give,
Objects gross and the unseen soul are one.

The Buddhas

In the realm of absolute (*paramārtha*) truth we may speak only of the Dharmakāya as void. But there exists also for us a realm of relative (*samvritti*) truth where the Absolute is made manifest by name and form; to the dwellers in heaven as Sambhogakāya, the Body of Bliss, and to those on earth as Nirmānakāya, the Body of Transformation.

The Sambhogakāya is the Buddha or Buddhas regarded as God in heaven, determined by name and form, but omniscient, omnipresent, and within the law of causality, omnipotent. A Buddha, in this sense, is identical with

[1] *The Forty Questions.*

[2] *The Supersensual Life*, Dialogue I. Closely parallel to a passage of the *Avatamsaka Sūtra:* "Child of Buddha, there is not even one living being that has not the wisdom of the Tathāgata. It is only because of their vain thought and affections that all beings are not conscious of this."

the Brāhmanical 'Īsvara,' who may be worshipped under various names (*e.g.* as Vishnu or as Siva), the worshipper attaining the heaven ruled by him whom he worships, though he knows that all of these forms are essentially one and the same. The Mahāyāna does in fact multiply the number of Buddhas indefinitely and quite logically, since it is the goal of every individual to become a Buddha. The nature of these Buddhas and their heavens will be best realized if we describe the most popular of all, whose name is Amitābha, or Amida.

Amitābha Buddha rules over the heaven Sukhāvati, the Pure Land or Western Paradise. With him are associated the historical Gautama as earthly emanation, and the Bodhisattva Avalokitesvara as the Saviour (Plate R). The history of Amitābha relates that many long ages ago he was a great king, who left his throne to become a wanderer, and he attained to Bodhisattvahood under the guidance of the Buddha, that is, the human Buddha then manifest; and he made a series of great vows, both to become a Buddha for the sake of saving all living things, and to create a heaven where the souls of the blessed might enjoy an age-long state of happiness, wisdom and purity. The eighteenth of these vows is the chief source of the popular development of Amidism, as the belief of the worshippers of Amitābha is styled. This vow runs as follows:

"When I become Buddha, let all living beings of the ten regions of the universe maintain a confident and joyful faith in me; let them concentrate their longings on a rebirth in my Paradise; and let them call upon my name, though it be only ten times or less: then, provided only they have not been guilty of the five heinous sins, and have not slandered or vilified the true religion, the desire of such beings to be born in my Paradise will be surely fulfilled. If this be not so, may I never receive the perfect enlightenment of Buddahood."

This is a fully developed doctrine of salvation by faith. The parallel with some forms of Christianity is very close. Amitābha both 'draws' men to himself, and 'sent' his son Gautama to lead men to him, and he is ever accessible through the holy spirit of Avalokitesvara. The efficacy of death-bed repentance is admitted; and in any case the dying Amidist should contemplate the glorious figure of Amitābha, just as the dying Catholic fixes his eyes upon the Crucifix upheld by the priest who administers extreme unction. The faithful Amidist is carried immediately to heaven, and is there reborn with a spiritual body within the calyx of one of the lotuses of the sacred lake. But those of less virtue must wait long before their lotus expands, and until then they cannot see God. Those who have committed one of the five heinous sins, and yet have called on Amitābha's name, must wait for countless ages, a period of time beyond conception, before their flowers open; just as, according to Behmen, those souls that depart from the body "without Christ's body, hanging as it were by a thread," must wait for the last day, ere they come forth. Another Mahāyānist idea, that the heaven of a Buddha is coextensive with the universe, is also to be found in Behmen, who, to the question, "Must not the soul leave the body at death, and go either to heaven or hell?" answers, "There is verily no such kind of entering in; forasmuch as heaven and hell are everywhere, being universally extended." Strictly speaking, the heaven of Amitābha cannot be identified with Nirvāna, but is a 'Buddha-field,' where preparation for Nirvāna is completed.

The following Table will exhibit the complete scheme of Mahāyāna Buddhology:

ĀDIBUDDHA

	Central	East	South	West	North
Buddhas:	Vairocana	Akshobya	Ratnasambhava	Amitābha	Amoghasiddha
Bodhisattvas:	Samantabhadra	Vajrapāni	Ratnapānī	Avalokitesvara or Padmapāni	Visvapāni
Earthly Buddhas:	Kakusandha	Konagammana	Kassapa	Gautama	Metteya

The Mahāyāna pantheon, however, is extended far beyond this simple scheme, to include more than five hundred divinities: in the words of Lafcadio Hearn, "a most ancient shoreless sea of forms incomprehensibly interchanging and intermingling, but symbolizing the protean magic of that infinite Unknown that shapes and reshapes for ever all cosmic being." Of all these divinities some further account is given below, but there must be mentioned here Prajñāpāramitā, the Bodhisattvas Manjusrī (Plate DD) and the Chinese Ti-tsang and Kwannon (kwanyin, Plates GG, HH), and also the Tārās or Saviouresses who are feminine divinities, recognized from about the sixth century A.D. as embodying the principle of Grace in the Bodhisattvas. The full development of this pantheon takes place during the first twelve centuries A.D., though its beginnings are earlier. Its final elaboration in Lamaistic Buddhism continues later.

We must now consider the Nirmānakāya, the plane of those Buddha-appearances which are emanated or projected from the Sambhogakāya as magical earthly apparitions, a doctrine of revelation in response to the spiritual needs of sentient beings. We have already seen that at an early stage of Buddhism Gautama is already made to affirm that he is not a man, but a Buddha; here, in a development similar to that of Christian Docetism, we find the view put forward that the earthly Buddhas are not living men, but ghosts or forms of thought, acting as vehicles of the saviour-will which led the Bodhisattva to the abyss of Buddhahood. In part, no doubt, this represents an attempt to get over the logical difficulty presented by the continued survival of the person Gautama for many years after the attainment of that enlightenment which cuts the connecting bonds of the spiritual compound known as personality; this continuance has also been aptly compared to the continued spinning of the potter's wheel for some time after the hand of the potter has been removed, the final physical death of the body being likened to the subsequent stopping of the wheel.

Convenient Means

Intimately associated with the doctrine of emanation is that of Convenient Means (*upāya*): "the Heart of Wisdom abiding in the Unity creates particular means of salvation" (Nāgārjuna). The knowledge of these means is one of the perfections of Buddhahood, and is the power of response to the infinite variety of the spiritual needs of sentient beings. The various forms which the divine Tathāgata assumes, revealing himself in the right place, at the right time, and never missing the right opportunity and the right word—these manifestations constitute the Nirmānakāya. To a certain extent the doctrine of upāya corresponds to the ready wit of such teachers as Buddha or Christ, who with little effort so effectually render aid to those who seek them, and no less effectually confound their opponents: admirably illustrated, for example, in Gautama's dealing with Gotamī the Slender, and in many well-known anecdotes of Jesus. Of either it may be said,

He is the Answerer,
What can be answer'd he answers, and what cannot be answer'd he shows how it cannot be answer'd.

This is also a doctrine of the graduation of truth: faiths are not divided into the true and the false, but are so many rungs of the ladder, so many separate ladders, that lead to One Unknown. The doctrine of upāya implies the perfect understanding of human needs by that divine intelligence that knows no need in itself, save that implied in the saying, *Eternity is in love with the productions of time*—the only reason we can allege for the desire of the One to become many. This perfect understanding, "as of father with son, comrade with comrade, lover with mistress,"[1] does not clash with the intellectual recognition of the gods as man-made, and this the Hindus have beautifully reconciled with the idea of Grace, in the adoration "Thou that doest take the forms imagined by Thy worshippers"—addressed, indeed, by Saivas to Siva, but no less appropriate to the thought of the Mahāyāna. The doctrine of upāya is comparable also with the thought, "He makes himself as we are, that we may be as He is." The arts and religions of the world are all so many upāyas—one source, one end, only with diversity of means.

A second Mahāyāna school, in some respects divergent from the Mādhyamikā school of Nāgārjuna, is the Yogācāra school of Asanga and Vasubandhu. Here three kinds of knowledge are recognized in place of two; but two of these three are merely a subdivision of relative

[1] *Bhagavad Gītā*, xi, 44.

knowledge, into positive error and relative knowledge properly so-called. We have thus in place of *samvritti* and *paramārtha satya*:

(1) *Parikalpita satya*, for example, when we mistake a rope for a snake.

(2) *Paratantra satya*, for example, when we recognize the rope as a rope.

(3) *Parispanna satya*, when we recognize that 'rope' is a mere concept, and has no being as a thing in itself.

Of which (1) and (2) are together samvritti and (3) is paramārtha.

The Yogācāras also maintain a form of idealism which differs from the absolute agnosticism of the Mādhyamikas. According to the former, there does really exist a cosmic, not impersonal, Mind, called *Ālaya-vijñāna*,[1] the All-containing, or Ever-enduring, Mind. All things in the universe rest in, or rather consist of this substrate. It is sometimes confused with the Suchness; but actually it corresponds rather to the *saguna* (qualified) than the *nirguna* (unqualified) Brahman of the Brāhmans. It provides the basis for a sort of Platonic idealism; for, according to the Yogācāras, it is in this Cosmic Mind that the germs of all things exist in their ideality. In other words, the objective world consists entirely of mind-stuff, and it is the illusion born of ignorance that projects the real ideas into an external and phenomenal universe.

III. CH'AN, OR ZEN BUDDHISM

We have so far set forth the Mahāyāna according to the Mādhyamika school of Nāgārjuna and the Yogācāra school of Asanga, with illustration of the Sambhogakāya according to the sect of the Amidists, and with some notice

[1] Hence the Yogācāras are commonly spoken of as Vijñānavādins.

of other special cults, particularly that of Avalokitesvara. We shall now notice at greater length another phase of the Mahāyāna, likewise of Indian origin, and of somewhat later development in China and Japan. This is the school of Bodhidharma, known in China as Ch'an, and in Japan as Zen Buddhism, from the Indian word *Jhāna* or *Dhyāna* already explained. This Ch'an, or Zen Buddhism, though in a practical and more or less intimate way associated with the cult of Amitābha, represents the more philosophical and mystic aspect of the Mahāyāna, and is essentially indifferent to iconolatry and to scriptural authority. This phase of Mahāyāna is little determined by special forms, and can scarcely be said to have any other creed than that the kingdom of heaven is in the heart of man. This school of thought most fully represents the Mahāyāna as a world religion; for however attractive and picturesque may be the imagery of Amitābha's Western Paradise, however tender the legendary histories of the deified Buddhas and Bodhisattvas, these visions of a material and sectarian paradise, and these personal divinities can claim universal acceptance no more than those of any other theistic system. Ch'an Buddhism differs from the orthodox and popular Mahāyāna of the theistic Sūtras just as the teaching of Christ and of the Christian mystics differs from the systematic Christianity of the Churches. Furthermore, it is in close alliance with Taoist philosophy, and constitutes not merely a religion, but the essential culture of the Far East, finding full expression not only in belief, but practically in life and art.

Ch'an Buddhism was founded in China by the patriarch Bodhidharma, claimed to be the twenty-eighth in apostolic succession from Gautama, in the year 527. This great man, whose Chinese ministry lasted for only nine years, and whose personality has yet impressed itself so deeply on the memory of the Far East, was of a taciturn and even *farouche* disposition, and little inclined to suffer fools gladly. He spent the nine years of his life in China (A.D. 527–536) in the Shao Lin monastery, near Loyang, achieving little popularity, and earned the nick-name of the 'Wall-gazing Brāhman.' The essence of his doctrine asserts that the Buddha is not to be found in images and books, but in the heart of man. His followers, as the name of the school implies, lay great stress on meditation; they avoid the slavish worship of images, the fetters of authority, and the evils of priestcraft.[1]

The fundamental principle of Ch'an, or Zen Buddhism, may be summed up in the expression that *the Universe is the scripture of Zen*,[2] or more philosophically, the identity of the Many and the One, of Samsāra with the Brahman, This with That. Actual scripture is worthless in the letter, and only valuable for that to which it leads; and to that goal there are other guides than the written page or spoken word.

[1] It must not be supposed, however, that the wide diffusion of Ch'an ideas in China has done away with ritual worship, or even with superstition. The creed of the Chinese layman, as in other countries, is "often crude, irrational, and superstitious; he is liable to mistake symbol for objective truth; and he is apt to assume that faith is a sufficient guarantee of historic fact."—R. F. Johnston, *Buddhist China*, p. 96. The Ch'an and Amidist parties, respectively philosophical or mystic, and devotional, are closely allied—gorgeous shrines are often attached to Ch'an monasteries—very much as Christian mysticism is associated with the iconolatry of the Roman church. The Chinese Buddhist leans to one side or the other according to his temperament and spiritual needs.

[2] He, therefore, is the true Teacher 'who makes you perceive the Supreme Self *wherever the mind attaches itself*' (Kabīr): for 'Whatever thing, of whatsoever kind it be, 'tis wisdom's part in each the real thing to see' (*Kurral*, xxxvi, 5). All is in all.

It is related, for example, of the sage Hüen Sha that he was one day prepared to deliver a sermon to an assembled congregation, and was on the point of beginning, when a bird was heard to sing very sweetly close by; Hüen Sha descended from his pulpit with the remark that the sermon had been preached. Another sage, Teu Tse, one day pointed to a stone lying near the temple gate, and remarked, 'Therein reside all the Buddhas of the past, the present, and the future.' The face of Nature was called 'The Sermon of the Inanimate.'

As we have already indicated, some of these conceptions may be traced back to very early Buddhist origins, and it would be easy likewise to point to Western parallels. When the Zen teachers point to the rising and setting of the sun, to the deep sea, or to the falling flakes of snow in winter, and thereby inculcate the lessons of Zen, we are reminded of One who bids us consider the lilies, which toil not, neither do they spin, and who bids us not to be anxious for the morrow. When the mysterious visitors to the Chinese island of Puto, being asked to explain their religious beliefs, reply, "Our eyes have seen the ocean, our ears have heard the winds sighing, the rain descending, the sea waves dashing, and the wild birds calling,"[1] we are reminded of Blake, exclaiming, "When thou seest an eagle, thou seest a portion of genius. Lift up thy head!" and "The pride of the peacock is the glory of God."

The lines already quoted—a complete poem in the Japanese original—

Granted this dewdrop world be but a dewdrop world,
This granted, yet . . .

[1] R. F. Johnston, *Buddhist China*, p. 388.

are purely of the Zen tradition, though not perhaps its most profound expression. That most profound intuition is of the one Suchness that finds expression in the very transcience of every passing moment: the same indivisible being is ever coming to expression, and never expressed, in the coming to be and passing away of man and of the whole world moment by moment; it is the very heart of 'culture' and religion to recognize the eternal, not as obscured, but as revealed by the transient, to see infinity in the grain of sand, the same unborn in every birth, and the same undying in every death. These thoughts find constant expression in the poetry and art inspired by Zen thought. The Morning Glory, for example, fading in an hour, is a favourite theme of the Japanese poet and painter. What are we to understand by the poem of Matsunaga Teitoku?

The morning glory blooms but an hour, and yet it differs not at heart
From the giant pine that lives for a thousand years.

Are we to think of the morning glory as a type and symbol of the tragic brevity of our life, as a *memento mori*, a reminder of impermanence, like the wagtail's tail? We may do this without error: but there lies beyond this a deeper meaning in the words of Matsunaga, something more than a lamentation for the very constitution of our experience. According to the commentary of Kinso:

"He who has found the way in the morning may die at peace in the evening. To bloom in the morning, to await the heat of the sun, and then to perish, such is the lot appointed to the morning glory by Providence. There are pines, indeed, which have lived for a thousand years, but the morning glory, who must die so soon, never for a moment forgets herself, or shows herself to be envious of others. Every morning her flowers unfold, magically fair, they yield the natural virtue that has been granted to them, then they wither. And thus they perform their duty faithfully. Why condemn that faithfulness as vain and profitless?

"It is the same with the pine as with the morning glory, but as the life of the latter is the shorter, it illustrates the principle in a more striking way. The giant pine does not ponder on its thousand years, nor the morning glory on its life of a single day. Each does simply what it must. Certainly, the fate of the morning glory is other than that of the pine, yet their destiny is alike in this, that they fulfil the will of Providence, and are content. Matsunaga thought his heart was like their heart, and that is why he made that poem on the morning glory."[1]

Closely consonant with Matsunaga's poem is Henry King's *Contemplation upon Flowers*. The student will, indeed, find that nearly every thought expressed in Buddhist and Hindu literature finds expression in the Western world also; and it could not be otherwise, for the value of these thoughts is universal, and therefore they could not be more Oriental than Western; the East has advanced beyond the West only in their wider and fuller acceptance.

Brave flowers that I could gallant it like you,
And be as little vain!
You come abroad, and make a harmless show,
And to your beds of earth again.
You are not proud: you know your birth:
For your embroider'd garments are from earth.

[1] R. Petrucci, *La Philosophie de la Nature dans l'Art d'Extrême-Orient.*

And with this contrasts the futile longing of man for an eternity of happiness:

> *You do obey your months and times, but I*
> *Would have it ever Spring:*
> *My fate would know no Winter, never die,*
> *Nor think of such a thing.*
> *O that I could my bed of earth but view*
> *And smile, and look as cheerfully as you!*

And so it is that the Sermon of the Woods should teach us spontaneity of action, to fall in with the natural order of the world, neither apathetic nor rebellious, but possessing our souls in patience.

PART V : BUDDHIST ART

I. BUDDHIST LITERATURE

Language and Writing

WE may safely assume that Gautama's teaching was communicated to his disciples in Māgadhī, the spoken dialect of his native country. The oldest contemporary documents of Buddhist literature, the Edicts of Asoka, are written in a later form of the sister dialect of Kosala.[1] The Hīnayāna Buddhist scriptures, the Theravāda Canon or old Buddhist Bible, are preserved to us only in the literary dialect known as Pāli; while the later Mahāyāna texts of the Mahāyāna are compiled to us in Sanskrit, and preserved in that form, or in the early Chinese translations. Pāli and Sanskrit in Buddhist circles play the part which was taken by Latin in the Christian Church of the Middle Ages. Pāli is a literary form based on Māgadhī, gradually developed, and perhaps only definitely fixed when the scriptures were first written down in Ceylon about 80 B.C.

How can we speak of authentic scriptures which were not put into writing until four centuries after the death of the teacher whose words are recorded? That is possible in India, though not in Europe. In the time of Gautama, a very long period of literary activity was already past, and the same activity still continued. Vedic literature, in particular, with the exception of the later Upanishads, was already ancient, while the work of the great compilers of epic poetry, and of the grammarians and lawmen, is only

[1] *The Edicts of Asoka*, though veritable Buddhist literature, are not included in the scriptural canon, and are here referred to in a separate chapter, p. 180 *seq.*

a little later, and this literature has been faithfully transmitted to the present day. There existed also a great mass of contemporary popular poetry in the form of ballads and romances, tales and proverbs, part of which is preserved and embedded in Buddhist and Sanskrit literature, such as the Pāli Jātakas and the Brāhmanical epics. And yet it is unlikely that any written books existed much before the time of Asoka.

Writing was first introduced to India about the eighth century B.C., probably by merchants trading with the cities of the Euphrates valley, but for a long time the idea of the written word was regarded in literary circles with much disfavour. One curious illustration of this appears in the fact that books are not included in the list of personal property allowed to be possessed by the Brethren. The Indians had long since elaborated a system of remembered literature, which, given the certainty of a regular succession of teachers and disciples, secured the transmission of texts as well, and perhaps better than the written page. Because of this mnemonic system, the lack of external means of record had not been felt. Study consisted, therefore in hearing, and in repeating to oneself, not in the reading of books. This tradition has survived in considerable vigour to the present day; it is no uncommon thing to meet with Pandits who can repeat from memory a body of sacred literature of almost incredible extent, and it is still believed that "oral instruction is far superior to book-learning in maturing the mind and developing its powers." It hardly needs to be pointed out that many great thinkers, both ancient and modern, have shared this view. Plato suggests that the invention of letters "will produce forgetfulness in the minds of those who learn it, through neglect of memory, for that, through trusting to writing, they will remember outwardly by means of foreign marks, and not inwardly by means of their own faculties;" while Nietzsche exclaims that "He that writeth in blood and proverbs, doth not want to be read, but to be learnt by heart." In point of fact the principal literary form of the age of Gautama is that of the *Sūtra* or *Sutta*, a 'string' of *logia* to be learnt by heart; and almost all early Indian literature, even the literature of law and grammar, is compiled in verse.

Another reason for regarding writing with disfavour was that the written text becomes accessible to all, while the Brāhmans at any rate wished to withhold the esoteric doctrine from those not qualified to understand or to make good use of it, and other matter from those who would perhaps encroach on their professional rights. The system of mnemonic education and pupillary succession was also so well organized that there was no fear that the well-trained 'rememberer' would ever forget what he knew; the only recognized dangers were that certain texts might fall out of favour and so be finally lost, as has inevitably happened with a great part of early Indian literature, or that some accident might interfere with the pupillary or 'apostolic' succession. Moreover, the means of making durable books had not yet been devised in the time of Gautama. On the other hand it is clear from the mode of publication of Asoka's edicts that a fairly general knowledge of writing, a literacy perhaps about the same as that of modern India, had been attained by the third century B.C.

The Buddhist canon was first written down in Pāli about 80 B.C., in the reign of King Vattagāmani, in Ceylon. It is worth while to quote the words of the Sinhalese chronicle on this important event:

"The text of the Three Pitakas and the commentary thereon did the most wise Bhikkhus hand down in former times orally, but since they saw that the people were falling away (from the orthodox teaching), the bhikkhus met together, and in order that the true doctrines might endure, they wrote them down in books."[1]

These texts have been faithfully transmitted to modern times by successive copyists. On the other hand it is quite certain that a considerable part already existed in the same form in the time of Asoka, for some of the texts are referred to by name, and with quotation, in the Edicts. Without entering upon a long discussion, it will suffice to say that some parts of the texts almost as certainly go back to an earlier period, and record the sayings and doctrine of Gautama as remembered by his immediate disciples. The orthodox Hīnayānists, however, are not justified in asserting that the Pāli canon was actually fixed, still less that it was written down, at the 'First Council' immediately following the death of Gautama; the Buddhist Bible, like the Christian, consists of books composed at different ages, and many or most of the books are compilations of materials by many hands and of various periods.

The Pāli Canon

The Pāli canon consists of 'Three Pitakas,' or 'Baskets.' The *Vinaya Pitaka* is concerned with the rules of the Order of Brethren. It is subdivided as follows:

- Suttavibhanga
  - Pārājika
  - Pācittiya
- Khandakā
  - Mahāvagga
  - Cullavagga
- Parivāra

[1] *Mahāvamsa*, ch. xxxiii.

A. CALLING THE EARTH TO WITNESS (THE ASSAULT OF MĀRA)

Cave painting at Dambulla, Ceylon (18th century)

PLATE T

B. BUDDHIST LIBRARY, KANDY, CEYLON

We need not repeat here what has been said elsewhere regarding the organization of the Order of bhikkhus. But it is of interest to note that the first chapter of the *Mahāvagga* contains some of the oldest parts of the Buddha legend, relating in dignified archaic language how Gautama attained enlightenment, determined to preach the Law, and gained his first disciples. Here also the First Sermon of the Buddha, at Benares, and the well-known Fire Sermon are given, and the ordination of Rāhula is also related. In the *Cullavagga* are found the stories of the merchant Anāthapindika who dedicated a park to the Order; of Devadatta, Gautama's cousin and enemy, the first schismatic; the establishment of the order of Sisters; and a number of edifying anecdotes, all connected with the history or constitution of the Order.

We have already quoted the First Sermon of Gautama, in which are set forth the essentials of the Dhamma, the Four Ariyan Truths and the Eightfold Path. Here we transcribe, with some abbreviation, the almost equally famous sermon in which the transient life of the individual, subject to grief and tormented by desires is likened to existence in the midst of a fire.

"Then said the Exalted One to his disciples: 'Everything, O disciples, is in flames. And what Everything, O disciples, is in flames? The eye, O disciples, is in flames, the visible is in flames, the knowledge of the visible is in flames, the contact with the visible is in flames, the feeling which arises from contact with the visible is in flames, be it pleasure, be it pain, be it neither pleasure nor pain, this also is in flames. By what fire is it kindled? By the fire of desire, by the fire of hate, by the fire of fascination, it is kindled; by birth, old age, death, pain, lamentation, sorrow, grief, despair, it is kindled: thus I say. The ear is in flames, the audible is in flames, the knowledge of the audible is in flames, the contact with the audible is in flames, the feeling which arises from contact with the audible is in flames, be it pleasure, be it pain, be it neither pleasure nor pain, this also is in flames. By what fire is it kindled? By the fire of desire, by the fire of hate, by the fire of fascination, it is kindled; by birth, old age, death, pain, lamentation, sorrow, grief, despair, it is kindled; thus I say. The sense of smell is in flames'—and then follows for the third time the same series of propositions;—'the tongue is in flames; the body is in flames; the mind is in flames';—each time the same detail follows unabridged. Then the address goes on:

"'Knowing this, O disciples, a wise, noble, hearer of the word becomes wearied of the eye, he becomes wearied of the visible, he becomes wearied of the knowledge of the visible, he becomes wearied of contact with the visible, he becomes wearied of the feeling which arises from contact with the visible, be it pleasure, be it pain, be it neither pleasure nor pain. He becomes wearied of the ear'—and then follows one after the other the whole series of ideas as above. The address concludes:

"'While he becomes wearied thereof, he becomes free from desire; free from desire, he becomes delivered; in the delivered arises the knowledge: I am delivered; rebirth is at an end, perfected is holiness, duty done; there is no more returning to this world; he knows this."[1]

It should be noted that this address is delivered by Gautama to an assembly of Brethren already initiated and ordained, already familiar with the thought of origination and decease. A somewhat different method is

[1] Condensed from Oldenberg. Another version above, p. 42.

employed in addresses to uninitiated laymen, such as the 80,000 village elders sent by King Bimbisāra to the Buddha for instruction. There is in a much more popular style—milk for babes. When in another place the Buddha is accused of favouritism, inasmuch as he teaches the more profound doctrine to his disciples and more simple matters to the public, he draws an analogy from the operations of a farmer, who devotes the most care to his most productive fields (the Brethren), somewhat less attention to the less fertile fields (the Buddhist laity), and less still to the barren soil (those who do not accept the Good Law).

While Discipline is dealt with in the *Vinaya Pitaka*, the *Sutta Pitaka*, the 'Basket of Suttas' is our chief source for the Buddha's Gospel as expounded in argument and dialogues. Here also are included the "Psalms of the Brethren and Sisters," the most important literary production of early Buddhism, and the *Jātakas*, which embody the largest and oldest collection of folklore extant. The *Sutta Pitaka* is divided as follows:

1. *Digha Nikāya*; 2. *Majjhima Nikāya*; 3. *Samyutta Nikāya*; 4. *Anguttara Nikāya*; and 5. *Khuddaka Nikāya*. The last, again, includes, 1. *Khuddakapātha*; 2. *Dhammapada*; 3. *Udāna*; 4. *Itivuttaka*; 5. *Suttanipāta*; 6. *Vimānavatthu*; 7. *Petavatthu*; 8. *Theragāthā*; 9. *Therīgāthā*; 10. *Jātaka*; 11. *Niddesa*; 12. *Patisambhidāmagga*; 13. *Apadāna*; 14. *Buddhavamsa*; and 15. *Cariyāpitaka*.

The first of the *Digha Nikāya* Suttas is called the Perfect Net. In this net are supposed to be caught and exposed each and all of sixty-two different philosophies which proceed from the ancient animistic conception of soul as a subtle, permanent entity within the body, and independent of the life of the body. These various eel-wrigglers, as Gautama calls them, he says are all of them trapped in the net of the sixty-two modes: "this way and that they plunge about, but they are in it; this way and that they may flounder, but they are included in it, caught in it. Just, brethren, as when a skilful fisherman or fisher-lad should drag a tiny pool of water with a fine-meshed net he might fairly think: 'Whatever fish of size may be in this pond, every one will be in this net; flounder about as they may, they will be included in it, and caught'; just so is it with these speculators about the past and future, in this net, flounder as they may, they are included and caught."

It is unfortunate that in all these cases we hear only one side of the argument, which always appears to leave no way of escape for the 'skilled absolutist.' If ever Gautama met his match we should like to hear what passed on such an occasion.

Of more enduring interest is the Sutta upon the *Fruits of the Life of a Wanderer*. Here, moreover, we do not get a purely Buddhist, but rather an Indian point of view. The whole Sutta constitutes a reply to the question, what advantage is the life of a recluse? King Ajātasattu of Magadha points out the gain that men derive from their worldly occupations, and wishes to know what corresponding fruit, visible here and now, the members of a religious Order obtain. Gautama replies that the fruit of the life of the member of an Order may be seen in:

1. The honour and respect shown to such men by others in the world; even the king, for example, would show respect to a man who had formerly been a slave or a servant, if he adopted the homeless life. 2. The training in mere morality, as kindness, honesty, chastity, etc.

3. Confidence, freedom from fear, etc., born of conscious rectitude. 4 and 5. Recollectedness and self-possession. 6. Contentment with little. 7. Emancipation from the Five Hindrances: Covetousness, ill-temper, laziness, anxiety and perplexity. 8. The consequent joy and peace. 9. Practice of the Four Jhānas. 10. Insight arising from knowledge. 11. The power of projecting mental images. 12. Five modes of mediumship and clairvoyance (thought-reading, audition, etc.);[1] and finally 13 (which alone is distinctively Buddhist), realization of the Four Truths, destruction of the Flood of Passion, attainment of Arahatta.

The argument concludes:

"Thus with the pure Heavenly Eye, surpassing that of men, he sees beings as they pass away from one state of existence, and take form in another; he recognizes the mean and the noble, the well-favoured and the ill-favoured, the happy and the wretched, passing away according to their deeds."[2]

And the recluse perceives the Four Ariyan Truths,

"and he knows Rebirth has been destroyed. The higher

[1] These are practices generally, but by no means always, condemned in early Buddhist scriptures.

[2] I quote this passage on the Heavenly Eye (*Dibba-cakkhu*)—omniscient vision of all that comes to pass in the Kāmaloka and Rūpaloka—because the same idea in a less mythical form frequently recurs in Indian writings, with reference to the intuition of men of genius generally; it can be paralleled elsewhere, *e.g.* Chuang Tzu: "The mind of the sage being in repose becomes the mirror of the Universe, the speculum of all creation," and William Morris: "It seems to me that no hour of the day passes that the whole world does not show itself to me." Buddhists also recognize the *Dhamma-cakkhu* (Eye for the Truth) and *Panna-cakkhu* (Eye of Wisdom). In Hindu mythology these three modes of 'vision' are symbolized by the third eye which opens on the brow of Siva.

life has been fulfilled. What had to be done has been accomplished. After this present life there will be no beyond!

"Just, O king, as if in a mountain fastness there were a pool of water, clear, translucent, and serene; and a man, standing on the bank, and with eyes to see, should perceive the shellfish, the gravel and the pebbles and the shoals of fish, as they move about or lie within it: he would know: 'This pool is clear, transparent and serene, and there within it are the shellfish, and the sand and gravel, and that the shoals of fish are moving about or lying still.'

"This, O king, is an immediate fruit of the life of a recluse, visible in this world, and higher and sweeter than the last. And there is no fruit of the life of a recluse, visible in this world, that is higher and sweeter than this."

The *Tevijja Sutta*, one of the very few which emphasize the advantage of rebirth in the Brahmā heavens, while leaving out of account the fundamental idea of Arahatta, is remarkable for the beautiful description of the Four Sublime Moods which, if they are not the end of Buddhist culture, are at any rate its initiation:

"And he lets his mind pervade one quarter of the world with thoughts of Love, and so the second, and so the third, and so the fourth. And thus the whole world, above, below, around, and everywhere, does he continue to pervade with heart of Love, far-reaching, grown great, and beyond measure.

"Just, Vasettha, as a mighty trumpeter makes himself heard—and that without difficulty—in all the four directions; even so of all things that have shape or life, there is not one that he passes by or leaves aside, but regards them all with mind set free, and deep-felt love.

"Verily this, Vasettha, is the way to a state of union with Brahmā."

Exactly the same formula is repeated in the case of the three other moods, Compassion, Sympathy, and Impartiality.

The *Sigālavāda Sutta* consists of a discourse in which the Buddha lays down for a young layman the duties of those who live in the world, in general accord with the injunctions of Brāhmanical scriptures.

A Sutta of greater importance is the *Mahāparinibbāna*, the Great Sutta of the Full Release, in which the last days and last words of the Teacher are recorded. Some parts of this date back almost certainly to the memory of the Buddha's immediate disciples. Undoubtedly old, for example, is the famous saying:

"Therefore, O Ānanda, be ye lamps unto yourselves. Be ye your own refuge. Hold fast to the Norm as your Light, fast to the Norm as your Refuge."

So too the description of Ānanda's overwhelming grief, leaning against a door-post and weeping, until the Master sends for and speaks to him words of consolation. Many of the verses scattered through the prose, and marking moments of heightened emotion, must be ancient. In all these more ancient passages the Buddha speaks entirely as a man to man; but elsewhere in the same work supernatural powers and portents are freely introduced. A number of quotations from this Sutta have already been given in earlier chapters.

The *Pāyāsi Sutta* maintains an argument in favour of the existence of a soul quite contrary to the real genius of early Buddhist thought. It is true the upholder of the Buddhist position is the venerable Kumāra Kassapa, and not Gautama himself; still it is taken to be the Buddhist position, and it is very curious to see the sceptical Pāyāsi inquiring: "But who lets Master Kassapa know all these things: that there are Three-and-Thirty Gods, or that the Three-and-Thirty Gods live so many years? We do not believe him when he says these things." This is evidence that some of the early Buddhists, at least, took very seriously their pantheon of minor divinities.

The Majjhima Nikāya contains a number—152—of sermons and dialogues which are shorter than those of the Digha Nikāya.

The Samyutta Nikāya contains fifty-six groups of Suttas dealing with connected subjects or persons. The *Mārasamyutta*, and the *Bhikkunisamyutta* for example, numbers four and five in the series, contain a group of legends in which Māra the Tempter appears to the Buddha, to his disciples, or to one or other of the Sisters, and endeavours to shake their faith. These Suttas are cast in the old form of *conte fable*, an alternation of prose and verse, the Indian name of which is *ākhyāna*. Amongst these ballads are some of the most beautiful of old Indian poems; we recognize in them also many of the elements of a primitive drama, the material from which drama may have developed, but we cannot speak of them as early Buddhist dramas in themselves, for they are neither sufficiently elaborated, nor was any such worldly activity as the drama tolerated in the rule of the Brethren. Only at a considerably later date (Asvaghosha) do we find Buddhist poets creating admittedly dramatic works. Of the spiritual ballads now under consideration, the following of Gotamī the Slender—the story of whose conversion has already been given (p. 148 f.) —will serve as a good example:

"Thus have I heard. The Master was once staying at

Sāvatthi, in the Jetta grove, the park of Anāthapindika. Sister Kisā Gotamī dressed herself early, and taking the alms-bowl beneath her robe, went to Sāvatthi to beg her food. And when she had gone about Sāvatthi and returned with what she had collected, and had duly eaten, she entered the Dark Wood, and sat her down at the foot of a tree thinking to pass the day there.

"Then the evil Māra, desiring to arouse fear, wavering, and dread in her, desiring to make her to desist from her concentred thought, went up to her. And he addressed Kisā Gotamī in the verse that follows:

> '*How comes it thou dost sit with tear-stained face*
> *Like to some mother that has lost her child?*
> *Here dwelling all alone within the forest depths*
> *Is it, perhaps, a man thou lookest for?*'

"Then Gotamī the Slender reflected: Who is this, whether human or not-human, who has spoken such a verse? And it came into her mind: It is the evil Māra, who seeks to arouse in me fear, wavering, and dread, and would make me to desist from my concentred thought; he has spoken the verse. And when the Sister Kisā Gotamī knew that it was Māra, she replied to him in the verse that follows:

'Tis sooth indeed that I am she whose child is lost for ever:[1]
While as for men, they are not hard to find!
I do not weep nor wail, nor have I any fear of thee, my friend:
Love of the world is utterly destroyed, the gloom is rent in twain,
And I have overcome the hosts of Death
And here I dwell, from all the Deadly Floods emancipate.'

[1] The words 'for ever' convey the thought that while Gotamī had lost her child, yet, being an Arahat, never again would she suffer the like loss.

"Then Māra vanished thence, sorry and dejected, thinking: Sister Gotamī knoweth me."

The *Anguttara Nikāya* is a very extensive work, containing at least 2308 Suttas. These are classified in sections, numbered one to eleven, the Suttas in each section dealing with such things of which there are as many as the number of the Sutta itself. Thus in the Second Section the Suttas speak of the two things which a man should avoid, the two kinds of Buddhas, the two virtues of the forest-life; in the Third Section the Suttas speak of the trinity of Thought, Word, and Deed, and the three sorts of monks; in the Fourth Section, the four things which lead to a cessation of Becoming, the four that lead to Purgatory, the four that lead to Paradise, and so forth; in the Eighth Section, the eight ways in which man and woman mutually hinder each other, and the eight causes of an earthquake; in the Tenth Section, the ten powers of a Buddha. Needless to point out, the arrangement is formal and pedantic, and the general tone is also somewhat dry. One of the best passages, however, is that which speaks of the Three Messengers of the Gods—Old Age, Illness, and Death—of whom King Yama asks the misdoers who fall into Purgatory, thus:

"'O man, did you not see the first of Death's messengers visibly appear among men?'

"He replies: 'Lord, I did not.'

"Then, O Brethren, King Yama says to him: 'O man, did you not see among men a woman or a man, eighty or ninety or hundred years of age, decrepit, crooked as the curved rafter of a gable roof, bowed down, leaning on a staff, trembling as he walked, miserable, with youth long fled, broken-toothed, grey-haired and nearly bald, tottering, with wrinkled brow, and blotched with freckles?'

"He replied, 'Lord, I did.'

"Then, O Brethren, King Yama says to him: 'O man, did it not occur to you, being a person of mature intelligence and years: "I am also subject to old age, and in no way exempt. Come now, I will act nobly, in deed, word, and thought?'"

"He replies: 'Lord, I could not. Lord, I did not think.'

"Then, O Brethren, King Yama says to him: 'O man, through thoughtlessness you failed to act nobly in deed, word, and thought. Verily it shall be done unto you, O man, in accordance with your thoughtlessness. . . . It was you yourself who did this wickedness, and you alone shall feel its consequences!"

From the literary point of view we may remark three characteristics of the Suttas so far considered. First of all, *the repetitions*, of which an example will be found in the Fire Sermon quoted above. It is almost impossible to put such texts before a modern reader without condensation, and without the use of the conjunction 'and,' and without pronouns, as they are in the original, to say nothing of the tedious reiteration of every phrase and every shade of thought.

"The periods of these addresses," says Professor Oldenberg, "in their motionless and rigid uniformity, on which no lights and shadows fall, are an accurate picture of the world as it represented itself to the eye of that monastic fraternity, the grim world of origination and decease, which goes on like clockwork in an ever uniform course, and behind which rests the still deep of the Nirvāna. In the words of this ministry, there is heard no sound of working within . . . no impassional entreating of men to come to the faith, no bitterness for the unbelieving who remain afar off. In these addresses, one word, one sentence, lies beside another in stony stillness, whether it expresses the most trivial thing or the most important. As worlds of gods and men are, for the Buddhist consciousness, ruled by everlasting necessity, so also are the worlds of ideas and of verities: for these, too, there is one, and only one, necessary form of knowledge and expression, and the thinker does not make this form but he adopts what is ready to hand . . . and thus those endless repetitions accumulate which Buddha's disciples were never tired of listening to anew, and always honouring afresh as the necessary garb of holy thought."

The Buddhist authors were perhaps so much impressed by and so pleased with the excellent doctrine, that they did not feel the repetitions wearisome, they could not hear too often the hard-won truths that had set them free. We have a glimpse of this point of view in one of Asoka's Edicts, where the Emperor says:

"Certain phrases have been uttered again and again by reason of the honeyed sweetness of such and such a topic, in the hope that the people may act up to them."

The early Buddhists had no wish to make their scriptures interesting, and it is very true that they 'have but one taste.' At the same time it is most likely that this extremely serious and indeed heavy style, made eloquent only by its very seriousness—it is not to be denied that the method of line upon line has a certain cumulative impressiveness, a kind of noble austerity and patience, a 'sublime monotony'—really reflects the manner of speech of the Buddha himself. For Gautama is not—like Jesus —a poet and a mystic, but a psychologist:[1] he does not

[1] If Gautama was indeed a mystic, as the Mahāyānists claim, it is then to Buddhaghosha and other of the Pāli authors whom we must regard as chiefly responsible for 'Pāli Buddhism.'

PLATE U

THE BUDDHA TEACHING

Gilt bronze, Laos, in Gupta style, but probably mediæval

Collection of Mr Victor Golonbew

speak to uneducated fishermen, but to practised metaphysicians, and in an atmosphere of controversy: he makes no personal appeal, he speaks with well-considered purpose rather than enthusiasm or fervour, and he is concerned to leave no loophole for possible or deliberate misunderstandings. He feels, indeed, some apprehension lest in future the most profound sermons should be neglected in favour of more artistic and attractive compositions:

"Some there are," he says, "who hearken willingly to the works of followers of mine who are poets, poetasters, *littérateurs*, or mystics . . . and who allow the sermons of the Tathāgata, of profound import, transcendent, and devoted to the doctrine of the Void, to be forgotten."

We may thus believe that the more poetical and literary books were only little by little and with some difficulty admitted to the canon; and this is probably the explanation of the fact that they are for the most part gathered together in one Nikāya, the *Khuddaka*, which was most likely included in the authoritative scripture at a comparatively late date, though of course it contains abundance of ancient matter side by side with the younger.

The second characteristic which we remark in the Suttas so far discussed is the *dialectic method* of the Buddha's argument. The manner of his speech is always courteous and friendly:

"The method followed is always the same. Gautama puts himself as far as possible in the mental position of the questioner. He attacks none of his cherished convictions. He accepts as the starting-point of his own exposition the desirability of the act or condition prized by his opponent. . . . He even adopts the very phraseology of the questioner. And then, partly by putting a new and (from the

Buddhist point of view) a higher meaning into the words; partly by an appeal to such ethical conceptions as are common ground between them; he gradually leads his opponent up to his conclusion. This is, of course, always Arahatship."[1]

This is the method of the Socratic dialogue; and we may also take it that in the Dialogues extant we have at least as much of the actual teaching of Gautama preserved, as Plato gives of the teaching of Socrates. The method, however, presupposes an acquaintance with the point of view of the Buddha's opponents, since, as Professor Rhys Davids justly remarks, the *argumentum ad hominem* can never be quite the same as a general statement made without reference to the opposite view. There is also the disadvantage that the argument is made to lead to a foregone conclusion, and though the logical sequence may be indisputable, the twisting of words in a new sense sometimes 'corners' the opponent without meeting his real position. We do not really hear both sides of the case. As Professor Oldenberg truly comments: "Those who converse with Buddha are good for nothing else but simply to say 'Yes,' and to be eventually converted, if they have not yet been converted." Subject to this limitation, and apart from the wearisome repetitions, we can nevertheless recognize that the Dialogues are skilfully constructed and couched in language of restraint and dignity.

A third special characteristic of the Suttas is the constant use of simile and parable. A simile, indeed, is not an argument; but it often serves better to convince the listener than any sequence of close reasoning. Many of the similes are well-found, and additional to their value

[1] Rhys Davids, *Dialogues of the Buddha*, i, p. 206.

for edification, they throw a strong light on the everyday life of ancient India, very welcome to the historian of manners. Those which refer to the crafts are of special interest: we read, for example:

"Just, O king, as a clever potter or his apprentice could make, could succeed in getting out of properly prepared clay any shape of vessel he wanted to have, or an ivory carver out of ivory, or a goldsmith out of gold: such, O king, is the Skill which is an immediate fruit of the life of a recluse."—*Samañña-phala Sutta.*

And with reference to the practice of breathing exercises, and mindfulness:

"Even as a skilful turner, or turner's apprentice, drawing his string at length, or drawing it out short, is conscious that he is doing one or the other, so let a Brother practise inhaling and exhaling."—*Mahā Satthipatthāna Sutta.*

A favourite simile is that of the oil-lamp:

"Just, O Brethren, as an oil-lamp burns oil and wick, and a man from time to time adds more oil and renews the wick, this oil-lamp thus fed with fuel burns for a much longer time—so, Brethren, waxes Craving in the man who finds his pleasure in things of the world, that in sooth are nought but bonds."—*Samyutta Nikāya.*

Another favourite simile is that of the lotus, for

"'Just as the lotus born of watery mud, grows in the water, rises above the water, and is not defiled by it: so have I arisen in the world, and passed beyond the world, and am not defiled by the world,' says Gautama."—*Samyutta Nikāya.*

The lotus has thus become a symbol of purity; and in iconography, when an apparitional character had been given to the figure of the Buddha, and in the case of other superhuman beings, the lotus pedestal or seat is a mark of other-worldly and divine origin or nature. Needless to say the lotus, in literature, is the source of many other similes and metaphors, for the most part not specifically Buddhist.

In general also, the lotus stands for anything that is excellent and well-liked:

"The boy Vipassi, Brethren, became the darling and beloved of the people, even as a blue or rose or white lotus is dear to and beloved of all, so that he was literally carried about from lap to lap."—*Mahāpadāna Sutta.*

In another place the true spiritual life is compared to a lute, of which the strings must be neither too loosely nor too tightly stretched; by this is indicated the internal balance and harmony of the ideal character. The teaching of salvation, again, is compared to the healing work of the physician, who removes from a wound the poisoned arrow, and applies the curing herbs. Sometimes the similes are humorous, as when it is pointed out that if a man should milk a cow by the horns, he would get no milk; or if one should fill a vessel with sand and water, and churn it ever so much, sesamum oil would never be produced; just so a monk will never reach his goal unless he goes the right way about it.

In other cases the parable is not merely valueless as argument, but absolutely futile. When, for example, it is desired to expose the social and spiritual pretensions of the Brāhmans, Gautama inquires if a fire should be lighted by a Brāhman, a Kshattriya, a Vaishya and a Sūdra: would the fires lit by Brāhmans and Kshattriyas alone give light and heat, or would the fires lit by outcasts, hunters and sweepers, not also yield their light and heat? The king with whom Gautama speaks can naturally only answer that the fires will not differ in their properties. But what has this to do with a discussion for or against the Brāhmanical scheme of social differentiation? That all men have many things in common does not prove that all men are alike in every particular, nor does it disprove the advantage of hereditary culture: the whole discussion, like so many others which turn upon analogy, is neither here nor there.

The contents of the *Khuddaka Nikāya* are very varied. Most of the works in this collection of aphorisms, songs, poems, and fables have some artistic and literary as well as an edifiying character, and thus it has the greatest importance in the literary history of India. Here also greater relative stress is laid on ethics, and the more profound doctrine occupies less space. The *Mangala Sutta*, for example, mentions the honouring of parents and the cherishing of wife and children as amongst the most auspicious actions. It is, however, the *Dhammapada* in which the ethical aphorisms are chiefly assembled. This book is better known in Europe than any other Buddhist scripture, and has been often translated. It is, indeed, worthy of the notice it has attracted, and of the eulogy of Oldenberg:

"For the elucidation of Buddhism nothing better could happen than that, at the very outset of Buddhist studies, there should be presented to the student by an auspicious hand the *Dhammapada*, that most beautiful and richest collection of proverbs, to which anyone who is determined to know Buddhism must over and over again return."

This proverbial wisdom gives a true picture of Buddhist thought and feeling, but expressed in terms of emotion and poetry which lend to the themes of transcience and to the formulæ of the psychologist a tragic poignancy that is often lacking in the set dialogues.

"How can ye be merry, how can ye indulge desire? Evermore the flames burn. Darkness surrounds you: will ye not seek the light?

"Man gathers flowers; his heart is set on pleasure. Death comes upon him, like the floods of water on a village, and sweeps him away.

"Man gathers flowers; his heart is set on pleasure. The Destroyer brings the man of insatiable desire within his clutch.

"Neither in the region of the air, nor in the depths of the sea, nor if thou piercest into the clefts of the mountains, wilt thou find any place on this earth where the hand of death will not reach thee.

"From merriment cometh sorrow: from merriment cometh fear. Whosoever is free from merriment, for him there is no sorrow: whence should fear reach him?

"From love cometh sorrow[1]: from love cometh fear: whosoever is free from love for him there is no sorrow: whence should fear reach him?

"Whoso looketh down upon the world, as though he gazed on a mere bubble or a dream, him the ruler Death beholdeth not.

"Whosoever hath traversed the evil, trackless path of the Samsāra, who hath pushed on to the end, hath reached the shore, rich in meditation, free from desire, free from hesitancy, who, freed from being, hath found rest, him I call a true Brāhman."

[1] This truth, which has so deeply penetrated Indian thought, is balanced by a recognition of the impossibility that the majority of men should for fear of sorrow refrain from love, and expressed with tragic beauty in a well-known Indian refrain, which may be translated—

Belovèd, had I known that love brings pain,
I must have proclaimed, with beat of drum, that none should love.

The thought of transcience constantly overshadows every other:

"Those bleached bones, which are thrown out yonder, like gourds in the autumn, seeing those, how may any man be merry?

"Esteeming this body like a bubble, regarding it as a mirage, breaking the tempter's flower-shafts, press on to the bourne where the monarch Death shall never see thee more."

Those who have thus attained exclaim:

"In perfect joy we live, without enemy in this world of enmity; among men filled with enmity we dwell without enmity.

"In perfect joy we live, hale among the sick; among sick men we dwell without sickness."

We read also:

"All men tremble at punishment, all men love life; remember that thou art like unto them, and do not slay nor cause to slay.

"Victory breeds hatred, for the conquered is unhappy. He who has given up both victory and defeat, he the contented, is happy.

"'He abused me, he beat me, he defeated me, he robbed me,' in those who do not harbour such thoughts hatred will cease.

"For hatred does not cease by hatred at any time: hatred ceases by love, this is an old rule."

It should be noticed that the *Dhammapada* is an anthology, rather than a single work; many of the sayings can be closely paralleled in other Indian books such as the *Mahābhārata* or *Hitopadesa*, and not more than half can be regarded as distinctively Buddhist.

The *Udāna* and the *Itivuttaka* consist of prose and

verse, and contain a collection of sayings of the Buddha. The simple ethical aspect of the Dhamma, for example, is given as follows:

"To speak no ill, to injure not,
To be restrained according to the precepts,
To be temperate in food,
To sleep alone,
To dwell on lofty thoughts,
This is the Law of the Buddha."

The *Sutta-nipāta* is a collection of five Suttas wholly in verse. The *Vasettha Sutta*, for example, returns to the old question of what constitutes a Brāhman, whether birth or character. In connexion with this discussion, there is a remarkable passage affirming the unity of the human species, a view in accord with most (though not all) of modern authorities. The passage runs, after mentioning the marks of distinction between quadrupeds, serpents, birds, etc.:

"As in these species the marks that constitute species are abundant, so in men the marks that constitute species are not abundant.

"Not as regards their hair, head, ears, eyes, mouth, nose, lips or brows, . . . nor as regards their hands, feet, palms, nails, calves, thighs, colour, or voice are there marks that constitute species as in other species.

"Difference there is in beings endowed with bodies, but amongst men this is not the case; the difference amongst men is only nominal."

And, therefore—

"Not by birth is one a Brāhman, nor is one by birth no Brāhman . . . but by effort, by religious living, by self-restraint and by temperance, by this one is a Brāhman."

Amongst all works of the *Khuddaka Nikāya*, however, the

"Psalms of the Brethren and Sisters" (*Therā-therī-gāthā*) stand foremost in literary and human interest. In skilful craftsmanship and beauty these songs are worthy to be set beside the hymns of the Rig Veda, and the lyrical poems of Kālidāsa and Jayadeva. Each of the songs is ascribed by name to some member of the Sangha who attained to Arahatta in the lifetime of Gautama, and the later commentary often adds a few words by way of a biography of the author. But we cannot place very much reliance on the names, although their citation does not mislead us in presupposing a great variety of authors in this collection. It is interesting to note that analysis reveals certain psychological differentiation as between the songs of the Brethren and those of the Sisters: in the latter there is a more personal note, and more of anecdote; in the former more of the inner life, and more descriptions of natural beauty. The burden of all the songs is the calm delight, the peace beyond words to which they have attained, who have left the world and are free from desires and from resentment; each Psalm, as it were, is a little song of triumph—like the Buddha's song of the builder of the house, which is here ascribed to the Arahat Sivaka—pertinent to the individual experience of the one that speaks.

These songs are a personal expression of all those ideals and aims which are spoken of in the more 'profound' texts. On the part of the Brethren, very often the theme is one of extreme misogyny: the true hero is he who bars his heart from 'all that emanates from woman.' More than one picture of a woman's corpse in the charnel field is presented with unpleasant detail; and there at least a woman becomes of some use, for her decaying body teaches the lesson of disgust; nowhere else can she be aught but a fetter and a hindrance to those who would set themselves to righteous duties. It would perhaps be unfair to contrast this point of view with the Brāhmanical ideal of marriage as undertaken by man and woman precisely for the joint performance of social and religious duties; for we are here concerned with monasticism, and Brāhmanical ascetic literature can provide its own misogynistic texts to compare with those of Buddhism. The following may serve as an example of the Thera's songs: [1] Of Candana it is said that when a child was born to him, he left his home for the Order, and dwelt in the forest. One day, hearing that he was engaged in meditation in the charnel field, his wife endeavoured to win him back to the household life. It was in vain; and this was the Arahat's 'witness':

In golden gear bedecked, a troop of maids
Attending in her train, bearing the babe
Upon her hip, my wife drew near to me.
I marked her coming, mother of my child,
In brave array, like snare of Māra laid.
Thereat arose in me the deeper thought:
Attention to the fact and to the cause.
The misery of it all was manifest;
Distaste, indifference, the mind possessed;
And so my heart was set at liberty.
O see the seemly order of the Norm!
The Threefold Wisdom have I made my own,
And all the Buddha bids me do is done.

[1] The translations are quoted from the admirable versions of Mrs Rhys Davids (*Psalms of the Brethren*, 1913). The much more interesting Nature poems of the Brethren are quoted above, p. 166 *seq.*

The following is an extract from the "Psalm of Revata":

Since I went forth from home to homeless life,
Ne'er have I harboured conscious wish or plan
Un-Ariyan or linked with enmity. . . .
With thought of death I dally not, nor yet
Delight in living. I await the hour
Like any hireling who hath done his task.
With thought of death I dally not, nor yet
Delight in living. I await the hour
With mind discerning and with heedfulness.
The Master hath my fealty and love,
And all the Buddha's bidding hath been done.
Low have I laid the heavy load I bore,
Cause for rebirth is found in me no more.
The Good for which I bade the world farewell,
And left the home to lead the homeless life,
That highest Good have I accomplished,
And every bond and fetter is destroyed.

Far more poetic than the verses inspired by the Brethrens' fear of woman as the subtlest form of worldly snare, are those of the Sisters themselves, reflecting on the passing away of their own youth and beauty, and pointing for themselves the lesson of transcience; and amongst these none is more interesting than that of the courtesan Ambapālī, whose generosity to the Order we have already noticed; she was converted by the preaching of her own son, and studying the law of impermanence as illustrated in her own ageing body, she uttered the following verses (nineteen in all, of which I quote five):

Glossy and black as the down of the bee my curls once clustered.
They with the waste of the years are liker to hempen or bark cloth.
Such and not otherwise runneth the rune, the word of the Soothsayer.

Dense as a grove well planted, and comely with comb, pin and parting.
All with the waste of the years dishevelled the fair plaits and fallen
Such and not otherwise runneth the rune, the word of the Soothsayer.

Lovely the lines of my ears as the delicate work of the goldsmith.
They with the waste of years are seamed with wrinkles and pendent.
Such and not otherwise runneth the rune, the word of the Soothsayer.

Full and lovely in contour rose of yore the small breasts of me.
They with the waste of the years droop shrunken as skins without water.
So and not otherwise runneth the rune, the word of the Soothsayer.

Such hath this body been. Now age-weary and weak and unsightly,
Home of manifold ills; old house whence the mortar is dropping.
So and not otherwise runneth the rune, the word of the Soothsayer.

"And inasmuch as the Therī, by the visible signs of impermanence in her own person, discerned impermanence in all phenomena of the three planes, and bearing that in mind, brought into relief the signs of Ill (dukkha) and of No-soul (anattā), she, making clear her insight in her Path-progress, attained Arahantship."[1]

The words of Sundarī-Nanda, another of the Sisters, resume the same train of thought:

Now for the body care I never more, and all my consciousness is passion-free.
Keen with unfettered zeal, detached, calm and serene I taste Nibbāna's peace.

Another composite work, and one of the greatest significance for literary and social history, is the book of *Jātakas*, or histories of the previous births of Gautama. Originally consisting only of verses, to which the reciter must have added a verbal explanation, they are now preserved in the form of the Pāli *Jātakavannana*, where the verses are enshrined in a formal framework of which the chief parts are the introductory episode and the concluding identification of the characters; within these is the story proper, consisting of prose and verse. Each of these four elements, as Professor Rhys Davids points out, has had a separate history; the old Jātaka book contained the verses only; the necessary oral commentary which accompanied the quotation of the verses was subsequently written down and forms the prose story, which is summed up, as it were, and clinched by the old verses, and finally the

[1] Mrs Rhys Davids comments: "It is interesting to find these two ancient institutions, the hetaira of the community and the Wise Woman, with her monopoly of seeing things as they have been, are, or will be, combined in one and the same poem."

scholastic framework was completed. The Jātakas in this final form were not completed before the fifth century A.D. However, the stories so preserved, we have every reason to believe, closely follow an old tradition handed down from at least the third century B.C.; for a considerable number of these stories are illustrated in the well-known Bharhut sculptures, and are there labelled with their names, and in one case a half verse is also quoted. We learn from these sculptures that folk-tales and secular fables were adapted to an edifying purpose quite early in the history of Buddhism precisely as popular and secular art is adapted to Buddhist purposes in the sculpture themselves.

Beside this, we have to observe that although the stories are now converted to the purposes of Buddhist edification, they belong rather to Indian than to specifically Buddhist literature, and very few have a purely Buddhist origin. In point of fact the rule of the Order forbids the Brethren to listen to stories of kings and queens, wars, women, gods and fairies, and so forth, and some little time must have elapsed before the Buddhists could have come to believe that the Jātakas were really related by the Buddha himself. Then again, in the very fact of the stress that is laid upon the doctrine of the Bodhisattva, and in the emphasis laid upon the old 'resolve' of the Brāhman Sumedha (in the Jātaka), as well as in the introductory and other references to the twenty-four 'previous Buddhas,' the Jātaka book shows a considerable development of Buddhist scholasticism and theology, and might very well be described as a Mahāyānist scripture, notwithstanding it is included in the Pāli canon. Many of the stories are older than Buddhism, and notwithstanding that in their Buddhist garb they do not date from the time of Gautama, they give us a true picture of old Indian life of about the fifth century B.C. Apart from their literary value, this fact alone makes the Jātaka collection of great interest; beside which, this is the "most reliable, the most complete, and the most ancient collection of folk-lore now extant in any literature in the world."

The Jātakas vary greatly both in subject and in literary merit, and also in length; some are dry and witless, others point a merely common-sense moral, others elaborate the systematic doctrine of the previous Buddhas and the character of the Bodhisattva as exemplifying the ten great virtues (*Pāramitās*), while yet others are works of the finest art, setting forth with poignant intensity the drama of human emotion: some are fragments of epics, with the flavour of aristocracy, others are the work of unimaginative misogynists, others are popular ballads, and many are little more than nursery tales. All this is easily explained by the composite authorship of the collection, and the variety of class and occupation of those from whom the Order of the Buddhist Wanderers was recruited.

Amongst the simplest stories there are many fables of world-wide distribution, like the story of the ass in the lion's skin, stories of grateful beasts and thankless men; here also are tales of demons and fairies, cannibal kings and masters of magic, to delight the hearts of any child or childlike people. On the other hand are the formal epics, amongst which is the recension of some old Rāma ballad, such as constituted the basis of the *Rāmāyana*. But here we shall quote only one Jātaka at some length, the *Chaddanta Jātaka*, which is perhaps the most beautiful, and add also a short summary of another which is a great favourite, the *Vessantara Jātaka*, which sets forth the 'supernatural generosity' of the Bodhisattva in his last incarnation before the attainment of Buddhahood.

Chaddanta Jātaka

Introductory episode: A well-born girl of Sāvatthi, recognizing the misery of the worldly life, had adopted the homeless state, and was one day seated with others of the Sisters, hearing the Master's teaching; and the thought came into heart, 'Was I in some former life an attendant of his wives?' Then she remembered that in the time of the elephant Chaddanta, she herself had been his wife, and her heart was filled with joy. But 'Was I well or ill-disposed to him?' she thought, 'for the greater part of women are ill-disposed to their lords.' Then she remembered that she had borne a grudge against Chaddanta, and had sent a hunter with a poisoned arrow to take his tusks. Then her grief awoke, and her heart burned, and she burst into sobs and wept aloud. On seeing that, the Master smiled, and being asked by the company of the Brethren, 'What, Sir, was the cause of your smiling,' he said, 'Brethren, this young Sister wept for an injury she did me long ago.' And so saying he told a story of the past.

Once on a time the Bodhisatta was born as the son of the chief of a herd of elephants in the Himālayas. He was pure white, with red feet and face; when he grew up he became the chief of a great herd, and he worshipped private Buddhas. His two chief queens were Cullasubhaddā and Mahāsubhaddā. One year it was reported, 'The great sāl-grove is in flower'; and with all his herd he went to take his pleasure there. As he went along he struck a sāl tree with his forehead, and because Cullasubhaddā was standing to windward, twigs and dry leaves and red ants fell on her, while Mahāsubhaddā stood to leeward, so that flowers and pollen and green leaves fell on her. Cullasubhaddā thought, "He let the flowers and pollen fall on his favourite wife, and the twigs and red ants on me,' and she bore him a grudge. Upon another occasion, when a lotus with seven shoots had been offered to him, he presented it to Mahāsubhaddā.

Then Cullasubhaddā was still more estranged, and she went to a shrine of private Buddhas and made offerings of wild fruits, and prayed: 'Hereafter, when I pass away, I would be reborn as the daughter of a king, that I may become the queen of the King of Benares. Then shall I be dear to him, and may work my will, and I will have him to send a hunter with a poisoned arrow to kill this elephant and bring me his sixfold tusks.' And in time to come she becomes the chief queen of the King of Benares. She remembers her former life, and thinks: 'My prayer has been fulfilled.' She feigns sickness, and persuades the king to grant her a boon, which alone will restore her health and spirits; what the boon is she will tell when all the king's huntsmen are assembled. It is that some one of them should bring her the tusks of Chaddanta. She opens a window and points to the Himālayas in the North and says:

There dwells invincible in might,
This elephant, six-tusked and white,
Lord of a herd eight thousand strong
Whose tusks are like to chariot poles,
And wind-swift they to guard or strike!
If they should see a child of man
Their anger should destroy him utterly,

and she beheld in her heart the very spot where he was taking his pleasure, how

Fresh from his bath and lotus-wreathed,
He moves along the homeward track.
Vast is his brake and lily white,
And there before him walks a dear-loved queen.

Of all the huntsmen, one by name Sonuttara, who was a hideous lout and big and strong, undertook the task, and being furnished with all needful implements, he set forth on his way. It needed seven years of weary going to reach Chaddanta's haunts; but no sooner come there, than Sonuttara dug a pit and covered it with logs and grass, and donning the yellow robes of a man of religion, and taking his bow and poisoned arrow, he hid himself and lay in wait. Presently Chaddanta passed by, and Sonuttara wounded him with the poisoned arrow. But the elephant subduing his feelings of resentment, asked the hunter, 'Why have you wounded me? is it for your own ends or to satisfy the will of another?' The hunter answered that Subhaddā, the consort of the King of Benares, had sent him to secure the tusks. Chaddanta reflected, 'It is not that she wishes for the tusks, but she desires my death;' and he said:

Come now, thou hunter, and before I die
Saw through my ivory tusks;
And bid the jealous queen rejoice——
'Here are the tusks, the elephant is dead.'

So Chaddanta bowed his head, and Sonuttara began to saw the tusks; and when he could not cut them, the great elephant took the saw in his trunk and moved it to and fro till the tusks were severed. Then he gave up the tusks and said, 'I do not give you these tusks, my friend, because I think them of little value, nor to win the status of a god, but because the tusks of omniscience are a thousand times dearer to me than these; and may this worthy gift be the cause of my attaining Omniscience.' Then the hunter departed with the tusks; and before the other elephants reached Chaddanta he had died.

The hunter came then before the queen and said:

Here are his tusks, the beast is dead.

'Do you tell me that he is dead?' she cried; and he answered, 'Rest assured that he is dead, here are the tusks.' Then she received the six-rayed tusks, and laying them across her lap, and thinking, 'These are the tusks of him who was once my lord,' she was filled with sorrow so great that she could not bear it, but there and then her heart broke and she died the same day.

To make the story clear, the Master said:

She whom you used to see,
A Sister in the yellow robe,
Was once a queen, and I
The king of elephants, who died.

But he that took the shining tusks
Matchless on earth, of pure white,
And brought them to Benares town,
Has now the name of Devadatta.

"This story of the past the Master told out of his own knowledge, but for all its sorrow, yet he himself was free from pain and grief.

"And on hearing this discourse a multitude entered the First Path, and the Sister novice not long afterwards attained to Arahatta."

Summary of the Vessantara Jātaka

A son was born to Phusatī, the Queen-consort of the King of Sivi; he was named Vessantara, and the fortune-tellers predicted that he would be devoted to almsgiving, never satisfied with giving. He was married to his cousin Maddī, and they had a son and a daughter. Vessantara possessed also a magical white elephant, that brought rain wherever he went. At that time there was a drought and famine in Kālinga, and the men of that country, knowing of the elephant, and of Vessantara's generosity, sent an embassy of Brāhmans to ask for the elephant, As the Prince was riding through the city on the elephant, to visit one of his alms-halls, the Brāhmans met him by the way and craved a boon, nor would he refuse the elephant himself. He descended from his back, and bestowed him on the Brāhmans, together with all his priceless jewels and hundreds of attendants.

> *Then was a mighty terror felt, then bristling of the hair*
> *When the great elephant was given, the earth did quake for fear,*

and the people of the city reproached the Bodhisattva for his too great generosity. In order to avoid their anger, he was banished. Vessantara spent a day in bestowing gifts of elephants, horses, women, jewels, and food; then he went forth into exile, accompanied by Maddī and both the children, setting out in a gorgeous carriage drawn by four horses. On the way he gives the horses and chariot in alms; finally they reach a beautiful forest retreat, and there take up their abode in a hermitage.

While there a Brāhman visits Vessantara, and begs for

the children to be his servants, and they are freely given; they are subsequently brought by the same Brāhman to the city from which Vessantara had been exiled, and they are there ransomed by his parents. Next, Sakka appears to Vessantara in the shape of another Brāhman, and asks for his wife.

The Bodhisattva bestows his wife upon the seeming Brāhman, saying:

Weary am I, nor hide I that: yet in my own despite,
I give, and shrink not: for in gifts my heart doth take delight . . .
Both Jāli and Kanhājinā I let another take,
And Maddī my devoted wife, and all for wisdom's sake.
Not hateful is my faithful wife, nor yet my children are,
But perfect knowledge, to my mind, is something dearer far.

Sakka then reveals himself, and restores Maddī, and bestows ten boons; as the result of which Vessantara and Maddī are brought back to their paternal city, restored to favour, and reunited with their children, and finally Vessantara receives the assurance that he shall be born only once again.

Other Books of the Canon

The *Buddhavamsa* is a somewhat jejune recital of the histories of the twenty-four previous Buddhas, and the life of Gautama, represented to have been related by himself. The last book of the *Khuddaka Nikāya* is the *Cariyāpitaka*, a collection of thirty-five Jātakas.

The third division of the Pāli canon, the *Abhidhamma Pitaka*, need not be considered here at any length, for it differs from the Sutta literature already discussed only in being more dry, more involved, and more scholastic; originality and depth are comparatively lacking, and our knowledge of Buddhist philosophy would be little less if the *Abhidamma Pitaka* were altogether ignored.

Uncanonical Pāli Literature

If we proceed now to speak of the uncanonical Pāli Buddhist literature, we meet in the first place the well-known book of the *Questions of King Milinda*, which might very well indeed have been included in the canon, and is so included in Siam. The most often quoted, and very characteristic passage of the *Milinda Panha* is the 'chariot' discourse on anattā:

Nāgasena enquires of the king: "Pray, did you come afoot, or riding?" and there ensues the following dialogue:

"Bhante, I do not go afoot: I came in a chariot."

"Your majesty, if you came in a chariot, declare to me the chariot. Pray, your majesty, is the pole the chariot?"

"Nay verily, Bhante."

"Is the axle the chariot?"

"Nay verily, Bhante."

And so for the heels, the body, the banner-staff, the yoke, the reins, and the goad: the king admits that none of these, nor altogether constitute a chariot, nor is there any other thing beside these which constitutes a chariot. Then Nāgasena continues:

"Your majesty, though I question you very closely, I fail to discover any chariot. Verily now, your majesty, the word chariot is a mere empty sound. What chariot is there here?"

And the king is convinced that the word 'chariot' "is but a

way of counting, term, appellation, convenient designation, and name for pole, axle, wheels, chariot-body, and banner-staff." Nāgasena draws the parallel:

"In exactly the same way, your majesty, (my name of) Nāgasena is but a way of counting, term, appellation, convenient designation, mere name" for the several parts of the mind and body collectively regarded, while "in the absolute sense no Ego is here to be found."

The whole of the canonical Pāli Buddhist literature, together with the *Questions of Milinda*, are of Indian origin, notwithstanding they are preserved only in the Pāli texts of Ceylon and Burma and Siam. The remainder of the uncanonical Pāli literature, on the other hand, is almost entirely the work of the Sinhalese Brethren, or of Indian authors like Buddhaghosha who took up their residence in Ceylon. This learned monk came from a Brāhman family of Bodh Gayā, and being converted by the monk Revata to Buddhism, he came to Ceylon to study the Buddhist commentaries. There he resided at the Great Monastery at Anurādhapura, and as the first fruit of his studies composed the *Visuddhi Magga* or 'Way of Purity,' a lengthy compendium of Buddhist lore. For the most part Buddhaghosha adheres to the setting forth of the old Arahat ideal, as, for example, when he tells of a monk who is so far removed from the world that he takes his daily meals for three months at the house of his mother without once saying 'I am thy son, thou art my mother'; notwithstanding she desired news of her lost son very greatly. So good a laywoman was she, however, that when another of the Brethren informed her that he had thus visited the house unknown, she speaks of her son's behaviour as altogether praiseworthy. For the most part there is no important contribution to Buddhist doctrine, but on the other hand many legends and tales of wonder are preserved here and nowhere else; there is considerable stress laid on miracles performed by the saints. Buddhaghosha also compiled a commentary on the whole of the canonical literature; though it is doubtful if the Jātaka and Dhammapada commentaries are really his work. In any case, Buddhaghosha is *the* Buddhist commentator, before all others; his method is clear and penetrating, and the illustrative legends serve to lighten the more tedious summaries.

Two Buddhist Pāli works of very great importance, the *Dīpavamsa* and *Mahāvamsa*, are verse chronicles of Ceylon history. Notwithstanding that no distinction is here made between saga, legend, and *de facto* history, a considerable part, and especially the later part of these works, has a great historical value. We find, for example, a striking confirmation of the general accuracy of the tradition, in the fact that the chronicles mention amongst the names of Asoka's missionaries those of Kassapa-gotta and Majjhima as having been sent with three others to the Himālayas, while archæological exploration has unearthed from a stūpa near Sānchī a funeral urn bearing the inscription in script of the third century B.C.: 'Of the good man Kassapa-gotta, teacher of all the Himālaya region,' while the inside of the urn is inscribed 'Of the good man, Majjhima.'

Indian practice, however, deals with history as art rather than science; and perhaps the chief interest of the Ceylon chronicles appears in their epic character. The *Dīpavamsa*, probably of the fourth century A.D.—just before Buddhaghosha—is composed in very poor Pāli, and is altogether an inartistic production; it has only been preserved in Burma, while in Ceylon its place has been taken by the much finer book of the *Mahāvamsa*, composed by Mahānama toward the end of the fifth century.

"We are here able," says Professor Geiger, "in a way that elsewhere is not easy, to follow the development of the epic in its literary evolution. We are able to picture to ourselves the contents and form of the chronicle which forms the basis of the epic song, and of the various elements of which it is composed. . . . The *Dīpavamsa* represents the first unaided struggle to create an epic out of the already existing material. It is a document that fixes our attention just because of the imcompleteness of the composition and its want of style. . . . The *Mahāvamsa* is already worthy of the name of a true epic. It is the recognized work of a poet. And we are able to watch this poet in a certain measure at his work in his workshop. Although he is quite dependent on his materials, which he is bound to follow as closely as possible, he deals with them critically, perceives their shortcomings and irregularities, and seeks to improve and to eliminate."[1]

The hero of this epic is Dutthagāmanī, a national hero king of the second century B.C., whose renown in Southern Buddhist annals is second only to that of Asoka himself. The king's victory over the Tamil leader is related as follows:

"King Dutthagāmanī proclaimed with beat of drum: 'None but myself shall slay Elāra.' When he himself, armed, had mounted the armed elephant Kandula, he pursued Elāra and came to the south gate (of Anurādhapura). Near the south gate of the city the two kings fought: Elāra hurled his dart, Gāmanī evaded it; he made his own elephant pierce (Elāra's) elephant with his tusks, and he hurled his dart at Elāra; and the latter

[1] Geiger, *Dīpavamsa und Mahāvamsa* (1905), introduction.

fell there with his elephant. . . . On the spot where his (Elāra's) body had fallen he burned it with the catafalque, and there did he build a monument and ordain worship. And even to this day the princes of Lankā, when they draw near to this place, are wont to silence their music because of this worship."

With true Buddhist feeling the king is represented to have felt no joy in his great victory and the slaughter of the invader's hosts:

"Looking back upon his glorious victory, great though it was, he knew no joy, remembering that thereby was wrought the destruction of millions of beings."

On this the chronicle comments:

"Should a man think on the hosts of human beings murdered for greed in countless myriads, and should he carefully keep in mind the (consequent) evil, and should he also very carefully keep in mind that mortality is the (real) murderer of all of them—then will he, in this way, speedily win to freedom from sorrow and to a happy state."

One of his warriors took the robes of a monk, and the name of Theraputtābhaya, saying:

"I will do battle with the rebel passions, where victory is hard to win; what other war remains where all the realm is united?"

The death-bed scenes are related with deep feeling: the king has his couch brought where he can gaze upon his two great buildings, the 'Brazen Palace' monastery, and the Great Thūpa, the latter not yet complete. He is surrounded by thousands of the Brethren, but looking about, he does not see Theraputtābhaya, his old companion-in-arms, and he thinks:

"The Theraputtābhaya comes not now to aid me, now

that the death-struggle is begun, for methinks he foresees my defeat." But Theraputtābhaya appears, and the king is gladdened by his words:

"O great king and ruler of men, fear not. Save sin be conquered, death is unconquerable. All that has come to be must also pass away, and all that is is perishable; thus the Master taught. Even the Buddhas, never touched by shame or fear, are subject to mortality: therefore bethink thee, all that is is perishable, full of sorrow, and unreal. . . . O thou that art rich in merit, think upon all those works of merit done by thee up to this very day, and straightway shall all be well with thee!"

The book of meritorious deeds is accordingly read aloud and we are given the long list of the king's good works: amongst others, he has maintained eighteen hospitals for the sick.

"But all this giving while that I reigned, rejoices not my heart; only the two gifts that I gave, without care for my life, the while I was in adversity, these gladden my heart. . . . Twenty-four years have I been a patron of the Brethren, and my body shall also be a patron of the Brethren. In a place where the great Thūpa may be seen . . . do ye burn the body of me, the servant of the Brethren."

Continuators of the *Mahāvamsa* have brought the chronicles up to modern times, the whole work constituting a remarkable history of Buddhist culture in Ceylon.

The Sanskrit Texts

The remaining books of Pāli Buddhist literature we shall not discuss, but turn to consider the Sanskrit books of the Mahāyāna.

A considerable part of these corresponds to the books of the Pāli canon already described ; but they are not translations from Pāli, but rather parallel texts derived from the same Indian sources, the lost Māgadhī canon on which the Pāli books are based. On this account, although few of the Mahāyāna texts can be shown to be older in recension than the third or fourth century A.D., we can understand that they embody older materials, together with the new additions.

The *Mahāvastu*, indeed ('The Book of Great Events'), is still nominally a Hīnayāna work, though it belongs to the heretical sect of the Lokottaravādins who regard the Buddha as a supernatural being; the biography is a history of miracles. It is a compilation without any attempt at system. It contains also much that is properly Mahāyānist, such as an enumeration of the Ten Stations of a Bodhisattva, Hymns to Buddha, the doctrine that worship of Buddha suffices to achieve Nirvāna, and so forth ; but there is no characteristically Mahāyāna mythology.

A more famous and a more important work is the *Lalitavistara*, 'The History of the Play (of the Buddha)' —a title suggestive of the Hindu conception of Līlā or Play, the 'Wonderful Works of the Lord.' This is a Buddha biography with elaborate mythology, and stress is laid on faith as an essential element of religion. The general trend of the *Lalitavistara* is well known to Western readers, for it has formed the basis of Sir Edwin Arnold's beautiful poem, *The Light of Asia*. Its contents have also been closely followed in the famous sculptures of Borobodur; and from the subject matter of Gandhāra art we can infer with certainty that the *Lalitavistara* or some very similar text must have already been known in the first and second century A.D. In itself, however, the work is not yet a true Buddha-epic, but contains the germ of an epic.

Asvaghosha

It is from such ballads and anecdotes as are preserved in the *Lalitavistara* that Asvaghosha, the greatest Buddhist poet, has composed his masterly *Buddha-carita*, the 'Course of the Buddha.' Asvaghosha is indeed not merely a Buddhist poet, but one of the greatest of Sanskrit poets, and the chief forerunner of Kālidāsa. We have no certain knowledge of his date, but it is most probable that he flourished during the first century A.D., and in any case he must be regarded as a Father of the Mahāyāna. He must have been brought up as a Brāhman before becoming a Buddhist. The Tibetan biography informs us that "there was no problem he could not solve, no argument he could not refute; he overcame his adversary as easily as the storm wind breaks a rotten tree." The same authority tells us that he was a great musician, who himself composed and went about the villages with a troupe of singers and songstresses. The songs he sang spoke of the emptiness of phenomena, and the crowds who heard his beautiful music stood and listened in rapt silence. The Chinese pilgrim I-tsing, who visited India in the seventh century, speaks of his literary style as follows:

"He is read far and wide throughout the five Indies and the lands of the southern seas. He clothes in but a few words many and many thoughts and ideas, which so rejoice the reader's heart that he never wearies of reading the poem. Very profitable also it is to read this poem, for here the noble doctrines are set forth with convenient brevity."

The work as we have it is but a fragment, completed by other hands; yet it is a true Buddha-epic and the work of a true poet, who has created a work of art, informed with his own deep love of the Buddha and belief in the doctrine; it is a court epic in the technical sense, in a style somewhat more elaborate than that of the *Mahāvamsa*, but not yet at all immoderately artificial. The *Buddha-carita* is not only an important monument of specifically Buddhist literature, but exercised an unmistakable influence on the development of Brāhmanical classic Sanskrit.

When the divine child is born it is prophesied.

"The child is now born who knows that mystery hard to attain, the means of destroying birth. Forsaking his kingdom, indifferent to all worldly objects, and attaining the highest truth by strenuous efforts, he will shine forth as a sun of knowledge to destroy the darkness of illusion in the world. . . . He will proclaim the way of deliverance to those afflicted with sorrow, entangled in objects of sense, and lost in the forest-paths of worldly existence, as to travellers who have lost their way. . . . He will break open for the escape of living beings that door whose bolt is desire, and whose two leaves are ignorance and delusion, with that excellent blow of the good Law that is so hard to find. . . . And since I have not heard his Law, but my time has come to depart" (says the prophet) "my life is only a failure, I count even dwelling in the highest heaven a misfortune."

The young prince, as he grew up, was surrounded by every pleasure, whereby to hinder him from seeking the Wanderers' life; his father "arranged for his son all kinds of worldly enjoyments, praying 'Would that he may not be able to forsake us, even though he be hindered by mere unrest of the senses.'"

The prince is tempted by beautiful women, skilled in the arts of seduction:

"Come and listen to the notes of this intoxicated cuckoo as he sings, while another cuckoo sings as if consenting, wholly without care. Would that thine was the intoxication of the birds which the spring produces, rather than the dreams of a man of thought, ever pondering how wise he is!"

So they sing, voicing the spring-songs of the folk, and the resentment of women against a man's abstraction; but the Bodhisattva remains unmoved, preoccupied with the thought that death is the ultimate fate of all.

"'What is it that these women lack,' he asks, 'that they perceive not that youth is fickle? for this old age will destroy whatever has beauty. . . . Evidently they know nothing of death which carries all away, they are joyous in a world which is all pain, and so at ease and without distress they can sport and laugh. What rational being, who knows of old age, death and sickness, could stand or sit at his ease, or sleep, far less laugh? . . . If desire arises in the heart of the man, who knows that death is certain, I think that his soul must be made of iron, who restrains it in this great terror, and does not weep.'"

The following is from Yasodharā's lament when it is discovered that Prince Siddhārtha has become a Wanderer:

"If he wishes to abandon his lawful wife as a widow, and to become a religious, then where is his religion, wishing to practise a rule without his lawful wife to share it! It must be that he has never heard of the monarchs of old, his own forefathers, Mahasudarsa and others, how they went with their wives into the forest, since he thus wishes to adopt the religious life apart from me! He does not see that husband and wife are alike consecrated by sacrifices, purified by the performance of Vedic rites, and destined to enjoy the same fruits hereafter. . . . I have no such longing for the joys of heaven, nor are these hard for common folk to attain, if they be resolute; but my one desire is that my darling may never leave me either in this world or the next."

It is interesting to note the arguments adduced by the king's Brāhman family priest, and by a trusted counsellor, who are sent to persuade the Bodhisattva to return, offering him the kingdom itself in his father's place. The former points out:

"Religion is not wrought out only in the forests; the salvation of ascetics can be accomplished even in a city; thought and effort are the true means; the forest and the badge are only a coward's signs."

and he cites the case of Janaka and others; at the same time he appeals to the prince to take pity on his unhappy parents. The counsellor, with more worldly wisdom, argues that if there be a future life, it will be time enough to consider it when we come to it, and if not, then there is liberation attained without any effort at all; and moreover, the nature of the world cannot be altered, it is *sui generis* subject to mortality, and it therefore cannot be overcome by extinguishing desire:

"'Who causes the sharpness of the thorn?' he asks, 'or the various natures of beasts and birds? All this has arisen spontaneously; there is no acting from desire, how then can there be such a thing as will?'"

At the same time he reminds the prince of his social duties, his debt to the ancestors, to be repaid only by begetting children, by study, and by sacrifice to the Gods, and suggests that he should fulfil these social duties before retiring to the forest. To these subtle advisers the prince replies by offering the usual 'consolation' to sorrowing parents:

"Since parting is inevitably fixed in the course of time for all beings, just as for travellers who have joined company on a road, what wise man would cherish sorrow, when he loses his kindred, even though he loves them?"

He adds that his departure to the forest cannot be considered 'ill-timed,' for liberation can never be ill-timed. That the king should wish to surrender to him the kingdom, he says, is a noble thought, but

"How can it be right for the wise man to enter royalty, the home of illusion, where are found anxiety, passion, and weariness, and the violation of all right through another's service (exploitation)?"

To the metaphysical objections he replies:

"This doubt whether anything exists or not, is not to be solved for me by another's words; having determined the truth by discipline or by Yoga, I will grasp for myself whatever is known of it . . . what wise man would go by another's belief? Mankind are like the blind directed in the darkness by the blind. . . . Even the sun, therefore, may fall to the earth, even the mount Himālaya may lose its firmness; but I will never return to my home as a worldling, lacking the knowledge of the truth, and with sense only alert for external objects: I would enter the blazing fire, but not my house with my purpose unfulfilled."

In such a fashion Asvaghosha represents those stations in the life of every Saviour, which are familiar to Christians in the reply of Christ to his parents: Wist ye not that I must be about my Father's business? and in his refusal of an earthly kingdom and the status of a Dharmarāja, when these are laid before him by the Devil.

The passages so far quoted are primarily edifying: and notwithstanding the skill with which Buddhist thought is there expressed, there are others that will better exemplify Asvaghosha's epic diction and personal intensity of imagination. Of the two following extracts, the first describes an early meditation of the Bodhisattva, beneath a rose-apple tree; and the second, the gift of food which he accepts, when after five years of mortification of the flesh, he finds that mortification of the flesh will not lead him to his goal, and reverts to that first process of insight which came to him as he sat beneath the rose-apple. Here Asvaghosha proves himself a true poet; he has a saga-teller's power of calling up a vivid picture in a few words, he understands the heavy toil of the peasant and of the beasts of burden, and he represents the pure dignity of unsophisticated girlhood, in the person of the herdsman's daughter, with the same simplicity that Homer uses when he speaks of Nausicaa.

The prince went forth one day with a party of his friends, "with a desire to see the glades of the forest, and longing for peace:"

"Lured by love of the woods and longing for the beauties of the earth, he repaired to a place near at hand on the outskirts of a forest; and there he saw a piece of land being ploughed, with the path of the plough broken like waves on the water. . . . And regarding the men as they ploughed, their faces soiled by the dust, scorched by the sun and chafed by the wind, and their cattle bewildered by the burden of drawing, the all-noble one felt the uttermost compassion; and alighting from the back of his horse, he passed slowly over the earth, overcome with sorrow—pondering the birth and the destruction proceeding in the world, he grieved, and he exclaimed, 'This is pitiful indeed!' Then because he would be lonely in his thoughts, he hindered those friends who were following him, and went to the root of a rose-apple tree in a solitary place, of which the leaves were all a-tremble. There he sat upon the leafy ground, and the emerald grass; and meditating on the origin and destruction of the world, he laid hold upon the path that leads to constancy of mind."

Long years after, having vainly mortified the flesh, the Bodhisattva reflected:

"This is not the road that leads to passionlessness, or to liberation; that was verily the true path which I found beneath the rose-apple tree. But that is not to be achieved by one who has lost his strength . . . and making up his mind, 'This means involves the taking of food.' . . . Then, at that very time, Nandabalā, the daughter of the chief of the herdsmen, impelled by the gods (*i.e.* following a spontaneous and inexplicable impulse) and with a sudden joy uprising in her heart, came nigh; her arm was decked with a white shell bracelet, and she wore a dark blue woollen cloth, like the river Jamunā, with its dark blue water and its wreath of foam; and with joy increased by faith, and widely opened lotus-eyes, she bowed before the seer, and persuaded him to take some milk."

Asvaghosha's other works include the *Saundarānanda Kāvya*, which also deals with the life of Buddha, and exhibits some Mahāyāna tendencies which are not apparent in the *Buddha-carita*. The *Sutrālamkāra* is a collection of pious legends in prose and verse, in the manner of the Jātakas and Avadānas. An Alamkāra sāstra is also ascribed to him. More doubtful is the authorship of the

Vajrasuci, or Diamond-needle, a polemic against the Brāhmanical caste system, supported mainly by citations from Brāhmanical sources, such as the Vedas, the Mahābhārata, and the Laws of Manu. Finally there remains to be named the very important *Mahāyāna-sraddha-utpada*, or 'Awakening of Faith in the Mahāyāna,' a philosophical and mystical work dealing with the doctrines of the Tathāgata-garbha and Ālaya-vijñāna after the manner of the Yogāvaracāras and Asanga; but there are good reasons to think that this text may be of considerably later date; it was first translated into Chinese only in the sixth century, and is not known in the Sanskrit original.

Āryasūra

A poet of Asvaghosha's school is Āryasūra, the author of a famous Jātakamālā or 'Garland of Jātakas,' to be assigned, most probably, to the fourth century A.D. Jātakamālās of this type are selections of the old stories retold as homilies in artistic prose and verse, for the use of monkish teachers trained in the tradition of Sanskrit court prose and poetry. Of Āryasūra's work it has been well said:

"It is perhaps the most perfect writing of its kind. It is distinguished no less by the superiority of its style than by the loftiness of its thoughts. Its verses and artful prose are written in the purest Sanskrit, and charm the reader by the elegance of their form and the skill displayed in the handling of a great variety of metres. . . . Above all, I admire his moderation. Unlike so many other Indian masters in the art of literary composition, he does not allow himself the use of embellishing apparel and the whole luxuriant *mise en scène* of Sanskrit *alamkāra* beyond what is necessary for his subject" (Speyer).

I-tsing praises the *Jātakamāla* as among the works specially admired in his time. But more important is the fact that it is these versions of the Jātakas which are illustrated in the wall-paintings of Ajantā, and indeed, in some cases the pictures are inscribed with verse from Āryasūra's work; the painting and the literary work are in close harmony of sentiment.

The first story relates the Bodhisattva's gift of his own body for the nourishment of a hungry tigress, that she might not eat her own young, and it begins as follows:

"Even in former births the Lord showed his innate, disinterested, and immense love toward all creatures, and identified himself with all beings. For this reason we ought to have the utmost faith in Buddha, the Lord. This will be shown in the following great deed of the Lord in a former birth." Following each story is an injunction pointing out the moral. Many of the stories inculcate the duty of gentleness and mercy, by means of the relation of some anecdote regarding some helpful animal and an ungrateful man. The Ruru-deer, for example:

"'With his large blue eyes of incomparable mildness and brightness, with his horns and hoofs endowed with a gentle radiance, as if they were made of precious stones, that ruru-deer of surpassing beauty seemed a moving treasury of gems. Then, knowing his body to be a very desirable thing, and aware of the pitiless hearts of men, he would frequent such forest ways as were free from human company, and because of his keen intelligence he was careful to avoid such places as were made unsafe by devices of huntsmen . . . he warned also the animals who followed after him to avoid them. He exercised his rule over them like a teacher, like a father.'"

One day, however, he heard the cries of a drowning man,

and entering the stream he saved his life and brought him to the shore. At the same time the ruru-deer prayed the man to say nothing of his adventure, for he feared the cruelty of men. The queen of that country, however, happened at that time to dream of just such a deer; and the king offered a reward for the capture of such a creature. The man whose life had been saved, being poor, was tempted by the offer of a fertile village and ten beautiful women, and revealed to the king the secret of the beautiful deer. The king is about to let fly his arrow, when the deer asks him to stay his hand, and to tell who has revealed the secret of his forest home. When the wretched man is pointed out, the deer exclaims: 'Fie upon him! It is verily a true word, that 'better it is to take a log from the water than to save an ungrateful man from drowning.' Thus it is that he requites the exertions undertaken on his behalf!"

The king inquires why the deer speaks so bitterly, and the Bodhisattva (for such, of course, is the deer) replies: "No desire to pass censure moved me to these words, O king, but knowing his blameworthy deed, I spoke sharp words to hinder him from doing such a deed again. For who would willingly use harsh speech to those who have done a sinful deed, strewing salt, as it were, upon the wound of their fault? But even to his beloved son a physician must apply such medicine as his sickness requires. He who has put me in this danger, O best of men, it is whom I rescued from the current, being moved by pity. Verily, intercourse with evil company does not lead to happiness."

Then the king would have slain the man; but the Bodhisattva pleads for his life, and that he may receive the promised reward. Then the Bodhisattva preaches the doctrine to the king and his wives and the officers of the court as follows:

"Of the Law with the manifold duties dependent on it and its divisions: to abstain from injuring others, from theft, and the like, of this, I hold the shortest summary is 'Mercy toward every creature.' For consider, thou illustrious prince: If mercy to every creature should lead men to look on these as like to themselves or to the members of their own family, whose heart would ever cherish the baleful wish for wickedness? . . . For this reason the wise firmly believe that in Mercy the whole of Righteousness is comprised. What virtue, indeed, cherished by the pious is not the consequence of Mercy? Having this in mind, be intent ever to fortify thy mercy to all people, holding them as like thy son or like thyself; and winning by thy pious deeds thy people's hearts, mayst thou glorify thy royalty!"

"Then the king praised the words of the ruru-deer, and with his landholders and burghers he became intent on following the Law of Righteousness. And he granted security to all fourfooted creatures and to birds. . . .

("This story is also to be told when discoursing on compassion, and may be adduced when treating of the high-mindedness of the virtuous, and also when censuring the mischievous.")

Many of the Buddhist stories are thus in perfect accord with the words of the Western poet who says:

He prayeth best who loveth best
All things both great and small,

and indeed, the *Ancient Mariner* is just such a tale as the Buddhist Brethren of literary tastes would have made into a Jātaka.

Scarcely distinguishable from the Jātakas are the various Avadānas, which consist in general of Bodhisattva legends. Amongst these there should be noticed the Asoka cycle which forms a part of the *Divyāvadāna* or 'Heavenly Avadānas.' The finest of these legends is the pathetic story of Kunāla, the son of Asoka, whose eyes are put out by his wicked stepmother, without awakening in his heart any feelings of anger or hatred. I quote the summary of this story from the work of Oldenberg:

"Kunāla—this name was given to him on account of his wonderfully beautiful eyes, which are as beautiful as the eyes of the bird Kunāla—lives far from the bustle of the court, devoted to meditation on impermanence. One of the queens is burning with love for the beautiful youth, but her solicitation and the menaces of disdained beauty are alike in vain. Thirsting for revenge, she contrives to have him sent to a distant province, and then issues an order to that quarter, sealed with the slyly stolen ivory seal of the king, for the prince's eyes to be torn out. When the order arrives, no one can be prevailed upon to lay hands on the noble eyes of the prince. The prince himself offers rewards to any one who should be prepared to execute the king's order. At last a man appears, repulsive to look on, who undertakes the performance. When, amid the cries of the weeping multitude, the first eye is torn out, Kunāla takes it in his hand and says: 'Why seest thou no longer those forms on which thou wast just now looking, thou coarse ball of flesh? How they deceive themselves, how blamable are those fools, who cling to thee and say, "This is I."' And when his second eye is torn out, he says: 'The eye of flesh, which is hard to get, has been torn from me, but I have won the perfect faultless eye of wisdom. The king has forsaken me, but I am the son of the highly exalted king of truth: whose child I am called.' He is informed that it is the queen, by whom the command concerning him was issued. Then he says: 'Long may she enjoy happiness, life, and power, who has brought me so much welfare.' And he goes forth a beggar with his wife; and when he comes to his father's city, he sings to the lute before the palace. The king hears Kunāla's voice; he has him called in to him, but when he sees the blind man before him, he cannot recognize his son. At last the truth comes to light. The king in the excess of rage and grief is about to torture and kill the guilty queen. But Kunāla says: 'It would not become thee to kill her. Do as honour demands, and do not kill a woman. There is no higher reward than that for benevolence: patience, sire, has been commanded by the Perfect One.' And he falls at the king's feet, saying: 'O king, I feel no pain, notwithstanding the inhumanity which has been practised on me, I do not feel the fire of anger. My heart has none but a kindly feeling for my mother, who has given the order to have my eyes torn out. As sure as these words are true, may my eyes again become as they were;' and his eyes shone in their old splendour as before.

"Buddhist poetry has nowhere glorified in more beautiful fashion, forgiveness, and the love of enemies than in the narrative of Kunāla. But even here we feel that cool air which floats round all pictures of Buddhist morality. The wise man stands upon a height to which no act of man can approach. He resents no wrong which sinful passion may work him, but he even feels no pain under this wrong. The body, over which his enemies have power, is not himself. Ungrieved by the actions of other men, he permits his benevolence to flow over all, over the evil as well as the good. 'Those who cause me pain and those who cause me joy, to all I am alike; affection and hatred I know not. In joy and sorrow I remain unmoved, in honour and dishonour; throughout I am alike. That is the perfection of my equanimity.'"

The whole of the Buddhist Sanskrit works so far described stand in a half-way position between the Hinãyãna and Mahãyãna, the Awakening of Faith ascribed to Asvaghosha, of course, excepted, though leaning more and more to the Mahãyãna side, a tendency which finds expression in an increasing emphasis on devotion to the Buddha upon the Bodhisattva ideal.

Mahãyãna-sũtras

With the Mahãyãna-sũtras we reach a series of works that are entirely and wholly Mahãyãnist. There is of course no Mahãyãna canon, but at the same time there are nine books which are still highly honoured by all sects of the Mahãyãna alike. Amongst these are the *Lalitavistara* already mentioned, the *Ashtasahasrika-prajñãpãramitã*, and the *Saddharmapundarĩka*.

The last mentioned, the 'Lotus of the Good Law,' is perhaps the most important of these, and certainly of the chief literary interest. It may be dated about the end of the second century A.D. Here nothing remains of the human Buddha: the Buddha is a God above all other gods, an everlasting being, who ever was and for ever shall be; the Buddhist religion is here completely freed from a dependence upon history. The Lotus of the Good Law is rather a drama than a narrative; it is "An undeveloped mystery play, in which the chief interlocutor, not the only one, is Sãkyamuni, the Lord. It consists of a series of dialogues, brightened by the magic effects of a would-be supernatural scenery. The phantasmagorical arts of the whole are as clearly intended to impress us with the idea of the might and glory of the Buddha, as his speeches are to set forth his all-surpassing wisdom." Of literary interest are the numerous dramatic parables, such as that in which the Buddha is likened to a physician, whose many sons are struck down by an epidemic. He prepares for them a medicine, which some take, and are cured; the remainder are perverse, and place no faith in the preparation. Then the father departs to a far country—the individual Buddha, that is, passes away—and then it is that the forsaken and still ailing sons turn to the remedy that has been left for them, knowing that they have no other resource. The narrator understands very well that trait of human nature whereby the man of genius is seldom appreciated until after his death!

The *Karandavyuha*, which was translated into Chinese already in the third century A.D. is concerned with the praise of the Bodhisattva Avalokitesvara. The *Sukhāvativyuha* praises the Buddha Amitābha, and the Blessed Land or Western Paradise. A more philosophical sūtra, and one widely read in Japan at the present day, is the *Vajracchedika*, or Diamond-cutter, and this text will be familiar at least by name to many readers of the works of Lafcadio Hearn.

The following passage will illustrate its metaphysical character, and reminds one of the saying of Behmen, in answer to the disciple's inquiry, Whither goeth the Soul when the Body dieth?—"There is no necessity for it to go anywhither."

"And again? O Subhuti, if anybody were to say that the Tathāgata[1] goes, or comes, or stands, or sits, or lies down,

[1] In this book generally translated 'He-who-has-thus-attained.'

he, O Subhuti, does not understand the meaning of my preaching. And why? Because the word Tathāgata means one who does not go to anywhere, and does not come from anywhere; and therefore he is called the Tathāgata (truly come), holy and fully enlightened."

The very much more extended works known as the *Prajñāpāramitās* are filled with similar texts upon the Emptiness (*Sunyata*) of things. Works of this class are known, having in various recensions 100,000, 25,000, 8000, and some smaller numbers of couplets; the *Prajñāpāramitā* of 8000 couplets is the most commonly met with. They deal in part with the Six Perfections of a Bodhisattva (Pāramitās), and especially with the highest of these, Prajnā, Transcendent Wisdom. This wisdom consists in perfect realization of the Void, the No-thing, the Sunyata; all is mere name. In these works the repetitions and the long lists of particular illustrations of the general truths are carried to incredible lengths, far beyond anything to be found in the Hīnayāna Suttas. But let us remember that the single truth of the Emptiness of things, thus inculcated by repetition—a repetition similar to that of the endless series of painted and sculptured figures of the excavated churches and temple walls—is no easy thing to be realized; and the pious authors of these works were not concerned for an artistic sense of proportion, but with the dissemination of the saving truth. They did not believe that this truth could be too often repeated; and if, for example, as they claim in the *Vajracchedika*, it was known even to children and ignorant persons that matter itself could be neither a thing nor nothing, perhaps even the modern world might do well to consider the value of repetition as an educational principle. For in Europe it is not always remembered, even in scientific circles, that Matter exists only as a concept.

Nāgārjuna and Others

We have already mentioned the great Mahāyāna master Nāgārjuna, who flourished in the latter part of the second century, a little after Asvaghosha. Like the latter he was first a Brāhman, and Brāhmanical philosophy is evident in his work. If not the founder of the Mahāyāna, he is the moulder of one of its chief developments, the Mādhyamika school, of which the chief scriptures are his own *Mādhyamika sūtra*. In these he is chiefly concerned to demonstrate the indefinability of the Suchness (Bhūtathutā), and he expresses this very plainly in several passages of these sūtras, as follows:

After his passing, deem not thus:
'The Buddha still is here.'
He is above all contrasts,
To be and not to be.

While living, deem not thus:
'The Buddha is now here.'
He is above all contrasts,
To be and not to be.

and

To think 'It is' is eternalism,
To think, 'It is not,' is nihilism:
Being and non-being,
The wise cling not to either.

The work of Kumārajīva consists in his biographies of Āsvaghosha and Nāgārjuna, and a certain legendary Deva or Āryadeva; these biographies were translated into Chinese early in the fifth century A.D.

The works of Asanga, the great master of the Yogācāra sect, were translated into Chinese in the sixth century.

Shānti Deva

Most eminent amongst the later Mahāyāna poets is the sainted Shānti Deva, who is probably to be assigned to the seventh century. His *Shikshāsamuccaya*, or 'Student's Compendium' is a work of infinite learning, each verse being provided with an extensive commentary and exegesis: the work itself neither is, nor is meant to be, original or personal. The two first of its twenty-seven verses run as follows:

Since to my neighbours as to myself
Are fear and sorrow hateful each,
What then distinguishes my *self,*
That I should cherish it above another's?

Wouldst thou to Evil put an end,
And reach the Blessed Goal,
Then let your Faith be rooted deep,
And all your thought upon Enlightenment.

Far more poetical, and in Buddhist literature very noticeable for its burden of personal emotion, is the *Bodhicaryāvatāra*, or 'Way of Enlightenment,' where the loftiest note of religious art is again and again touched. This is perhaps the most beautiful of all poetic expressions of the Bodhisattva ideal, of self-dedication to the work of salvation, and the eternal activity of love.[1]

"Nothing new will be told here," says Shānti Deva, "nor have I skill in the writing of books; therefore I have

[1] This work has been compared to the *Imitation of Christ* of Thomas à Kempis; both are works of true devotion and true art, but the *Way of Enlightenment* is not an 'Imitation' of Buddha, but teaches how a man may become a Buddha.

done this work to hallow my own thoughts, not designing it for the welfare of others. By it the holy impulse within me to frame righteousness is strengthened; but if a fellow creature should see it, my book will fulfil another end likewise."

The following is a part of Shānti Deva's self-dedication (Pranidhāna) to the work of salvation:

"I rejoice exceedingly in all creatures' good works that end the sorrows of their evil lot; may the sorrowful find happiness! . . . In reward for this righteousness that I have won by my works I would fain become a soother of all the sorrows of all creatures. . . . The Stillness (Nirvāna) lies in surrender of all things, and my spirit is fain for the Stillness; if I must surrender all, it is best to give it for fellow-creatures. I yield myself to all living creatures to deal with me as they list; they may smite or revile me for ever, bestrew me with dust, play with my body, laugh and wanton; I have given them my body, why shall I care? Let them make me do whatever works bring them pleasure; but may mishap never befall any of them by reason of me. . . . May all who slander me, or do me hurt, or jeer at me, gain a share in Enlightenment. I would be a protector of the unprotected, a guide of wayfarers, a ship, a dyke, and a bridge for them who seek the further Shore; a lamp for them who need a lamp, a bed for them who need a bed, a slave for all beings who need a slave. . . . I summon to-day the world to the estate of Enlightenment, and meanwhile to happiness; may gods, demons, and other beings rejoice in the presence of all the Saviours!"

It is true that the old Buddhist love of loneliness and scorn of the flesh find expression again in Shānti Deva; but there is a sensitive intimacy in his gentle words that overcomes the coldness of the early Buddhist asceticism, and engages our sympathy without provoking disgust:

"Trees are not disdainful, and ask for no toilsome wooing; fain would I consort with those sweet companions! Fain would I dwell in some deserted sanctuary, beneath a tree or in caves, that I might walk without heed, looking never behind! Fain would I abide in nature's own spacious and lordless lands, a homeless wanderer, free of will, my sole wealth a clay bowl, my cloak profitless to robbers, fearless and careless of my body. Fain would I go to my home the graveyard, and compare with other skeletons my own frail body! for this my body will become so foul that the very jackals will not approach it because of its stench. The bony members born with this corporeal frame will fall asunder from it, much more so my friends. Alone man is born, alone he dies; no other has a share in his sorrows. What avail friends, but to bar his way? As a wayfarer takes a brief lodging, so he that is travelling through the way of existence finds in each birth but a passing rest. . . .

"Enough then of worldly ways! I follow in the path of the wise, remembering the Discourse upon Heedfulness, and putting away sloth. To overcome the power of darkness I concentre my thought, drawing the spirit away from vain paths and fixing it straightly upon its stay. . . .

"We deem that there are two verities, the Veiled Truth and the Transcendent reality. The Reality is beyond the range of the understanding; the understanding is called Veiled Truth.[1] . . . Thus there is never either cessation

[1] Veiled Truth, *i.e. samvritti-satya*, the saguna or aparā vidyā of the Vedānta, and the Reality, *i.e. paramārtha-satya*, the nirguna or parā vidyā of the Vedānta, the former a 'distinction of manifold things,' the latter truth 'which is in the unity' (Tauler).

PLATE W 322

FIGURES OF A YAKKHĪ OR DRYAD, AND OF A NĀGARĀJA OR SERPENT KING

Guardian spirits of the Great Thūpa at Bharhut (3rd–2nd century B.C.)

or existence; the universe neither comes to be nor halts in being.[1] Life's courses, if thou regardest them, are like dreams and as the plantain's branches; in reality there is no distinction between those that are at rest and those that are not at rest. Since then the forms of being are empty, what can be gained, and what lost? Who can be honoured or despised, and by whom?[2] Whence should come joy or sorrow? What is sweet, what bitter? What is desire, and where shall this desire in verity be sought? If thou considerest the world of living things, who shall die therein? who shall be born, who is born? who is a kinsman and who a friend, and to whom? Would that my fellow-creatures should understand that all is as the void! . . . righteousness is gathered by looking beyond the Veiled Truth."

II. SCULPTURE AND PAINTING

As little as Early Buddhism dreamed of an expression of its characteristic ideas through poetry, drama, or music, so little was it imagined that the arts of sculpture and painting could be anything other than worldly in their purpose and effect. The hedonistic prepossessions are too strong—and this is also true of other contemporary Indian thought—for any but a puritanical attitude toward the arts to have been possible to the philosopher. The arts were regarded as a sort of luxury. Thus we find such texts as the following:

---

[1] How like Bergson the thought that the universe never halts in being!

[2] "He who deems *This* to be a slayer, and he who thinks *This* to be slain, are alike without discernment; *This* slays not, neither is it slain." —*Bhagavad Gītā*, ii, 19.

"Beauty is nothing to me, neither the beauty of the body, nor that that comes of dress.[1]

"If a Brother or Sister sees various colours, such as wreaths, dressed images, dolls, clothes, woodwork, plastering, paintings, jewellery, ivory-work, strings, leaf-cutting, they should not, for the sake of pleasing the eye, go where they will see these colours and forms."[2]

Sisters were forbidden to look on 'conversation pictures' or love scenes; while the Brethren were only permitted to have painted on the monastery walls or the walls of their cave retreats the representation of wreaths and creepers, never of men and women. The hedonistic foundation of these injunctions is very clearly revealed in a passage of the later *Visuddhi Magga*—for the Hīnayāna maintains the puritanical tradition to the end, with only slight concession in admitting the figure of the Buddha himself—in a passage where 'painters and musicians' are classed with 'perfumers, cooks, elixir-producing physicians and other like persons who furnish us with objects of sense.'

'*Early Buddhist*' *Art*

It is only in the third and second centuries B.C. that we find the Buddhists patronizing craftsmen and employing art for edifying ends. From what has already been said, however, it will be well understood that there had not yet come into being any truly Buddhist or idealistic Brāhmanical religious art, and thus it is that Early Buddhist art is really the popular Indian art of the time

[1] Infinitely remote from a modern view, which was also current in Mediæval India, that 'the secret of all art . . . lies in the faculty of Self-oblivion.'—Riciotto Canudo, *Music as a Religion of the Future.*

[2] *Dasa Dhammika Sutta.*

PLATE X

FIGURE OF YAKKHĪ, A DRYAD

From decorated gateway of the Sānchi Stūpa (2nd century B.C.)

adapted to Buddhist ends, while one special phase of art, represented by the capitals of the Asoka columns (Plate P) and other architectural motifs is actually of extra-Indian origin.

Such non-Buddhist art as we have evidence of in the time of Asoka is concerned with the cults of the Nature spirits—the Earth Goddess, the Nāgas or Serpent Kings of the Waters, and the Yakkha kings who rule the Four Quarters. The Early Buddhist art of Bharhut and Sānchī, which is Asokan or a little later than Asokan, reflects the predominance of these cults in the low-relief figures of the Yakkha Guardians of the Quarters which the entrance gateways (Plate O) of the ambulatory are protected. The victory of Buddhism over the animistic cults—of course, only a partial victory, for these cults flourish even to-day—is suggested by the presence of these Nature spirits (Plate W) acting as the guardians of Buddhist shrines, just as in the story of Buddha's life, by the episode of the Nāga Mucalinda who becomes the Buddha's protector and shelter during the week of storms (Plate A6). The Nature spirits seem to be also represented with a purely decorative, or perhaps reverential intention, in the case of the dryad figures (Plate X) associated with trees on the upper part of the Sānchī gates. These beautiful and sensuous figures are of high æsthetic rank, powerful and expressive: but in their vivid pagan utterance of the love of life, how little can we call them Early Buddhist art!

Apart from the figures of Nature spirits and the representations of animals, decorative or protective, the art of the Sānchī gateways is devoted to the illustration of edifying legends, the stories of the Buddha's former lives (Jātakas) and of the last incarnation. In these delicately executed sculptures in low-relief we have a remarkable record of Indian life with its characteristic environment, manner, and cults, set out with convincing realism and a wealth of circumstantial detail. But though they tell us in what manner the holy legend was visualized within a few centuries of the Buddha's death, they are fundamentally illustrations of edifying episodes, and only to a very limited extent—far less, for example, than at Borobodur—can be said to express directly the Buddhist conceptions of life and death.

There is, however, one respect in which that view is perfectly reflected, and this is in the fact—strange as it may at first appear—that the figure of the Master himself is nowhere represented. Even in the scene which illustrates Siddhattha's departure from his home,[1] Kanthaka's back is bare, and we see only the horse, with the figures of Channa, and of the attendant Devas who lift up his feet so that the sound of his tread may not be heard, and who bear the parasol of dominion at his side. The Buddha, however, may be symbolized in various ways, as by the Wisdom Tree, the Umbrella of Dominion, or, most typically, by conventionally represented Footprints. It will be seen that the absence of the Buddha figure from the world of living men—where yet remain the traces of his ministry—is a true artistic rendering of the Master's guarded silence respecting the after-death state of those who have attained Nibbāna—"the Perfect One is released from this, that his being should be gauged by the measure of the corporeal world," he is released from "name and form." In the omission of the Buddha figure, then, this Early Buddhist art is truly Buddhist, but in nearly all

[1] Depicted on the central horizontal beam of the east Sānchī gate (Plate O).

Plate Y

STANDING IMAGE OF THE BUDDHA

Anurādhapura (2nd–3rd century A.D.)

else it is an art about Buddhism, rather than Buddhist art.

The Buddhist Primitives

We have explained above under the heading 'Beginnings of the Mahāyāna,' in what manner the Buddha came to be regarded as a personal god, and how the Early Buddhist intellectual discipline is gradually modified by the growth of a spirit of devotion which finds expression in worship and the creation of a cult. This may to a large extent reflect the growing influence of the lay community, and it is paralleled by similar tendencies in the development of other contemporary phases of belief. With what passionate abandon even the symbols of the 'Feet of the Lord' were adored will appear in the illustration (Plate Q) from the sculptures of Amarāvatī, a Buddhist shrine in southern India, lavishly decorated with carvings in low relief, mostly of the second century A.D. Feeling such as this could not but demand an object of worship more personal and more accessible than the abstract conception of one whose being lay beyond the grasp of thought, for "exceeding hard" in the words of the *Bhagavad Gītā*, "is the unshown way." Thus the Buddha, and together with him first one and then another of the Bodhisattva saviours, originally idealizations of particular virtues, came to be regarded as personal gods responsive to the prayers of their worshippers, and extending the vessel of their divine benevolence and infinite compassion to all who seek their aid. This was the human need which alike in Buddhist and Hindu churches determined the development of iconography.

The form of the Buddha image—the figure of the seated

yogī—was determined in another way. We have already under the headings of 'Yoga' and 'Spiritual Exercise,' explained the large part that is played, even in Early Buddhism, by the practice of contemplation. At a very early date, probably already, in fact, in the time of Buddha, the seated yogī, practising a mental discipline or attaining the highest station of Samādhi, must have represented to the Indian mind the ultimate achievement of spiritual effort, and the attainment of the Great Quest. And so, when it was desired to represent by a visible icon the figure of Him-who-had-thus-attained, the appropriate form was ready to hand. It is most likely that images of the seated Buddha were already in local and private use as cult objects, but it is not until the beginning of the Christian era that they begin to play a recognized part in official Buddhist art,[1] and the Buddha figure is introduced in narrative sculpture.

It is very probable that examples of these earliest Buddhist primitives are no longer extant, but even if that be so, the splendid and monumental figures of Anurādhapura and Amarāvatī of perhaps the second century A.D., still reflect almost the full force of primitive inspiration. Of these figures there is none finer—and perhaps nothing finer in the whole range of Buddhist art—than the colossal figure at Anurādhapura illustrated in Plate K. With this figure are to be associated a standing image of Buddha (Plate E) and one of a Bodhisattva, and these again are closely related to

[1] As pointed out by M. Foucher, the image on the Kanishka reliquary 'indicates an already stereotyped art . . . and this votive document suffices to throw back by at least a century the creation of the plastic type of the Blessed One, and thus to take us back to the first century before our era.'—*L'Origine grecque de l'Image du Bouddha*, Paris, 1913, p. 31.

PLATE Z

A. GAUTAMA BUDDHA
Bronze, Ceylon, 6th century

B. GAUTAMA BUDDHA
Bronze, Ceylon, 9th century A.D.

C. AVALOKITESVARA BODHISATTVA
Bronze, Ceylon, 7th–8th century A.D.

D. BODHISATTVA
Bronze, Chinese, 9th century A.D.

A, B, Colombo ; C, Author's Collection ; D, Getty Collection

the standing Buddha figures of Amarāvatī. In these austere images the moral grandeur of the Nibbāna ideal finds its own direct expression in monumental forms, free of all irrelevant statement or striving for effect, and these are prototypes that are repeated in all subsequent hieratic Buddhist art.

Græco-Buddhist Sculpture

From these works we must return to a consideration of the slightly earlier, better known and far more abundant art of Gandhāra, generally called 'Græco-Buddhist.' This art is so called because, apart from the seated Buddha form, which must of course be wholly Indian, the leading types of the Buddhist pantheon—viz. the standing Buddha figure, the reclining type, the figures of Bodhisattvas and of other Buddhist divinities, as well as the types of composition of some of the scenes of the Buddha's life, and likewise certain details of architectural ornament, are either directly based upon or strongly influenced by Græco-Roman prototypes. Gandhāra art is in fact a phase of provincial Roman art, mixed with Indian elements, and adapted to the illustration of Buddhist legends. The influence of the western forms on all later Indian and Chinese Buddhist art is clearly traceable: but the actual art of Gandhāra gives the impression of profound insincerity, for the complacent expression and somewhat foppish costume of the Bodhisattvas, and the effeminate and listless gesture of the Buddha figures (Plate AA) but faintly express the spiritual energy of Buddhist thought. From the western point of view also the art must be regarded as even more decadent than that of Roman art within the Roman Empire: for truly, "in the long sands and flats of Roman realism the stream of Greek inspiration was lost for ever," and there is no better evidence of this than the art of Gandhāra. It is of interest to observe also the manner in which certain Indian symbols are awkwardly and imperfectly interpreted, for this affords proof, if that were needed, that the types in question are of older, and Indian origin. A clear case is that of the lotus seat which is the symbol of the Buddha's spiritual purity or divinity. The seated Buddha of Gandhāra is insecurely and uncomfortably balanced on the prickly petals of a disproportionately small lotus, and this defect at once destroys the sense of repose which is above all essential to the figure of the yogī—who is likened in Indian books to the flame in a windless spot that does not flicker—and in immediate conflict with the Yoga texts which declare that the seat of meditation must be firm and easy (*sthira-sukha*). We see before us the work of foreign craftsmen imitating Indian formulæ which they did not understand. We cannot think of this as an original and autochthonous art, despite its historical interest, and it is certainly not primitive in the sense in which this word is used by artists.[1]

Iconography

We may digress here to describe the chief types of Buddha image. The seated figure has three main forms, the first representing pure Samādhi, the highest station of ecstasy —here the hands are crossed in the lap in what is known as *dhyāna mudrā*, the 'seal of meditation' (Plate K); the second, in which the right hand is moved forward across the right knee to touch the earth, in what is known as the *bhumisparsa mudrā*, the 'seal of calling the earth to witness' (Plates Ta, Zb); the third with the hands

[1] "In primitive art you will find . . . absence of representation, absence of technical swagger, sublimely impressive form."—Clive Bell, *Art*, p. 22.

PLATE A A 330

THE FIRST SERMON (TURNING THE WHEEL OF THE LAW)

Gandhāra, 1st–2nd century A.D.

British Museum

raised before the chest in the position known as *dharma-cakra mudrā*, the 'seal of turning the wheel of the law' (Plates B, C, AA). In a fourth type the right hand is raised and the palm turned outward, making the gesture known as *abhaya mudrā*, the 'seal of dispelling fear.' The last pose is characteristic for standing figures, where the left hand grasps the end of the robe (Plates E, Y). In Bodhisattva figures the right hand is very often extended in the *vara mudrā* or 'seal of charity' (Plate R), while the left hand holds an attribute, such as the lotus of Avalokitesvara (Plates R, Za). But the variety of Bodhisattvas is great. Another characteristic pose is known as *vitarka mudrā*, the 'seal of argument,' indicating the act of teaching (Plate Zc). Other forms are generally self-explanatory, like the sword of wisdom which is held aloft by Manjusrī (Plate DD) to cleave the darkness of ignorance. It will also be noticed that the Buddha images have certain physical peculiarities, of which the most conspicuous is the *ushnīsha* or protuberance on the top of the skull. Technically this appears to be derived from a western form of headdress, but in significance it is to be classed with the physical characters attributed by Indian physiognomists to the Superman, the Mahāpurusha. This *ushnīsha* serves to distinguish the Buddha figure from that of a mere Brother, for the heads of the Bhikkhu (Plate L) is always shaved bare and without the Buddha's bump of wisdom. The Buddha type (*e.g.* Plate E) is distinguished, on the other hand from that of the Bodhisattva, in whom the ushnisha is also evident, by the difference of costume: that of the Buddha is monastic, while that of the Bodhisattva is the full and jewelled garb of a king or god. In all three cases the ears are pierced and elongated, but the Bodhisattva alone wears earrings. The monastic costume of the Buddha and the Brethren consists of three strips of cloth, forming an undergarment (*antaravāsaka*) worn about the loins like a skirt, and fastened by a girdle, an upper garment (*uttarasanga*) covering the breast and shoulders and falling below the knees and a cloak (*sanghati*) worn over the two other garments. It is this outer cloak which is naturally most conspicuous in the sculptured images. In standing figures the drapery is treated with elaboration, and the more so the stronger the western influence—being based on the drapery of the well-known Lateran Sophocles, and amounting to absolute identity of design between the Græco-Christian Christ and the Græco-Buddhist Buddha: but in a majority of typically Indian figure the drapery is almost transparent, and indicated by a mere line. In Gupta images especially the whole figure is plainly revealed (Plates B, E). The upper robes are worn in two different ways, in the one case covering both shoulders, in the other leaving the right shoulder bare. Another conspicuous feature of Buddha images is the nimbus or glory, which assumes various forms, the early types being plain, those of the Gupta period elaborately decorated; this again appears to be a motif that is technically western, at the same time that it reflects the traditions regarding the 'Buddha rays' and the transfiguration, and from a visionary standpoint may be called realistic.

Classic Buddhist Art

The various types of Buddhist art to which we have so far referred, from this time onward draw closer and closer together, to constitute one national art and style

PLATE B B

THE BUDDHA

Cambodia, 13th–14th century

Collection of Mr Victor Golonbew

which extend throughout Indian in the Gupta period, and form the main foundation of the colonial and missionary phases of Buddhist art in Siam and Cambodia, Burma, Java, China, and Japan. One of the most marked characters of Gupta art is the fullness and suavity of all its forms, well exemplified in the two figures illustrated on Plates B, E; the latter of these is a standing figure from Mathurā, the other a seated image from the site of the old monastery of the Deer Park at Benares, where the first sermon was preached. It will be seen that by this time the foreign elements introduced by way of Gandhāra are completely absorbed and Indianized, and in the words of Professor Oscar Münsterberg, "developed under national and Buddhist inspiration into a new and genuine art." From Indian Gupta art there is an imperceptible transition to Indian classic, which is more *mouvementée* and distinguished by more slender forms and greater delicacy and mastery of technique. It is in the late Gupta and Early Classic painting of Ajantā that Indian Buddhist art which began with the creation of the seated figure, attains its final perfection and completes its cycle. These paintings, like the low reliefs of Sānchī and Bhārhut, chiefly illustrate the stories of the Buddha's former birth and last incarnation. There is indicated, however, a long development in doctrine and in technique. The Buddha figure is freely represented, but the hieratic type is generally subordinate to that of the Bodhisattva as the living and moving hero in the stories of human and animal life, where he exhibits every possible perfection of character. What is even more noteworthy is the fact that Ajantā painting does not echo the disparagement of life which is so conspicuous in the Pāli Suttas—where the world of living beings is so bitterly denounced as 'unclean'

—but represents this life with passionate sympathy for all its sensuous perfection. Praise of the beauty of women could not be more plainly spoken, and the sound of music is everywhere: no reference is made to age, and there is no insistence upon death or suffering, for human and animal life alike are always represented at the highest levels of experience. It is in quite another way that Buddhist ideals are here expressed—by the ever present sense of tragedy: for the very emphasis on youth and beauty is the revelation of their transcience. The life of the world is depicted with such transparency—"as if in a mountain fastness there were a pool of water, clear, translucent, and serene" —that it appears like the substance of a dream, too frail to grasp, however heaven-like its forms. And there moves through these enchanted scenes the figure of one whose heart is set on a more distant goal, and feels an infinite compassion for all born beings whose sweet delights are subject to mortality (Plate CC). It is just because the mediæval Buddhist consciousness has learnt so well to understand the value of the world that the figure of One who seeks to save all creatures from this radiant phenomenal life appears so tragic.

"'It is not that I do not value these my tusks,' says the Bodhisattva elephant in the *Chaddanta Jātaka*, 'nor that I desire the status of a god, but because the tusks of Infinite Wisdom are dearer to me a thousand times than these, that I yield you these, good hunter.'"

It is to be observed, too, that the spiritual Superman is never poor and despised, but always freely endowed with the lordship and the wealth of the world, he does not scorn the company of beautiful women. *Dharma*, *artha*, and *kāma*, social virtue, wealth, and the pleasures of the senses are his, and yet the Bodhisattva's thoughts are

PLATE C C

BODHISATTVA, PERHAPS AVALOKITESVARA

Ajantā fresco (6th–7th century A.D.)

not diverted from the fourth 'human end' of *moksha*, salvation. So far from the rich man representing the type of him who cannot enter the kingdom of heaven, riches and power are represented as the natural evidence of goodness; and without such riches and such power how could the Bodhisattva's supernatural generosity be sufficiently displayed?

Up to this point, of course, we have spoken rather of ethics than of art. It is not, however, the literally Buddhist subject-matter of Ajantā art that makes it so profoundly moving—we do not need to know what the paintings were about before we are able to feel their significance. Artists painted thus, not because they were Buddhists, but because they were artists. The intellectual and logical content, the narrative element is so entirely subordinate to direct emotion that it is sometimes difficult to realize that the subject of all the Ajantā paintings is really Buddhist. It is always easy for the artisan to illustrate a creed or a legend, but only when he is an artist is he able at the same time to express the deeper and fundamental reality upon which all creed and ritual are based. Certainly the Early Buddhists, who hated 'conversation pictures,' that is to say, love scenes such as we often see at Ajantā, and all who adhere to hedonistic views of art, might utterly condemn the whole work as worldly, or even fleshly. We have already seen, however, that dogmatic content has no necessary connexion with the spiritual significance of a work of art, for nothing could well be less spiritual than the conspicuously 'Buddhist' art of Gandhāra.

After the seventh century Buddhism declined in India proper, and continued to flourish only in Bengal, Nepal and Ceylon, and in the eastern colonies. The widely distributed and splendid monuments of Indian classic sculpture are thus—as at Elephanta, Ellora, and Māmallapuram—almost entirely Hindu in subject. It is only here and there that there survive a few precious relics of purely Indian Buddhist sculpture of the classic age. Probably the best of these is the little Sinhalese bronze of Avalokitesvara reproduced on Plate Zc, while the rather less impressive, but very gracious Sinhalese figure of Maitreya reproduced on Plate S may be a little later. The Nepalese figures of Buddha and Avalokitesvara, illustrated on Plates C, R, are closely related to Ajantā types, and range from the eighth to the eleventh century, and from the eleventh to the thirteenth century there are preserved several examples of beautifully illustrated Buddhist palm-leaf manuscripts in the same style. Subsequent to this the Buddhist art of Nepal is modified by Tibetan, Chinese, and perhaps also Persian influences. Buddhist art persisted in Magadha and Bengal only until the final victories of Islam involved the destruction of the monasteries in the twelfth century.

Colonial Indian Art

India has been the source of a colonial art of great importance, developed from the sixth century onward in Burma, Siam, Cambodia, Laos, and particularly in Java: and the great part of this colonial art is Buddhist. The most important school is the Javanese. Java was colonized by Brāhmanical Hindus in the early centuries of the Christian era and largely converted to Buddhism a little later; the two forms of belief existed side by side until the Muhammadan conquests of the fifteenth century. The largest and finest Buddhist monument is the stūpa of Borobodur; here the procession galleries are adorned by a series of some 2000 bas-reliefs illustrating the life of the Buddha

PLATE D D

MANJUSRĪ BODHISATTVA
Java (14th century A.D.)
Berlin

according to the *Lalitvaistara*, as well as various legends from the *Divyāvadāna* and the *Jātakas*. The reliefs are so extensive that if laid end to end they would cover a space of more than two miles. We have here a third great illustrated Bible, similar in range, but more extensive than the reliefs of Sānchī and the paintings of Ajantā. This is a 'supremely devout and spontaneous art,' naturally lacking the austerity and the abstraction of the early Buddhist primitives, but marvellously gracious, decorative, and sincere. The episodes represented are by no means so exclusively courtly as is the case at Ajantā, but cover the whole circle of Indian life alike in city and village. The narrative element is more conspicuous than at Ajantā, the craftsmen adhering closely to the book. But "every group and every figure are absolutely true and sincere in expression of face, gesture, and pose of body; and the actions which link the various groups and single features together are strongly and simply told, without effort or striving for effect—it was so, because so it could only be"![1] Buddhist art in Java continued to flourish for many centuries, and many works of great beauty are still preserved, both stone reliefs and sculptures in the round, and smaller and very delicate bronzes. Amongst the later works none are more impressive than the Manjusrī—the Bodhisattva who holds aloft the sword of wisdom—reproduced here on Plate DD, but I cannot agree that the well-known Prajñāpāramitā, though still beautiful, is 'one of the most spiritual creations of any art,' but much rather, as another critic has suggested, think of this comfortable and bejewelled gracious figure as 'all too human.'

[1] Havell, *Indian Sculpture and Painting*, p. 118. Many good reproductions will be found in the same volume.

The Far East

The Buddhist art of China is on another footing, for notwithstanding it repeats the forms of Indian art, China had already an old, and, from a technical standpoint, exceedingly accomplished art, and a profound philosophy of her own, before the Buddhist pilgrims and missionaries carried across the wastes of Central Asia the impulse to a new development of thought and of plastic art; thus, although there were at one time many thousands of Indians in China, and some of these were Buddhist artists, yet Chinese Buddhist art is not, like Javanese, entirely Indian, but essentially a new thing, almost as much Chinese as Indian.

The first introduction of Buddhism took place in the first century A.D. In the second century a golden statue, perhaps of the Buddha, was brought into China from the west; in the same century a Buddhist mission reached China from Parthia. Buddhism did not however immediately obtain a firm hold, and the Chinese were then as now partly Confucianist, partly Taoist and partly Buddhist. Naturally as the early Buddhist influences came through western Asia, early Chinese Buddhist art exhibits some relation to the Græco-Buddhist art of Gandhāra; but few traces of any work older than the fifth century now remain, and by that time the Græco-Roman elements were almost negligible, or traceable only in minor details of ornament and technique. Under the Northern Wei dynasty of the early fifth century, however, there is an immense artistic activity, and the mountains and caves of Tatong are carved with countless images of Buddhas and Bodhisattvas of all sizes, from miniature to colossal, and these works are the typical Chinese Buddhist primitives. One colossal figure

PLATE E E 338

BODHISATTVA

Chinese, school of Long-men (8th century)

Cologne

is some ninety feet in height and here the form is full and round, but some of the smaller figures are very delicate and slender. One of the features of immediate Indian origin is to be recognized in the gigantic figures of door-guardians represented as muscular giants protecting the entrances to the Buddhist caves. While in these figures the muscles are conspicuously developed and the body bare, the Buddha and Bodhisattva figures are always clothed and the details of the anatomy suppressed and generalized. Similar decorated caves are found at Long-men near the town of Honan, a later North Wei capital; these excavations and sculptures belong to the sixth century. The inscriptions recording the various donations show that these works were commissioned by the king, the queen, the nobles, and even by individuals of the lower classes. A great development of Buddhist sculpture also took place in Korea. These figures like those already described are hewn out of the living rock, in an environment of great natural beauty, far from the haunts of men. Buddhist art in India, as at Ajantā, and still more in the Far East, is constantly thus associated with naturally impressive scenes: and were it not for this love of Nature and for the institution of pilgrimage to sacred and far away sites, it would be difficult to account for the great part which is played in Chinese and Japanese art by landscape painting somewhat later.

It is from Korea that Buddhist thought and art were introduced to Japan in the sixth century. The new faith met with considerable opposition. The hero of the period of the first introduction of Buddhism to Japan is the renowned Prince Wumayado, who prepared the seventeen articles of the Japanese constitution, and wrote some remarkable commentaries on the Buddhist Sūtras, setting forth the teachings of Nāgārjuna: he is still worshipped by craftsmen and artisans as Patron of the Arts. The only remains of this period, however, are the colossal bronze Buddha of Ankoin, which has suffered many vicissitudes and is too much restored to afford a very definite idea of the earliest Japanese Buddhist art: and the famous temple of Horiuji near Nara, which is rich alike in contemporary sculpture and paintings. "We find in these works," says Okakura, "a spirit of intense refinement and purity, such as only great religious feeling could have produced. For divinity, in this early phase of national realization, seemed like an abstract ideal, unapproachable and mysterious, and even its distance from the naturalesque gives to art an awful charm." We are reminded here that all the early Buddhist art of the Far East is more purely hieratic and abstract than is the case, for example, at Ajantā, to which the painting at Horiuji is otherwise so closely related; and the explanation is not far to seek. For when the artists of the Far East, together with the new religion, "adopted the Indian formulas and symbols, they kept these separate from the ordinary practice of their art, and so developed a specialized hieratic quality, the rarest and most remote perhaps the art of the painter has ever expressed." Whereas, "to the Indian mind Buddha and his disciples were more actual figures, with positive relations to their own social world. The places where they lived and taught were to them definite places, to which they themselves could at any moment make pilgrimages,"[1] and thus there was not in India that "separation of social and religious traditions" which is apparent in Chinese art, as it is likewise evident in European religious sculpture and painting. Of

[1] W. Rothenstein, in *Ajanta Frescoes* (India Society), London, 1915.

PLATE F F 340

THE BUDDHA

Central figure of a triptych in the Tofukuji temple, Kyoto, Japan, ascribed to Wu Tao-tzu (Chinese, 8th century)

From Tajuna, Selected Relics of Japanese Art, Vol I

two early Japanese paintings of Samantabhadra and of Manjusrī, Mr Binyon remarks:

"The fluid lines of form and drapery are of an indescribable sweetness and harmony, as if sensitive themselves with life; the colour also discloses itself as part of the calmly glowing life within, veined with fine lines of gold, not as something applied from without. Such images, as these, of which this early Buddhist art has created not a few, images of the infinite of wisdom and of tenderness, not only express the serenity of the spirit, but have in a degree unreached in any other art the power of including the spectator in their spiritual spell: to contemplate them is to be strangely moved, yet strangely tranquillized."[1]

We must however return for a time to China, to consider the classic art of the T'ang epoch (A.D. 618–905), for this is the great creative age of the Far East, by which the whole future development both of Chinese and Japanese art is mainly determined: the part that Greece has played for Europe was played for Japan by China.

"The T'ang era stands in history for the period of China's greatest external power—the period of her greatest poetry and of her grandest and most vigorous, if not, perhaps, her most perfect, art. Buddhism now took hold on the nation as it never did before, and its ideals pervaded the imagination of the time. China was never in such close contact with India; numbers of Indians, including three hundred Buddhist monks, actively preaching the faith, were to be found in the T'ang capital of Loyang. And Buddhist ideas permeate T'ang painting."[2]

The T'ang sculpture is best displayed in the sculptured caves of Longmen, near Honan, similar in method to the

[1] Binyon, *Painting in the Far East*, ed. 2, p. 105.

[2] *Ibid.*

earlier excavations at Tatong; from these we reproduce here the central figure of a colossal Buddha (Plate F), and of the same school but unknown provenance the gracious and almost coquettish figure of a Bodhisattva (Plate EE), now in the museum at Cologne. Many other detached examples of T'ang Buddhist sculpture may be seen in the European and American museums. Intermediate in date between the Wei and T'ang periods is the monumental stele in black marble, in the collection of M. Goloubew, reproduced on Plate G. What little we know of the painting of the T'ang period is dominated by the great name of Wu Tao-tzu, of whom a few more or less authentic works are preserved in Japan. One of these, which if not actually the work of Wu Tao-tzu, is at any rate a masterwork of T'ang, is the beautiful Buddha figure of the Tofukuji temple in Kyoto, reproduced on Plate D. Another painting by a somewhat later artist, but thought to be after Wu Tao-tzu, is the Bodhisattva Kwanyin, the Indian Avalokitesvara, reproduced on Plate HH. At an early date the male Avalokitesvara was interpreted in China as a feminine divinity and saviouress, and there is a long and charming Chinese legend which recounts her life as an earthly princess. Since Kwanyin is a gracious saviouress who hears all cries and answers all prayers, it will readily be understood that she became one of the most popular of all Chinese and Japanese Buddhist divinities, and the subject of innumerable paintings. It will be noticed in our example (from the collection of Mr C. L. Freer, and reproduced by his kindness) that the goddess holds a basket with a fish in her outstretched hand, whereas in a majority of representations she carries a willow spray or a phial of the water of life.[1] A more

[1] The cult of Kwanyin and the significance of the fish are discussed by R. F. Johnston, *Buddhist China*, ch. xi.

PLATE G G

KWANYIN

Gilt bronze, mediæval Japanese

Collection of Mr H. Getty

famous work by Wu Tao-tzu was the 'Death of Buddha,' painted in A.D. 742, of which "We know at least the composition, for Wu Tao-tzu's design was repeated by more than one early master of Japan, and the original is described in Chinese books. In the British Museum is a large painting of this subject, by the hand of a great artist entirely modelled on the art of T'ang. Magnificent indeed is the conception. The whole of creation is wailing and lamenting around the body of the Buddha, who lies peaceful in the midst, having entered into Nirvāna, under a great tree, the leaves of which are withered where they do not cover him. Saints and disciples, kings, queens, priests and warriors, weep and beat their breasts; angels are grieving in the air; even the beasts of the field and the forest, the tiger, the panther, the horse, the elephant, show sorrow in all their limbs, rolling with moans upon the ground; and the birds cry. An ecstasy of lamentation impassions the whole work. What must have been the effect of the original?" [1]

Three hundred other painters' names of the T'ang period are known, but not their works. The greatest of these is Wang Wei, who is a painter of landscape, and probably supreme in China, as the Chinese are supreme in this art in the world. It should be remarked that the Chinese landscape painter's interests are far from topographical; he uses the familiar scenes or lonely mountains and forests to interpret and communicate a mood, or express a philosophic concept. It is in this way that landscape art, though it is not specifically Buddhist, lends itself to religious sentiment. There is a Sung painting of the thirteenth century called the *Evening Chime of the Distant Temple.* "A range of mountains lifts its rugged outline in the

[1] Binyon, *Painting in the Far East.*

twilight, the summits accentuated and distinct against the pale sky, the lower parts lost in mist, among which woods emerge or melt along the uneven slopes. Somewhere among those woods, on high ground, the curved roof of a temple is visible. It is just that silent hour when travellers say to themselves, 'The day is done,' and to their ears come from the distance the expected sound of the evening bell. The subject is essentially the same as that which the poetic genius of Jean François Millet conceived in the twilight of Barbizon, at the hour when the Angelus sounds over the plain from the distant church of Chailly."

But as another critic has remarked on this:

"What a difference in the treatment! Millet places Man in the foreground, explaining the content of the picture by human action, but the Chinese artist needs no figure, nothing but a hint; the spectator must complete the thought himself."

The world of Nature at this time had come to mean for the Chinese artist something other than we are accustomed to think of in connexion with European landscape. In one way he uses Nature's forms as the phrases of a philosophical language, likening mountain and mist, dragon and tiger, to the Great Extremes: so that while the modern critic can perhaps appreciate much of their purely æsthetic quality, it is only by an effort that he realizes the depth of suggestion and mystical significance which these monochrome brush drawings have for the Chinese student steeped in Buddhist nature lore and Taoist philosophy. Very often also even this underlying philosophical significance is, so to say, unexpressed. In any case, "The life of nature and of all non-human things is regarded in itself; its character contemplated and its

PLATE H H

KWANYIN

Chinese painting, 10th–12th century, after Wu Tao-tzu

Collection of Mr C. L. Freer

beauty cherished for its own sake, not for its use and service in the life of man. There is no infusion of human sentiment into the pictures of birds and beasts, of the tiger roaring in the solitudes, of the hawk and eagle on the rocky crag; rarely is there any touch of the sportsman's interest which has inspired most European pictures of this kind."[1]

Even the smallest flower, the most trivial insect can thus be represented with such intensity of vision as to seem a world in itself: and this world is a part of humanity, as man is a part of the world by nature. The world of nature is not merely an object of interest, but a perpetual expression of the one life. Those strange lines of Blake

The caterpillar on the leaf
Reminds me of my mother's grief

would have been immediately intelligible to every cultivated reader of mediæval Chinese and Japanese epigrams, and would have inspired, most likely, innumerable paintings, in which the caterpillar should be so represented as to set forth to the eye and still more to the heart of the spectator the essential unity of all existences. This is the 'Sermon of the Wild'; and to be sensitive to these prophecies and intimations is characteristic alike of poetry and painting in the later developments of the Mahāyāna. Thus in China as in India, but in a different fashion, thought expressed in art developed from an early hieratic formulation to a representation of the pure transparency of life.

[1] Binyon, *loc. cit.*

BIBLIOGRAPHY OF WORKS CONSULTED BY THE AUTHOR

ARNOLD, SIR EDWIN: *The Light of Asia.*

BARNETT, PROF. L. D.: *The Path of Light* (*Bodhicaryāvatāra of Sānti-Deva*), London, 1909.

BEAL, S.: *The Romantic History of Buddha.* London, 1875.

BEAL, S. A.: *Catena of Buddhist Scriptures.* London, 1871.

BINYON, L.: *Painting in the Far East.* (2nd ed.) London, 1913.

BURGESS, J.: *Amarāvatī and Jaggayyapeta.* London, 1887.

CHAVANNES, E.: *Mission Archæologique dans la Chine septentrionale.* 1909.

COOMARASWAMY, A.: *Arts and Crafts of India and Ceylon.* London, 1913.

Bronzes from Ceylon, chiefly in the Colombo Museum. Colombo, 1914.

Buddhist Primitives, "Burlington Magazine," Jan., March, 1916.

Mahāyāna Buddhist Images from Ceylon and Java. "Journal of the Royal Asiatic Society." 1909.

Mediæval Sinhalese Art. Campden, 1908.

COWELL, MAX MULLER, and TAKAKAKUSO.: *Buddhist Mahāyāna Sūtras* (*Buddhacarita of Asvaghosha*, etc.). Oxford (S.B.E.) 1894.

CUNNINGHAM, A.: *Mahābodhi.* London, 1892.

Stupa of Bharhut. London, 1879.

FOUCAUX, E.: *Rgya Tch'er Rol Pa* (*Lalita-vistara*). Paris, 1848.

FOUCHER, A.: *Étude sur l'iconographie bouddhique de l'Inde.* Paris, 1900, 1905.

L'Art gréco-bouddhique du Gandhāra. Paris, 1905.

La Porte Orientale du Stūpa de Sānchī. Paris 1910.

Le 'Grand Miracle' du Buddha à Srāvastī. "Journal Asiatique," 1909.

L'origine grecque de l' Image du Bouddha. Paris, 1913.

GARBE, R.: *Sāmkhya and Yoga* ("Grundriss der Indo-arischen Philologie"). Strassburg, 1896.

GEIGER, W.: *The Mahāvamsa.* London, 1912.

GEMMEL, W.: *The Diamond Sutra.* London, 1912.

GETTY, A.: *The Gods of Northern Buddhism.* Oxford, 1914.

GOLOUBEW, V.: *Peintures Bouddhiques aux Indes.* "Annales du Musée Guimet, Bibliothèque de Vulgarisation," Tome 40, Paris, 1914.

Bibliography

GRAY. J.: *Buddhaghosupatti.* London, 1892.

GRIFFITHS: *The Paintings of the Buddhist Cave-temples of Ajanta.* London, 1896.

HACKMANN, H.: *Buddhism as a Religion.* London, 1910.

HALL, FIELDING: *The Soul of a People.*

HARDY, S.: *A Manual of Buddhism.* London, 1860.

HARE, W. L.: *Buddhist Religion.*

HAVELL, E. B.: *Indian Sculpture and Painting.* L

HUBER, E.: *Sutrālamkāra of Asvaghosha.* Paris, 1908.

INDIA SOCIETY: *Ajanta Frescoes.* Oxford, 1915.

JOHNSTON, R. F.: *Buddhist China.* London, 1913.

KERN, H.: *Manual of Indian Buddhism* ("Grundriss der Indo-arischen Philologie"). Strassburg, 1896.

Saddharma Pundarīka (*The Lotus of the Good Law*). Oxford (S.B.E.), 1909.

LE COQ, A. VON: *Chotscho.* Berlin, 1913.

MAISEY, F. C.: *Sānchī and its Remains.* London, 1892.

MAX MULLER and FAUSBOLL: *Dhammapada and Sutta Nipāta.* Oxford (S.B.E.) 1881.

MÜNSTERBERG, O.: *Chinesische Kunst.* Erlangen, 1910.

NARASU, P. L.: *The Essence of Buddhism.* Madras, 1907.

NUKARIYA, K.: *The Religion of the Samurai.* London, 1913.

OKAKURA KAKUZO: *Ideals of the East.* (2nd ed.) London, 1904.

OLDENBERG, H.: *Buddha; his Life, his Doctrine, his Order* (English version by W. Hoey). London, 1882.

POUSSIN, L. DE LA VALLÉE: *Bouddhisme.* Paris, 1909.

The Three Bodies of a Buddha. "Journal of the Royal Asiatic Society." 1906.

RHYS DAVIDS, C. A. F.: *The Love of Nature in Buddhist Poems.* "Quest," April 1910.

Buddhism. (Home University Library.)

Buddhist Psychology. London, 1910, 1914.

Compendium of Philosophy (Anuruddha). London, 1910 (with S. Z. Aung).

Psalms of the Early Buddhists. London, 1909, 1913.

RHYS DAVIDS, T. W.: *Buddhism, its History and Literature.* London and New York, 1907.

Buddhism. S.P.C.K. London (many editions).

Indian Buddhism. (Hibbert Lectures, 1881.) London, 1897.

Bibliography

RHYS DAVIDS, W. T.:

Buddhist Birth Stories (Jātakas). London, 1880.

Buddhist India. London, 1903.

Dialogues of the Buddha. London, 1899, 1910.

Early Buddhism. London, 1908.

The Questions of King Milinda (S.B.E.), 1890, 1894.

SMITH, V. A.: *A History oj Fine Art in India and Ceylon*. Oxford. 1911.

Asoka. (2nd ed.)' Oxford, 1909.

SPEYER, J. S.: *The Jātaka Mālā of Āryasūra*. London, 1895.

STEIN, SIR A.: *Ancient Khotan*. Oxford, 1907.

Ruins of Desert Cathay. London, 1912.

STRONG, MAJOR D. M.: *The Udāna*. London, 1902.

SUBASINHA, D. J.: *Buddhist Rules for the Laity* (*Sigālawāda and Vyaggapajja Suttas*). Madras, 1908.

SUZUKI, D. T.: Asvaghosha's *Awakening of Faith in the Mahāyāna*. Chicago, 1900.

Outlines of Mahāyāna Buddhism. London, 1907.

WADDELL, A.: *Evolution of the Buddhist Cult*. "Imperial and Asiatic Quarterly Review," 1912.

The Indian Buddhist Cult of Avalokita and . . . Tārā . . . "Journal of the Royal Asiatic Society." 1894.

WARREN, H. C.: *Buddhism in Translations*. Cambridge (U.S.A.) 1906

WOODWARD, F. L.: *Pictures of Buddhist Ceylon*. Adyar, 1914.

WORSLEY, A.: *Concepts of Monism*. London.

GLOSSARY

Where a word is given in two forms, the first is Pāli, the second, within brackets, is Sanskrit. Elsewhere the distinction is indicated by the letters P and S. The Pāli and Sanskrit terms are, of course, cognate throughout.

Ahamkāra, S : the conceit of individuality, empirical egoism.

Akhyāna, S : an old literary form, viz. *conte fable*.

Alamkāra, S : rhetoric, poetic ornament.

Ālaya-vijñāna, S : Cosmic Mind or Reason, realm of the Platonic Ideas.

An-attā, P : the doctrine that there are no egos, or souls.

Anicca (anitya) : impermanence, transcience.

Antahkarana, S : inner actor, the inner man, the 'soul.'

Aparā vidyā, S : relative truth, esoteric truth.

Arahat, P : one who has attained to Arahatta.

Arahatta, P : the state of saving truth, the state of one who has attained Nibbāna, or walks in the Fourth Path of which the fruit is Nibbāna.

Ariya (ārya) : noble, gentle, honourable.

Ariyasaccāni (āryasatyāni) : the Four Noble Truths emunciated in Buddha's first sermon.

Arūpa-lokas, S : the Four Highest Heavens, transcending form.

Asubha-jhāna, P : meditation on the essential uncleanness of things.

Ātman, S : (1) taken by Buddhists in the sense of ego, or soul; (2) in Brāhmanism, the Absolute, unconditioned, spirit, Brahman; also the reflection of the Absolute in the individual.

Atta (artha) : aim, gain, advantage, profit.

Attā (ātman), P : self, soul, person, ego; a permanent unity in the sense of an 'eternal soul,' the existence of which is denied in the proposition 'an-attā.' *Attā* etymologically = ātman, but does not connote the unconditioned Ātman of the Brāhman absolutists.

Avidyā, S : ignorance, the contraction of Suchness into variety. The basis of *Tanhā*, and thus of the whole *Samsāra*.

Ignorance is the true 'First Cause' of Indian philosophy: but this 'First Cause' is 'first' only as 'fundamental,' not as temporal. Ignorance can be overcome by the individual consciousness, which is then 'set free," *vimutto*.

Bhakti, S : loving devotion.

Glossary

Bhakti mārga, S: the way of love, the means of salvation by devotion.

Bhavanga-gati, P, S: the ordinary unconscious life of the body, etc.

Bhikkhu, P: mendicant friar, 'Buddhist priest.'

Bhikkhunī, P: feminine of *Bhikkhu*.

Bodhi, P: wisdom, Suchness, intuition, illumination, inner light. Cf. Persian *'Ishq*.

Bodhi-citta, P: heart-of-wisdom, inward light, grace, 'shoot of ever-lastingnesse,' the divine spark of the Buddha-nature in the heart.

Bodhisatta (*Bodhisattva*): Wisdom-being. (1) Gautama before attaining enlightenment; (2) any individual self-dedicate to the salvation of others and destined to the attainment of Buddhahood.

Brahmā, S: the supreme personal god so called.

Brahmācārya, S: chaste life, especially of a Brāhmanical student.

Brāhman, S: a man of the *Brāhmana varna*, a Brāhman by birth, a philosopher, priest. Ethically, one who fulfils the ideal of a true Brāhman.

Brahman, *Brahma*, S: the Absolute, the Unconditioned, which is 'Not so, not so,' the Ground, the Undivided Self, the World of Imagination.

Buddha, P, S: Enlightened. (1) Siddhattha Gautama, after attaining enlightenment; (2) other individuals who have similarly attained Nibbāna; (3) any such individual considered as a supreme God, whose attainment of Buddhahood is timeless.

Buddhi, P, S: enlightenment, intelligence.

Cakka (cakra): 'wheel.' Symbol of sovereignty, hence the Wheel of the Good Law, of the Gospel.

Cariyā, P: 'course,' the succession of lives of a Bodhisattva.

Cetanā, P: will.

Citta, P: heart, Suchness.

Deva, P, S: any personal god, angel, *e.g.* Brahmā, Sakka.

Dhamma (dharma): Norm, gospel, law, righteousness, morality, religion; condition.

Dhamma-cakkhu, S: Eye for the truth.

Dharmakāya, S: law body, Logos, the supreme state of a Buddha; Absolute Being, the Ground; absolute knowledge.

Dibba-cakkhu, P: heavenly eye, omniscient vision of the Universe of Form (Rūpaloka and Kāmaloka).

Dosa, P: hatred, resentment, revenge, anger.

Glossary

Dukkha, P : evil, suffering, sin, imperfection. One of the Three Signs of Existence and one of the Four Ariyan Truths.

Hīnayāna : the 'Little Vessel,' a term applied by the Mahāyānists to the doctrines of early Buddhism. The *Hīnayāna* is set forth in the Pāli *Theravāda*. Sometimes, but not accurately, called Southern Buddhism.

Īsvara, S : Overlord, a Supreme Personal God. God in the general Christian sense.

Jaina, P, S : a follower of Mahāvīra, the Jina or Conqueror.

Jātaka, P, S : a birth-story, the history of some episode in the former life of the Buddha.

Jhāna (dhyāna) : meditation, the mental exercise so called, in particular the Four Ecstasies.

Jīva, Jivātman, S : the Supreme Ātman as particularized in the individual.

Jñāna, S : wisdom, the intellectual.

Jñāna mārga, S : the intellectual way, means of salvation by knowledge.

Kāma, P, S : love, lust.

Kāma-loka, P, S : the Six Heavens of the Lesser Gods, and the Five Lower Worlds.

Kamma (*karma*) : deeds, character, causality.

Karma mārga, S : the way of deeds, the means of salvation by disinterested activity.

Karunā (*karma*) : compassion, the bestowing virtue—the leading passion in a Bodhisattva.

Khandha (skandha) : 'aggregate,' the compound factors of consciousness.

Klesa, S : sin, prejudice.

Līlā, S : 'play,' the 'wonderful works of the Lord,' manifestation.

Mādhyamika, S, : a division of the Mahāyāna, mainly dependent on Nāgārjuna.

Magga (*mārga*) : way, path.

Mahāyāna, S : the 'Great Vessel,' the doctrines of the Mahāyānists, so-called by themselves. The *Mahāyāna* is set forth in the Sanskrit Buddhist texts. Sometimes referred to, but not accurately, as Northern Buddhism.

Māna, P, S : pride, conceit, any intrusion of the ego.

Manas, P, S : mind, soul ; ego.

Māyā, S : illusion, the power of creation or manifestation.

Mettā (maitri) : friendliness, goodwill, loving-kindness.

Moha, P: infatuation, delusion, prejudice, folly, sentimentality.

Muditā, P: sympathy, one of the Four Sublime Moods.

Mudrā, S: seal. Position of the fingers, hieratic gesture.

Nāga, P, S: a being having the dual character of man and serpent. Also an elephant, a wise man.

Nāginī, P, S: feminine of Nāga.

Nāma-rūpa, P, S: lit. name and form, which alone constitute an aggregate into a seeming personality or unit. Psychologically, 'an embodiment' without the idea of anything embodied: mind and body, or mind and matter. For *rūpa* in other senses, s.v.

Nibbāna (nirvāna): ethically, the dying out of lust, resentment, and illusion: psychologically, release from individuality. The Recognition of Truth. A state of salvation to be realized here and now; those who attain, are released from becoming, and after death return no more. *Nibbāna* does not imply the 'annihilation of the soul,' for Buddhism teaches that no such entity as a soul has ever existed. *Nibbāna* is one of many names for the *summum bonum*; it may be best translated as Abyss, Stillness, Void, or Nothing (not-thing-ness).

Nirguna, S: unconditioned, unqualified, in no wise.

Nirmānakāya, S: magical body, apparition, body of transformation, the earthly aspect of a Buddha.

Nishkāma, S: disinterested.

Nivritti mārga, S: the Path of Return.

Pacceka Buddha, P: one who attains enlightenment, but does not teach; a 'private Buddha.'

Pañña, P: wisdom, reason, insight.

Pañña-cakkhu, P: Eye of insight or wisdom.

Parā vidyā, S: absolute truth, esoteric truth.

Paramārtha satya, S: absolute truth.

Pāramitā, S: transcendental perfection, especially the perfected virtue of a Bodhisattva.

Paribājaka, P: a 'Wanderer,' a peripatetic hermit.

Parinibbāna (parinirvāna): 'full Nibbāna,' (1) identical with *Nibbāna*, *Arahatta*, *Vimutti*, *Aññā*, etc., (2) death of a human being who has previously realized *Nibbāna*, death of an *Arahat*: also simply 'dissolution.'

Paticca-samupāda, P: dependent origination, causality.

Prajñā, S: reason, understanding.

Glossary

Prajñā-pāramitā, S : supreme reason. Also personified as the 'Mother of the Buddhas,' *Tathāgata-garbha*. Cf. Persian *'Aql*. Regarded as the way out, she is the principle of analysis; as the way in, the principle of synthesis.

Prakriti, S : Nature, the corporeal world.

Pranidhāna, S : vow, self-dedication, firm persuasion, of a Bodhisattva.

Pravritti mārga, S : the Path of Pursuit.

Puñña (punya) : merit, good character.

Purusha, S : 'Male,' a personification of the Brahman or Ātman (Vedānta): an individual soul (Sāmkhya). Antithetic to Prakriti, 'spirit' as opposed to 'matter.'

Rāga, P, S : lust, passion, desire.

Rākshasa, S : a man-devouring demon.

Rūpa, P, S : form, shape. In a categorical sense, quality. See also *Nāmarūpa*.

Rūpa-lokas, P, S : the Sixteen Heavens conditioned by form, next the below Arūpa-lokas.

Saguna, S : conditioned, qualified.

Samādhi, P, S : tranquillity, self-concentration, calm, rapture. A state attained in Jhāna, and then equivalent to the transcending of empirical consciousness: also the state of calm which is always characteristic of the Arahrat.

Samana, P : wandering friar. The Buddha is often referred to as 'The Great Samana.'

Sambhogakāya, S : 'Enjoyment-body,' the heavenly aspect of a Buddha.

Sāmkhya, S : 'School of the Count,' a pre-Buddhist philosophy, so-called as 'reckoning-up' the twenty-five categories.

Samsāra, P, S : Becoming, conditioned existence, birth-and-death, eternal recurrence, mortality, corporeal existence, the vegetative world.

Samvritti satya, S : relative truth.

Sangha, P, S : the Order, the company or congregation of monks and nuns.

(*Sankhāra*) *Samskāra* : 'conformation,' impression of previous deeds, constituents of character.

Sañña, P : perception.

Sarraguna, S : in all wise, having all possible qualities.

Sati, P : recollectedness, conscience.

Sīla, P : conduct, morality.

Sūfī: a Persian mystic.

Sukha, P, S: good, pleasure, happiness, weal.

Sukhāvatī: the Western Paradise of Amitābha, the highest heaven, the 'Buddha field' where souls are ripened for Nirvāna.

Sutta (sūtra): 'thread.' A literary form, in Buddhist scriptures, words of the Buddha 'strung together' as a sermon or dialogue; in Hindu scriptures, a connected series of aphorisms.

Svabhāva, S: 'own-nature.' The self-existent, the source of spontaneity; a term analogous to 'I am that I am,' applied to the Supreme Buddha (Ādi-Buddha of the later Mahāyāna).

Sva-dharma, S: 'own norm,' peculiar duty of the individual or social group.

Tanhā (trishna): desire, coveting, craving, an eager wish to obtain or enjoy, interested motive. In this sense Buddhism teaches the extinction of desire (in Hinduism, 'renunciation of the fruits of works'), but *Tanhā* does not cover aspiration or good intention, which are included in the 'Right Desire' of the Eightfold Path.

Tao: the absolutist philosophy of the Chinese philosopher Laotse. The term Tao has a connotation similar to that of Nirvāna and Brahman.

Tapas, S: burning, glow, toil, torture.

Tārā: the feminine counterpart of a Bodhisattva, a saviouress.

Tathāgata, S: Thus-gone or Thus-come, He-who-has-thus-attained, a term used by the Buddha in speaking of himself.

Tathāgata-garbha, S: 'Womb-of-Those-who-have-thus-come.' The *Dharma-kāya*, or Suchness, as viewed from the standpoint of the relative and regarded as the origin of all things; mother of the Buddhas and all sentient beings; Nature as potential matter, Māyā, Prakriti; Prājñāpāramitā.

Tattva, bhūtatathatā, S: Suchness, Ground, Substrate, the inevitability and universality of things, the source of spontaneity. The quality of infinity in every particular, of the whole in the part.

Tāvatimsa: Heaven of the Thirty-three Gods, one of the Six Lower Heavens.

Thera, P: an elder; amongst the Brethren, an Arahat.

Theravāda, P: 'word of the elders.' By this term the early Buddhists distinguish their belief from that of the Mahāyānists. The *Theravāda* texts constitute the Pāli canon.

Therī, P: feminine of *Thera*.

Glossary

Thūpa (stūpa): a memorial mound, generally enshrining relics.

Tri-kāya, S: the Three Bodies, or modes, of a Buddha (Mahāyāna), viz. *Dharmakāya*, *Sambhogakāya*, and *Nirmānakāya*, q.v.

Tri-ratna, S, the 'Three Jewels.' In the *Hīnayāna*, the Buddha, the Dhamma, and the Sangha; in the *Mahāyāna*, the Buddhas, the Sons of the Buddhas, and the Dharmakāya.

Tusita, S: Heaven of Pleasure, one of the Six Lower Heavens.

Upadhi (*upādhi*): attributes, superimposed by the mind upon the unconditioned: individualizing determinations.

Upanishad, S: books of the later Veda, partly pre-Buddhist, where are found the leading texts of the Vedānta or Brāhmanical absolutist philosophy to which Buddhism is nominally opposed.

Upāya, P: means, accommodation.

Upekhā, P: impartiality, same-sightedness, one of the Four Sublime Moods.

Vānaprastha, S: a forest-dwelling hermit.

Varna, S: 'colour,' complexion. Combined with hereditary occupation, and the recognition of special social forms, 'colour' becomes caste, which was in process of development in the time of Gautama.

Vedanā, P: feeling.

Viññāna (*vijñana*): consciousness, mental activity.

Vimutti, *Vimokha (moksha)*: salvation, release, the summum bonum.

Vimutto: saved, released.

Vinaya, P: Rules of the Buddhist Order.

Yakkha (*yaksha*): a nature spirit.

Yogācāra, S: a division of the Mahāyāna, mainly dependent on Asanga.

INDEX

A

Index

Index

H

I

J

K

N

Q

R

S

Published by

Facsimile Publisher
Ashok Vihar, Delhi-110052 (India)
Website: www.facsimilepublishers.com

Distributed by

Gyan Books Pvt. Ltd.
5, Ansari Road, Daryaganj, New Delhi-110002 (India)
E-mail: books@gyanbooks.com, Website: www.gyanbooks.com

9 789333 197809